My Name is B-1259

I SURVIVED NINE NAZI CONCENTRATION CAMPS

Michael Brown

Based on the story of Elias Feinzilberg

ISBN-13: 979-8-218-30896-4

Other Books by Michael Brown

Historical fiction

'William & Lucy'

(A Tale of Suspicion and Love)

~

'The Girl Who Was Me Is Gone'

and its sequel, 'In the Company of Savages.'

(A Tale of Love and Passion)

~

Romantic Suspense

'The Girl from Fisher Island'

~

Romantic Comedy

'Loving You is Crazy'

Table of Contents

Dedication

To the memory of Elias and Esther Feinzilberg

Author's Note

This book came to fruition from a conversation with an old friend who asked me to write this almost inconceivable true story about his father, Elias Feinzilberg, a World War ll Holocaust survivor of nine concentration camps.

As I was about to start researching Elias's story, he passed away at the age of 104. With live interviews now impossible, I sought out transcripts of Elias's many lectures and interviews he gave to groups interested in the Holocaust during his retirement years in Jerusalem. I created his dialogue by reading Elias's words as he survived from one camp to the next. In one of these death camps, he crosses paths with a young woman who eventually becomes his wife.

With the rise of antisemitism and Holocaust deniers worldwide, every generation needs to be reminded that six million Jews were imprisoned in ghettos and camps, tortured and killed simply because they were Jewish. Unless humanity is diligent and has periodic reminders of these atrocities, the past can and will repeat itself.

It is my hope Elias's story will be part of the warnings:

Never Again. Never Forget.

"The fact I stayed alive does not imply that a part of me did not die."
—Elias Feinzilberg

Acknowledgment

My gratitude goes to Jacob and Patty Feinzilberg. It was Jacob who first came to me and asked me to write his father's memoir.

I also wish to thank Jay Kenhoff, my entertainment attorney, literary agent, and scholar, for his excellent suggestions and wise counsel.

And a special thanks to all of you who took the time to read this manuscript in its earlier form and make valuable suggestions. My son, Casey Brown, Jerry London, Gilbert Valdesuso, Ron and Linda Day, Esther Farber, Michael Ornstein, Michael Markman, Larry and Sharon Poston, Cliff and Vickie Mylett, Arieli-Chai Hagit, and my wife, Holly Brown, who patiently read many versions of this book adding her always valuable suggestions.

Chapter 1

I was born in Tarczyn, Poland, on October 22nd, 1917. My father told me there is a religious significance associated with October, known as 'Cheshvan.' Cheshvan is the only month that does not have any holidays or special mitzvot, which are our rules and commandments. We are taught it is "reserved" for the coming of *Moshiach,* our Jewish Messiah, a righteous scion of King David. He will rebuild the Holy Temple in Jerusalem, gather the Jewish people from all corners of the earth, and return them to the Promised Land.

While pleased to be born during such an auspicious month, I am aware this belief in Cheshvan has sustained my people throughout a 2,000-year exile fraught with pogroms, expulsions, and persecutions with our ancestors' firm belief in a better time to come, and their trust that they will be resurrected to witness this day. This belief has carried me through some difficult situations and given me hope.

The Torah has taught me that this physical world is merely a strategic challenge the soul must battle and transcend en route to a heavenly paradise. The physical has no intrinsic worth; it retains no value once its function has been fully served—it is a means to a spiritual end and constitutes the very purpose of creation.

My birth name is Eliyahu Faizylber. My father's name is Yaakov Faizylber. We children, five sisters and one brother call him 'Tate,' and my mother is Golda, or 'Mame.'.

I am twenty-two and the eldest sibling in our family. I am followed by my sisters, Guena (20), Reizl (17), Hanche (15), Pearl (10), and the twins: sister Rivka and brother Avigdor 'Avi' (8).

After living in Tarczyn for two years, we finally settled in Lodz. There are about a quarter of a million Jews living in Lodz out of an overall population of slightly more than 600,000. It is the third largest city in the country after Warsaw, our capital, and Krakow.

The neighborhood we live in is called "Baluty." It is, in fact, a large and integral part of the city. Our neighbors are working class. Everyone lives in a modest rented apartment or a small house.

My family's financial situation is standard. There is money for food but little else. Each of us has one set of clothes. When they are torn, there are no new ones; we use seamstresses to repair everything we wear.

I began my religious classes at the age of three. I was sent to Cheder, a religious school. There are no religious schools for girls in Baluty. While at Cheder, I studied the Torah, the Five Books of Moses, the foundation of all Jewish instruction and guidance. These classes taught me to look deeper, beyond one's outward appearance and behavior, beyond a person's intellect, into the depths of the heart, to find the divine spark of unconditional love.

When I was older, my sisters and I went to a local Polish public school. Before entering school, my parents changed my first name to 'Elias' although I am 'Eli' to my family. The reason for my name change was antisemitism is and was prevalent in Lodz, and they didn't wish me to be harassed or harmed. For similar reasons, Tate changed our surname from Faizlber to Feinzilberg. We have since kept that name.

From the age of thirteen to fourteen, Tate wanted me to go to a yeshiva, a Jewish educational institution focusing on the study of Rabbinic literature, primarily the Talmud and halacha (Jewish law), while Torah and Jewish philosophy are studied in parallel.

Since Tate is always working, I went with Mame to the yeshiva for the first time, and the head of the yeshiva turned his back on us. For reasons of modesty, he did not want to see my mother and told me to come back with my father. I told him that Mame was religious and there was no reason why he should not want to talk to her, but the yeshiva head insisted.

Mame did not like it and would rather I start working than study in a place like this. She recommended I learn a profession. Since Lodz is a city with many textile manufacturers, and next to us is a knitting workshop, I learned to knit sweaters.

Starting on Friday at sundown and continuing until Saturday at sunset, everything is closed to observe the Sabbath, and then on Sunday night, I go out with my friends to plays or to the cinema. Jews are not allowed to purchase tickets, but I have a workmate who looks like a Gentile who buys us tickets. Sometimes, when we are in the theater, a few Gentiles hear us speaking Yiddish and harass us, so we flee to safety.

Poles, I must explain, are taught at a young age that Jews crucified Jesus. I recall Jewish friends going to the theater and being beaten for no reason other than being Jews. But despite everything, I keep going to the theater and enjoying it.

Over the years, I've come across many cases of antisemitism. Once, I was in the park with a friend when a group of Polish gentiles beat us up simply because we were Jewish. There are places in Lodz I avoid as misguided Christians who forget the tenets of their religion and harass and beat every Jew they come across.

At Easter, which marks the resurrection of Jesus, if Jews walk in Christian neighborhoods, they could be attacked. In Churches, during Christian holidays, the priests slander and speak ill of us, exacerbating the problem.

My family and friends usually avoid trouble by staying home on Christian feast days. As for our Polish government, before World War I, the most powerful in Europe, it is riddled with antisemitic politicians. While we have Jewish representatives in parliament, they have hardly any influence. There are almost no Jews admitted to universities, and very few are allowed to study medicine, engineering, or law.

To get back to me, the most earth-shaking event in my life to date happened on November 9th, 1938, at night and continued through the 10th. Even now, as I recall *Kristallnacht,* the night of broken glass, shivers course down my spine.

German rioters, led by Hitler's Brownshirt youths, destroyed hundreds of synagogues and Jewish institutions throughout Germany, Austria, and the Sudetenland. Synagogues were burned throughout the night in full view of the public and local firefighters, who had received orders to intervene only to prevent flames from spreading to nearby buildings.

Hitler Youth members shattered shop windows of an estimated 7,500 Jewish-owned commercial establishments and looted their wares. Brownshirt youths roamed the streets, attacking Jews in their houses and forcing Jews they encountered to perform acts of public humiliation. Jewish cemeteries became particular objects of desecration in many regions.

The official figure for Jewish deaths, released by German officials in the aftermath of Kristallnacht, was 91, but witnesses suggest there were hundreds of deaths, especially if one counts those who died of their injuries in the days and weeks that followed the pogrom. Police records also document a high number of rapes and suicides in the aftermath of the violence.

Alarm spreads throughout Lodz like an infectious virus. Although this did not happen in my city, we all know it's a harbinger of things to come. Fear invades our hearts and remains there…as we await the inevitable.

And now, on September 1st, 1939, our worst apprehensions come to pass as the Wehrmacht's overwhelming forces cross into Poland, and our two countries are now at war. After the heavy shelling and bombing of Warsaw, the Polish government fled the country. Shortly after that, on September 27th, we surrendered, and all formal resistance ends on Oct. 6th.

I am aware of this unsettling news as Tate, and I walk along Limonowski Street. Tate left the textile factory where he works six days a week early this Friday as it is our custom to meet and shop for food before the Sabbath. By Jewish tradition, it is prohibited to cook on the Sabbath. Consequently, we have been shopping for our Kosher supper that Mame will prepare in just a few hours.

I hear a rumble like distant thunder. A flicker of movement draws my attention to the end of the street. I miss a step and almost fall. Tate glances at me and then turns to see what I am staring at.

Three Mercedes convertibles, their tops down, carry high-ranking officers in black be-ribboned uniforms bearing the Nazi's silver skull and crossbones emblems. They spearhead a long column of armored vehicles, tanks, motorcycles, some with sidecars.

Rooted in place, Tate and I adjust the small packages we carry and exchange troubled glances as the convertibles and the rest of at least twenty tanks roll past us, their iron tracks clattering over cobblestones, juddering the sidewalk beneath our feet—the helmet and goggle-wearing motorcycle drivers and their machine gun-carrying passengers in those odd-looking sidecars motor by.

After these come impressive-looking foot soldiers, marching four abreast, as far as the eye can see. They all seem to be giants in their steel helmets, green Waffen uniforms, ammunition belts, tall boots, and rifles slung over their shoulders. A cavalry brigade of more than 100 horseback riders, animals snorting, follow. Other, larger draft horses pull equipment and ammunition carriages. This invasion, for that's what this undoubtedly is, proceeds up the street, spewing smoke and dust, permeating the air with smells of horse dung and acidic diesel fuel.

I have never seen such a display of sheer military power. It appears the entire German Army is entering our city of Lodz on October 12th.

Pedestrians all over the street have stopped to gape. More people come out of shops and apartments to gawk, and we remain silent. I feel a growing dread as if a plague is descending upon the earth, spreading disease into all corners of our lives, a poison about to destroy life as we know it.

Incredulously, several Polish Christians begin yelling, "Heil Hitler. Heil Hitler."

Are these fools insane? I ask myself. Do they not know the nature of these Nazis?

My Jewish neighbors keep silent. Their expressions are grim, withholding expletives they dare not utter. Watching this ongoing spectacle of German military strength, Father and I pull our overcoats tighter on this cold fall day. Tate's overcoat is dark blue, and mine is grey. We each wear short-brimmed caps that would have matched the color of our coats if they weren't so faded. Beneath our head caps are our traditional Jewish kippah, the small circular head covering that's also called a yarmulke.

Tate, who is of medium height like me, wears iron-rimmed spectacles. He strokes his short, grey-streaked beard, a sign of thoughtful consideration as we watch these invaders marching past us.

As I gaze at their faces, very few appear to be my age. Most seem to be in their late teens, some even younger. Aren't these soldiers reputed to be the so-called Master Race? It's difficult for me to believe these same men/boys would obey orders to shoot and kill innocent men, women, and children without a thought of protest.

Observing this formidable display of evil, for that's what I believe they represent, I think, *How can anyone, especially unarmed Jews, fight against such a strong combat force? Impossible.*

I fear these monsters will devour us all.

Unfamiliar gloom settles over me like a heavy shroud. I am frightened, not so much for myself but for my family and friends.

Having sensed the shiver in my bones, Tate places a reassuring hand on my shoulder. "It will be all right. We're non-combatants. We will be safe. Life will go on."

Will it?

I doubt anything will ever be the same again.

"Mother is waiting," Tate says, interrupting my musings. "Come, Eli."

Clutching my packages, I follow Father along the sidewalk with the harsh sounds of marching soldiers and weaponry reverberating in my ears.

Chapter 2

Tate and I climb the stairs to our second-floor apartment, and I enter to find the family huddled around two windows facing the street, holding curtains aside as they attempt to catch glimpses of the spectacle unfolding two blocks away.

Mame and Guena are with Reizl at one window, while Hanche, Pearl, and the twins, Rivka and Avi, stand before the other window.

My mother wears a modest gray dress and her ever-present light blue tichel, a scarf married Jewish women traditionally wear to cover their hair, especially when venturing outside the home. My little brother, Avi, wears his home-sewn tan shirt and brown pants. My sisters all have sweaters on over dresses of pastel colors that fall below their knees. They are speaking in hushed undertones as they peer down at the Germans.

"Hello, my family," Tate says as we touch the Mezuzah nailed on the right side of the doorframe and kiss our fingers as is our custom.

I was eight before I learned the four-inch-tall by a-one-inch-wide brass cylinder with the tiny nine-branch candlestick embossed on its cover contained a piece of parchment with two verses. "Hear, O Israel, the Lord is our God, the Lord is One," and the commandment to "Love God with all of your heart."

Tate closes the door behind us and announces, "We come bearing food for Sabbath."

"Yaakov," Mother says, turning from the window. "Thank God you and Eli are safe. The soldiers … we were worried."

My sisters and Avi all begin talking at once—a cacophony of voices—asking Father what he thinks of the German invasion, what it will mean to our family, and whether we will be persecuted because we are Jews?

Tate holds up a hand. When the voices taper off, he says, “I am afraid nothing good will come of this.” He shrugs philosophically. “We will have to wait and see. We will talk after supper.”

Tate crosses to Mother and kisses her cheek. He gestures to our wrappings and adds, “Eli and I bring surprises.”

“Thank you, *mein zeeskeit*,” Mame says, calling him her sweetheart with a wan smile. “You continue to make miracles.”

Obviously thankful for the distraction our packages have brought, Tate heads for the kitchen with Mame, me, and my siblings following. Besides the combined parlor/kitchen, our home has three small bedrooms. Avi and I share one, my mother and father have their own room, and my five sisters occupy the largest bedroom. With the convenience of chamber pots, we all share the single bathroom on the first floor below us without getting into too many disagreements with our neighbors. It is tight living, but we are content and relatively happy.

Besides its sink, running water, and squat little icebox, our kitchen area’s main feature is Mame’s cast-iron stove. The original occupants left it behind when they moved out many years ago. It is still in good condition and gives off enough heat when she is cooking to warm the front of our apartment. Coal is expensive, so we light up the stove only to cook our meals on the coldest days.

Tate and I place our bundles on the long kitchen table as Mame joins us. There is seating for all of us, with two mismatched benches and Tate’s armchair at the far end—a chair that squeaks every time he sits.

My siblings crowd in as Mame begins to unwrap packages. Carrots appear, along with a fat onion, a jar of milk, four eggs, and a packet of flour, which I know Mother will mix with a pinch of kosher salt and sugar to make noodles.

Mame's face lights up as she unwraps two medium-sized pieces of pike and whitefish. "Oh, Yaakov, I was worried I wouldn't be able to make Gefilte Fish for Sabbath."

"God provides," he responds simply.

"And now we have enough ingredients to bake two loaves of challah."

"Yes!" Hanche exclaims. "I love the smell of bread baking."

"Can I have two fish balls?" Avi asks.

"Me too," Rivka, his twin, adds.

As my other sisters chime in with their requests, I am almost salivating as I imagine a dinner of Gefilte fish, noodles with carrots and onions, and freshly baked challah bread. Mame will begin cooking almost immediately as she likes to have supper prepared well before sunset. Like my siblings, I, too, anticipate the yeasty aroma of baking bread filling our apartment.

I look around and see that our shopping is a success and has momentarily diverted everyone's attention from the threat outside.

"Oh, Yaakov…" Mame's face lights up as she lifts the contents of the last small package—chocolate—her favorite delicacy.

My siblings all ask at once, "Can I have a bite? Just a little piece, please, please."

Mame smiles. "I can't hear a word you're saying."

We all protest as she sniffs the prized morsels, inhaling deeply. "Heavenly... How did you ever manage?"

Tate suppresses a smile. "The fish or the chocolate?"

"Both. But mostly the chocolate."

I answer for us, "Mr. Swartz set the fish aside for us, knowing we would be stopping by."

"The chocolate…" Mame says.

"Ah," Yaakov says. "Ada, at the fish shop, made it herself and saved it, especially for you."

"Bless her. I will write a note and thank her for her thoughtfulness."

Suddenly, the parlor windows rattle and shake, and we exchange startled looks. Shocked into silence, we listen. A deep, reverberating rumble, ever-increasing, engulfs the apartment. All I can think of is the coal mines of Lodz are exploding, shaking the earth. No, I'm not hearing explosions. It's something else.

The decibels increase. We dash to the parlor windows and yank back the curtains. We gasp.

The sky is crowded with hundreds, maybe thousands of Luftwaffe bombers and squadrons of Messerschmidt fighter planes. I've been told the Luftwaffe is the aerial branch of the Wehrmacht, the armed forces of Nazi Germany. They fly in V formations, stretching across the sky as far as the eye can see. In my mind's eye, they resemble dark-winged vultures as their shadows pass over our upturned faces. Their altitude is earth-shakingly low, clearly displaying the Luftwaffe's black iron cross insignia on their fuselages. It's a warning as if to say, 'Look at us, we are the mighty German Air Force. We rule the skies. We are invincible.'

The thundering engines are obviously meant to intimidate and frighten. It works, and a chill courses down my spine. At this moment, I feel the Germans are indeed the superior military race, unbeatable, not only on land but also in the air. What chance does the small population of Jews in our city have to survive against the mightiest fighting force in Europe?

"Why have the Germans come to Lodz?" Pearl asks.

Tate frowns. The question requires a complicated answer. He finally says, "I'm afraid they have thoughts of conquest in mind."

It's more insidious than that.

From the stories I've heard, Adolf Hitler fervently hates Jews, and it's common knowledge he has promoted this hatred since his rise to power in 1933. Once he gained control over Germany, he commanded that all Jewish businesses be boycotted, and all Jews be dismissed from civic-service posts. In that very same year, the writings of Jewish authors were burned in communal ceremonies across the country. Businesses were commanded to no longer service Jews. Then, in Sept. 1935, the new Nuremberg Laws ordered that only Aryans could be full German citizens, and it became illegal for Aryans to marry or have intercourse with Jews.

I swallow hard, suspecting that Hitler's actions will only worsen over time.

"Tate," I say. "We must leave Poland."

"Yes, Tate," Pearl adds. "We have to go someplace where people don't hate us."

"If it were that easy," Tate replies, "we'd be already gone. Your mother and I have been discussing such a move for over a year, but moving costs money we don't have."

Not wishing to add to my father's financial woes, I keep quiet, thinking, as the eldest, it is time for me to do something dramatic. For the past few weeks, I have been mulling over a plan to get a higher-paying job, and now, with the arrival of the Germans, I feel a new sense of urgency. My current place of employment is at a Jewish home for refugees, and while the work is satisfying, the salary is negligible. I need to find a better position in a city that reserves the best jobs for Christians.

A thought comes to me: I'll just become a Christian. In name only, of course. It shouldn't be too difficult, as aside from Yiddish, I speak fairly good street Polish, having learned it at school, even though I had to drop out after the seventh grade to help support our growing family. I have also learned Christian prayers by heart from some of my Catholic friends. I can make the sign of the cross and utter the words, '*Jezus Krisus. Matka Boska.*' Even my old work clothes will work as many Christians wear similar garments as they are in the same financial straits as my family.

My plan is set. I will quit my job tomorrow. No, I will wait until I am hired and on a new job, then I will quit the Jewish home for refugees and break the news to the family. With a new rise in salary,

I am confident I will be able to save enough money to help us relocate to a friendly country where Jews are tolerated.

Of course, if the Nazis discover my subterfuge, I will probably be shot, but I believe God will protect me, and I am determined to proceed. That settled, and I tune back into the family's conversation.

"...and if the Germans hate us," Rivka says, "Why don't they just pay us to leave?"

"Rivka," Tate says, "that's a very good question."

"It's cheaper just to kill us," Avi says from where he and Mother stand in the kitchen doorway.

"Avi," Mame replies, chastening him. "No talk of killing, please."

"Well," Pearl says. "From a financial point of view, he's right."

Tate raises a hand. "Enough of such morbid subjects."

"Where will we go if we leave Lodz?" Hanche asks.

"There are possibilities," Tate says. "Jews are accepted and treated as equals in Romania, Lithuania, Portugal, even Japan. Russia is open to Jews, but they can't be trusted. I've heard they send us to Siberia to work as slaves."

"Maybe Switzerland?" little Avi suggests.

"Yes, it's very pretty," responds Rivka. "It has beautiful mountains and—"

"Switzerland is only for the rich," Mame interrupts.

"Children, as I said before, your mother and I will discuss this subject later tonight."

"That reminds me, someone has to make supper." Mother leaves us and enters the kitchen area. She takes a handful of carrots to the sink and begins peeling.

Father follows her, offering, "May I help peel?"

"No, no, there's only one peeler." After a moment, she says, "Yaakov, I don't like being at the mercy of these anti-Semitics."

"The Poles are anti-Semitic too," he says, moving beside her.

"Not nearly to the same extent. We have Polish friends whose company we enjoy, and our children, for the most part, get along and play together. Yes, there are exceptions, Yaakov, but the Germans are another breed. Hitler is a sick, dangerous man; he plans to drive the Jews out of Poland or worse."

"Golda, I am as worried as you are. But, for the moment, we must wait and see what this occupation means for us. One thing in our favor: Jews are a labor force. The Nazis need us to fuel their war machine."

"I wouldn't count on it," Mame says. "Hate blinds common sense."

"True, Golda, but always remember, I will protect you and our family with every ounce of my strength." Yaakov leans in and kisses her gently on the side of her neck.

She turns quickly and kisses him full on the lips. Then, looking into his eyes, she says, "I know you will, *mein zeeskeit*. I love you. I love you with every fiber of my body. I know you'll do what's best for the family."

He smiles. "I will try."

Gratified and a little embarrassed to have been eavesdropping on my parents from the archway, I turn to my siblings. "Guena, will you play something for us?"

"Yes, Guena," Avi begs.

"Please, please," adds Rivka.

Mother and Father step to the front room, their faces brightening. "Yes," Mame says. "Chase away those dreadful sounds outside."

"Play, Guena," Father urges. "A little music to remind us of our heritage."

My sister, who never needs much encouragement to play her violin, says, "Since you have all asked so nicely, I will. But only if Reizl and Hanche help Mother with supper."

"I don't need help. Please, play Guena."

We find seats as Guena opens the brown leather case holding her violin and withdraws the beautiful instrument formerly owned by a Russian violin maestro who lives on the floor below us. When the maestro discovered Guena's love of music, he offered her free violin lessons. Our parents thought it was a magnanimous offer and allowed her to accept. Guena was nine at the time.

Over a decade later, when the maestro passed away, he left the violin to my sister with a note informing my parents that she was the most gifted student he had ever taught and that he expected them to continue her studies because Guena was sure to become a concert violinist.

Now, at nineteen, Guena has already played in several prestigious recitals and, as her new instructor says, will soon be a candidate for the Warsaw Orchestra, Poland's finest.

Guena lifts the violin to her chin, hovers the bow above its strings, pauses for a dramatic moment, and then begins to play 'Chiribim Chiribom.' The lyrics of this piece have been in our home since before I was born.

Music has always affected me; my mother says it turns me into a mensch. This piece touches my heart, transporting me into another more ethereal and fervent dimension than my everyday self. When moved by the harmonies of music, I can become a poet, a lover, a soldier, another person who is ready to write beautiful sonnets, fall into bed with a lusty woman, or charge into battle and fight to the death. Not a bad thing. So, when I find myself humming with the lyrics I know so well, my mind plays with my emotions.

Germany's invasion of Poland terrifies me, not so much for myself, but for my family. How dare they invade Lodz, a peaceful city! With fear and anger wrestling with one another, I wonder how today's events will affect us. Will the Jewish population be persecuted as they are in Germany? Very likely, I believe.

My thoughts are distracted as Pearl begins to sing along in her small, pretty voice. A moment later, Reizl and Hanche are harmonizing. The twins, Avi and Rivka, also begin to sing.

'Come on, kids, let's sing
All together a song,
A ... tune
With cheerful words.
Us mom's cooking noodle soup,
Dumplings and porridge
Come Purim,
We turn spinning tops
Chiribim, chiribom
Once our Rebbe was walking along the road.
Suddenly out of nowhere
It rained heavily.
Shouts our Rabbi the cloud:
"Stop pouring water!"
All the Hasidim came out dry-
Only-
The Rebbe is completely soaked
Chiribim, chiribom.'

I feel a tug in my heart. Now I hear my frog of a voice as I join my sisters—eliciting a raised eyebrow from my mother, but then she smiles.

My father's deep baritone joins the chorus. Mother takes his hand in hers and sings along, leaning into him, her pillar of strength.

At moments like this, I forget all the disagreements I have ever had with my siblings. A unifying spirit has taken hold of me and reminds me of the value of family and the love between us. Perhaps it's the troubling times that have awakened my sentimental feelings. Whatever it is, I am moved to sing louder.

Guena flashes me a disturbing look but then ignores me and plays on.

Music is a necessary balm, binding us together and fulfilling our need to momentarily escape these troubled times. As we sing, tears well and run, dropping like lost dreams. My family's faces are wet, and rivulets stream down their cheeks. Those of us who are sitting stand, and we all join hands. We form a circle and begin to dance.

My heart aches as I realize this may be the last family time we enjoy together in Lodz. Our lives are about to be altered by a force as evil as any I have ever imagined. It is impossible to fathom the heartbreak and horrors the Germans must be planning for us, but I know this moment is special, and one may never be repeated.

Guena's fingers dance on the neck of her instrument, her bow flies, and my parents and siblings are a blur. I clench my eyes, squeezing tears as I attempt to push aside premonitions that pierce my mind as sharply as if a dagger has penetrated my skull—I can see the hilt—it is crowned by a swastika.

Chapter 3

The Sabbath starts as an uneventful day, with my parents and siblings observing our age-old tradition of spending time focused on Yahweh. It is not a time to discuss the commonplace or even the eventful incursion and threat of the Germans. This is when we study the Torah and learn God's Word. If Yahweh commands that a person refrain from commerce, pleasures, and work on the Sabbath, it follows that conversations involving these things should also be avoided. Our actions, thoughts, and discussions on this day should, in some fashion, reflect on God and honor Him.

Tate and Mame take us all to our neighborhood temple, where we pray for our people, our city, and for the peace in the world. I also pray especially for my parents; they are under a great deal of stress as they struggle to protect and feed us. I worry about them. Now, more so than ever. What would I do if I were in their position with seven children to raise? I don't really know. I sometimes think they're miracle workers simply to feed us.

Generally, on the Sabbath, I can hardly wait until sundown when I can go outside and meet with my friends and perhaps watch a play or see a film in the movie theater. This evening, though, I do something I never do. I go for a walk by myself.

It's a unique feeling to really pay attention to my surroundings. For the first time, I become aware of what is happening to Lodz and to the Jews in our community. I see Jewish-owned shops and markets that have been closed. I notice older Hassidic Jews in their distinctive black outfits scurrying around, not walking but moving rapidly on the sidewalks as if they're afraid of being molested.

I notice groups of young Polish men loitering. They look like toughs to me, like the Dankowski gang of thugs that live a few blocks away and make it a practice to harass and rob Jews. One thing I really become aware of is that there are no single young women on the streets, be they Jewish or Christian.

I realize that my neighborhood has changed, and not for the better. God only knows what's going to happen to us now with the Nazis in charge. Already, they are adding fear to our neighborhood with their antisemitic rules and regulations.

I think I've seen enough for tonight. I'm going home. I should have joined my friends and gone to see a movie.

***

The following morning, Tate and I, having risen before the rest of the family to go to work, are in the kitchen with Mother, eating our usual bowl of porridge for breakfast.

"Eli," Tate says. "Your mother and I discussed our situation last night now that the Germans have arrived."

I notice mother and father exchange worried looks. My heart goes out to them. I wish there is something I could say or do that would help our vulnerable situation, but I can think of nothing.

Tate continues, "Because we lack the funds for our family to travel, we have no choice but to stay in Lodz. We realize the German threat is real, especially after Kristallnacht, but the sad fact is we have no alternative."

Knowing how my parents must be feeling, I have to try and help. I suggest, "Tate, perhaps we can move out to the country where we have relatives. We could stay with them."

Mame offers a weak smile at my trying to be helpful. "That was among the first things we discussed, Eli. But with the size of our family, it would be an unbearable hardship to place on relatives who would take us in. We can't do that to anyone."

Tate adds, "And even if someone did take us in, Eli, you and I would be out of work. So, we are stuck here with no options."

Tate's right. I can see my parent's depression on their drawn faces.

Suddenly aware I'm not breathing, I take in a breath and affect a lopsided grin. It's a façade, but I can't let my parents see my hopelessness since it will only make them feel worse.

I say, "I'm going to look for a better-paying job. I can save the extra money I earn and buy us train tickets, 4th class, of course. We can go to Portugal or Spain or wherever Jews are not persecuted, just so long as it's out of Poland."

It's a fantasy, of course. But mother and father are silent, not wishing to dishearten me. I feel blessed to have such parents.

"A good idea, Eli," Mame says with a solemn smile. "In the meantime, we'll make do. We always have. The Germans can't stay here forever."

I don't respond, but I consider: what if they do stay here forever? What happens to us then?

While this troubling thought filters through my mind, I remember my father talking of a speech given by a man named David Ben-Gurion. He is the leader of British-ruled Mandatory Palestine. He was born in Ptonsk, Poland, not too far from where we live, and migrated to Eretz, Israel, several years ago.

He recently returned to Poland to enlist Jews to immigrate to the Holy Land. He warned us that there is a great danger for us living here. But before we could leave, it would be necessary for us to undergo training to learn how to work the earth so we could make a living as farmers in Israel. Once this training is completed and with the financial help of Zionist sponsors, we could travel. But, Tate and I were unable to take time off from our jobs to take the course. So, that opportunity has slipped by.

"Time to go," Tate announces as he rises from the table.

Within minutes, we are out the door and walking down the street. Coming toward us, I see Jan Katzenel, an old family friend. He is the grey-haired writer for the Yiddish newspaper *Lodzer Naje Folkscagtung*.

He tips his hat to us as he hurriedly approaches. "Shalom, Yaakov, Eli," he says.

We exchange 'good mornings,' and Tate asks, "Any news on the German occupation?"

"Yes, some good, some not so good. The German Army that has bivouacked on the outskirts of Lodz is pulling out, leaving for the Western Front first thing in the morning."

Can this be true? If so, it's surprising and amazing news. But what did Jan mean when he said he had 'not so good' news?

As if anticipating my question, Jan says, "As soon as the Wehrmacht forces move out, they are being replaced by SS and Gestapo troops for a virtual occupation."

"*Mein Got*," Tate responds, the color draining from his face.

I've heard stories about the SS and their treatment of Jews, and we all know they are far worse than Wehrmacht troops, and the Gestapo is reputed to be even worse than the SS. These new arrivals will have a devastating effect on the Jews of Lodz.

"I am sorry to be the bearer of such news, but my article on the subject will be in print tomorrow for everyone to read."

Tate asks, "Do you have any idea how long this *occupation* is going to last?"

"Hitler's plans?" Jan shakes his head. "We have yet to find out. But from everything I've heard, the Fuhrer plans to annex Poland."

"We're a sovereign country," I protest.

"We're a *conquered* country," Jan corrects me, "subject to the will of our conqueror. *'To the victor belongs the spoils'* is an old adage Adolf Hitler is certain to uphold. My suggestion is for every able-bodied Jew to leave this country as soon as possible. Now, I must be off to write my story and warn every Jew in Lodz of the coming apocalypse. These are terrible times." He tips his hat to us. "Shalom."

"Shalom," Tate and I respond as Jan hurries away.

I glance at Tate. His face is drawn, his worry lines more pronounced. Aware of his burdens, I know he is thinking of us, his family, and realizing there is very little, if anything, he can do to change the tides of war. I feel we're on a sinking ship with no life preservers.

***

Two days later, Tate and I are again walking to work when people suddenly begin to hurry and run past us. Approaching Limonowski Street, I hear voices.

"Nazis."

"SS."

"Gestapo."

The commotion continues with people exiting shops, apartments, and places of work. We quicken our step, and as we turn the corner, we stop in our tracks.

Two black Mercedes convertibles are driving up the cobblestone street toward us. The cloth tops are down, revealing two high-ranking Nazi officers sitting in the back of each vehicle. The men in the first car wear the black uniforms of the dreaded Gestapo, with their silver skulls and crossbones displayed on caps and collars. Each man wears a Swastika armband.

The bemedaled officers in the second Mercedes wear the dark green uniforms of the Waffen-SS infantry.

Following, in long lines, four abreast, are the regular SS infantry. They wear dark green uniforms with steel helmets, ammunition belts, and tall boots. Most carry long rifles, but the first ranks hold short-barreled submachine guns.

The shouts and greetings of "Heil Hitler!" from our Polish neighbors when we met the Wehrmacht Army's arrival a few days ago are missing. The crowd seems to sense these troops are an entirely different group of invaders.

The Gestapo and SS officers' faces are stoic, and their forbidding demeanor makes me believe the stories I've heard of their brutality toward Jews. I look at my father, and I can read his thoughts;

they are mine, too. These men are the perpetrators of antisemitism and the indiscriminate slaughter of innocents, and now they are in our city.

There are no tanks, field artillery, or munitions. But there are supply trucks, at least a dozen of them. It dawns on me this is the occupation force. They are planning to stay in Lodz.

My eyes are riveted to this marching hoard of invaders, an approaching thunderstorm, a tempest that is certain to bring loss and sorrow. Several soldiers gaze in my direction. Their expressions are as cold as ice.

I shiver. I've never seen killers before, but their soulless eyes tell me this is what they must be. It doesn't take much imagination for me to visualize one command from their superiors, and they will turn their weapons on us and unleash a rain of death.

I can't take my eyes off these devils, for I am certain that's what they are, as they march rhythmically up the street—my street. The crowds around Tate and I stare with ashen faces at the menace permeating the air.

"We should go," Tate says, touching my arm. "We'll take the back streets."

I nod, and with a last look at the invaders, we backtrack to a side street and proceed to our places of work.

As we walk along the cobblestones, I am more and more certain that my family is in grave danger. By circumstance and lack of funds, every Jew in Lodz is trapped in a city about to be governed by anti-Semitic Nazis. My question now is, what happens next?

***

It's Friday, the day before Sabbath once again. Having worked my customary half-day, I arrive home to find my mother, brother, and sisters sitting around the kitchen table, unusually quiet, with anxious faces. I don't see Father. "Where is Tate?" I ask, unbuttoning my overcoat.

"He came home and went right away to the synagogue to hear the latest news," Mame answers.

Halfway out of my overcoat, I slip it back on.

"Where are you going?" Mame asks.

"To the synagogue. I'm curious to find out what the Germans are up to."

"It's too dangerous," Mame responds. "There are SS patrols out on the streets."

"I'm going," I reply with resolve. "I have to make sure Tate is safe."

Mame looks at me for a long moment, then nods. "Go. But be careful. We don't know yet what these demons are planning."

I button up my overcoat. "I'll be careful."

"Eli," Guena says. "I'll go with you."

"I want to go too," Hanche adds, and then all my siblings are asking to accompany me.

"No," Mame says. "No one is leaving except for Eli."

As the protests continue, Mame adds firmly, "Eli will go alone."

Minutes later, I am on Limanowski Street, hurrying toward our synagogue, a fifteen-minute walk. The afternoon is cold with a grey, overcast sky. The sidewalk is covered with two inches of fresh snow that fell overnight.

The streets are alive with German armored vehicles, a few Polish sedans filled with families and luggage, and isolated groups of Polish citizens scurrying along the sidewalks as if to avoid an imminent deluge. The Nazis could be that storm.

A motorcycle and sidecar manned by SS soldiers drive by, and the Aryans give me the eye. I pray they won't stop and hassle me.

Six blocks later, I turn the corner onto Wiznera Street and almost collide with a very large SS soldier with three companions.

My heart jumps. This soldier is enormous, almost a foot taller than my 5 foot 6 inches, and he must outweigh me by seventy or eighty pounds. Even though I am strong and seldom intimidated, this giant gives me the creeps and his face doesn't help—he resembles a snarling Rottweiler.

I manage to say, "Excuse me."

The soldier growls something in German I don't understand.

Shaking, I mutter one of the few Aryan phrases I know, "*Ich spreche kein Deutsch*," which I hope translates to 'I don't speak German."

There must be something wrong with my pronunciation as Rottweiler-face stares blankly.

I try Yiddish, knowing it is close to his language. "I do not speak German."

The soldier's lip curls.

I quickly add what I hope is an acceptable smile and move to step around him. My arm is grabbed by what feels like an iron clamp. Wincing, I try not to cry as his fingers dig into my flesh.

He leans in close to me.

I press my thighs together, praying I won't embarrass myself by peeing.

"Juden?" he asks in a voice tainted with the smell of beer.

I move my lips, but no words come out.

"*Ich spreche kein Deutsch*?" he taunts, throwing my words back at me.

All I'm capable of is a nod.

His mouth turns into a snarl. "Juden?"

I am going to pee.

The SS soldier barks out a laugh. He lets go of my arm, but before I can escape, he knocks my cap off and sneers at my yarmulka. "Ya, Juden," he proclaims to his companions.

"Ja. Ja. Ja," they respond like baying hounds.

Rottweiler-face grabs my yarmulka off my head, holds it in front of me, and then spits on it.

I gasp. Shock and horror transfix me. Also, a spark of anger ignites.

He throws my yarmulka to the sidewalk. He grins and then stomps on it, grinding it through the snow and into the cobblestones.

His guttural snigger inflames me.

His companions join in, laughing hilariously.

Heat streaks up my neck, flushing my cheeks. Rottweiler-face suddenly punches me on the side of my left eye.

Seeing stars, I stagger in the slush but manage to keep upright. Ears ringing, I stare defiantly at him.

Rottweiler-face pushes his canine-like face close to mine and swears, spittle flying, "*Schwien*! *Schau mich ja nicht an*!"

His words, I believe, translate to, "Swine! Do not look at me!"

I keep staring.

He lashes out, his fist smashing into my mouth.

Blood spurts from my split lip. Furious but not stupid, I look down, humiliated and angry.

Then, having had his fun, he turns away, and he and his companions saunter off, their chortles burning my ears.

My brain afire, I stoop and retrieve my cap and yarmulka. I wipe off snow and grit. I replace the yarmulka on my head, followed by my hat, which I pull down hard. My heart is thundering. I suddenly realize I am going to do something stupid. Will I be killed? Possibly. No, make that probably.

I look behind me. I am two hundred feet from the corner of Czarwona Street. I know there is an alley fifty feet beyond, and after that, another one. With a slim hope of survival, but no longer caring, I unbutton my overcoat, knowing it will give me an advantage if these brutes chase after me, as they will be hampered by their buttoned-up greatcoats. Buoyed by the knowledge that I am one of the fastest runners in my neighborhood, I scoop up a large handful of snow and squeeze it tightly into a ball. Taking a breath, I throw the snowball as hard as possible and yell, "Hey!"

Rottweiler-face turns to look—the snowball hits his face!

I did it!

Snarling, wiping slush from his face, he grabs his rifle, unslinging it.

And me, I'm laughing and crying and running as fast as I can.

I hear the huge German bellowing indecipherable words as his companions laugh hysterically.

Running, slipping, almost falling on the icy sidewalk, I can't resist a quick look.

The big soldier is working the bolt action on his rifle, chambering a round.

Oh, God...

I resume full speed ... another forty feet, until I reach the corner.

Will I make it?

I know I cannot outrun a bullet. My heart sinks. I can almost feel the lead projectile slamming into my back, ending my life.

What have I done? Tate, Mame, my brother, my sisters, I am so sorry—

BANG!

The brick wall of the building beside me sparks as the bullet hits and ricochets off.

Almost to the corner, I hazard another look.

Rottweiler-face's rifle is being held to the side by one of his laughing comrades, who must have pushed the barrel just as Rottweiler-face pulled the trigger!

Thank God for one good German, I think, my feet slipping as I round the corner.

Ahead of me, the snow-covered sidewalk and road are relatively empty in this section of Lodz except for a few pedestrians carrying luggage—and luckily, not a soldier in sight.

Chest burning, I reach the next corner, turn onto the street, and release a breath. I slow my run to a trot and then to a brisk walk. I touch my split lip, and my fingers come away bloody, but I can feel the cut is small.

I know I dare not slow down as I turn another corner. I must put distance between myself and the irate SS soldier. He is sure to come after me. Although, by the time he rounds the first corner, it will be too late. I will have lost him in the maze of streets that lay ahead.

Later, when I see I am not being followed, I begin to laugh. Ouch! It hurts, but I laugh anyway until tears stream down my cheeks—even though my left eye socket aches where the putz's first punch hit me—I still laugh.

To increase my odds of escaping, I decide to walk several blocks out of my way to reach the synagogue, and I am on Sarego Street now, a snow-covered, tree-lined avenue nestled between two stately boulevards where many upper-class Poles and Jews live. The rich who inhabit these elegant homes and mansions are owners of textile mills, politicians, bankers, successful lawyers, doctors, and wealthy businessmen, a far cry from my neighborhood of small shop owners, clerks, and laborers in the textile factories and coal mines.

As I walk along, I am struck by the large number of families exiting their homes, most adults carrying a suitcase.

A group of high-ranking Gestapo and SS officers stand in the street beside two large Mercedes, supervising what appears to be evictions.

The ranking Gestapo officer is pointing his baton at a beautiful mansion as SS soldiers hustle a Hasidic family, a father, a mother, and four young children, out of the front door.

The husband wears a large, wide-brimmed hat, a long black coat, and a thick beard with stringy curls bouncing on each side of his face as he leads his family down a row of steps. The woman is dressed conservatively in a dark blue overcoat that covers her dress and a matching silk tichel to cover her hair. The soldiers are roughly prodding them with rifles, hassling them for no apparent reason.

Approaching another Hasidic couple with their children in tow, I hold up my hand. "Excuse me," I say, stopping them. "Where is everyone going?"

Large blue eyes behind iron-rimmed glasses appraise my disheveled appearance.

Inadvertently, I raise a hand to the side of my face where I was hit. I wince. A lump has blossomed around my eye. I know from experience it will soon be black and blue. The Hasidic man's gaze drops to my sweat-soaked shirt, apparent beneath my open overcoat. He backs up a step, saying, "Jews are being evicted from our homes, our valuables stolen. I don't know about the neighbors, but we're on our way to the train station. We're leaving Lodz. We won't be returning."

The woman, red-eyed from crying, adds, "The Nazis banged on our door and demanded we leave immediately, ordering us to carry only one suitcase each for all our possessions. We had only ten minutes to leave! We've left everything, my family's antiques, paintings, silver, photos, all our clothes. Those animals are in our house now, stealing everything. These people are barbarians."

"Heartless swine," the husband adds. "If we refused to leave, they said they would shoot us, our children too. I didn't believe them until I heard shots from next door. They killed our neighbors, the entire Leipzig family, including three young children, and murdered them in cold blood for not vacating fast enough. We're leaving this madness. If you value your life, I suggest you do the same as fast as you can."

At a loss for words, I simply nod and watch as they move off down the snow-covered street.

I gaze around. Other Jews, young and old, homeless now, frightened, are carrying scant possessions, straggling along the street as sadly as if in a funeral procession.

The speed and cold efficiency of the Reich's assault upon our Jewish residents is shocking. It's only been a bit more than a week since the Germans entered Lodz, and already they are evicting Jews, robbing them, beating them, and shooting those who argue or refuse to evacuate. Shooting them! It's murder. A living nightmare.

A rare emotion steals into my psyche—hate. It pumps venom through every artery, permeating my being. I am shaking, yet at the same time, I am also awed by the Nazis' expert organization, their discipline, and their terrifying effectiveness.

I walk on, passing more evicted families who seem dazed as they hold onto a few possessions, dragging their packs, deserting their homes, leaving behind memories of years of their lives, cringing like beaten dogs.

Unable to respond with more than gritted teeth, I head for Bankowa Park, with its large expanse of greenery. I need to cleanse my mind to see lawns, flowers, trees, and water ponds. I can only hope this example of eviction of the wealthy and well-to-do from their homes doesn't extend to my much poorer neighborhood.

Buoyed by that somewhat guilty but hopeful thought, I realize I can save time by cutting through the park's common area to the synagogue.

As I approach Bankowa Park, I stop abruptly, almost slipping on the slushy trail. Before me, covering a huge snow-covered area of the park, are the SS and Gestapo's supply trucks, all parked in symmetrical quadrants resembling a giant game board laid out like deadly chess pieces. Beyond these trappings, I see workers clearing snow from dozens of tents. Amid this display of Nazi might, soldiers are hustling about, as busy as worker ants. I suddenly realize these men won't want to be sleeping out in the open for long. They will all soon be taking over additional Jewish properties. No home or apartment is safe.

Worried I may be drawing unwanted attention to myself, I hasten to a familiar trail that leads through Bankowa's woods, circumventing the open spaces. Fortunately, I have the snowy path to myself.

Minutes later, having successfully evaded the enemy, I sigh with a feeling of accomplishment and walk out onto Leibniz Street. I quicken my steps, striding three blocks to our modest two-story, red-bricked synagogue. Finding the front of the building deserted, I hurry up the steps.

As I enter, I am immediately confronted by a large room full of Polish, Hebrew, and Yiddish-speaking Jews, all talking at once. I recognize many, having seen them in my neighborhood.

I spot Father by the podium at the front of the room. He is talking to two of his oldest friends, Aaron Orlanski and Ira Golabek.

I move toward them, picking my way through the crowd, nodding to acquaintances, who give me odd looks. I self-consciously touch my cut lip, which still bleeds a bit. There's nothing I can do about it or the wet, perspiration-soaked shirt that sticks to my chest like another layer of skin.

"Shalom," I announce as I join Father and his friends.

Tate's eyebrows arch. "Eli, what has happened to you? Your lip is cut and bleeding and you have a red bump by your eye."

How to explain? I give it a try. "A thug hit me. Actually, it was an SS soldier."

"Pig!" Ira Golabek declares.

"Why did he hit you?" Aaron Orlanski asks.

"Well, he hit me *after* I stared at him when he asked me not to." I won't worry Father by telling him about my yarmulka episode and that I was almost killed.

He shakes his head. "Eli, these are dangerous times. You must be more careful. Use the brains God gave you." Concern wrinkles his forehead. "Besides the bump and the cut lip, you are okay?"

"I'm fine. I'm good."

"Don't mention this to your mother."

"I won't," I reply, knowing it's best if I don't tell Father about the snowball incident either.

I add, "On the way here, I came down Sarego Street. The neighborhood is being taken over by Nazis. Jews are being evicted so SS officers and soldiers can move into their homes. And those who refuse to leave are shot on the spot." I pause, taking a breath. "We must do something to stop them, Tate."

"Yes, I agree," Father says. "These evictions and killings are happening all over Lodz. That's why we're here, to discuss our options. We're forming a committee to see what we can do to stop them. Rabbi Huberband should be here any moment now. He's been speaking to the German commanding officers and our Hitler-loving Mayor, Werner Ventzki. The Rabbi will tell us what to expect and how we can fight back without being murdered in the process."

"A waste of breath and time," Aaron states. "We must leave Lodz. I read Jan Katzenel's piece in the newspaper. He states in no uncertain terms that these Nazi anti-Semites are out to kill us and wipe us off the face of the earth. Poland is going to end up as part of Germany. That's Hitler's plan. You all know how Nazis treat Jews there."

Raised voices attract our attention to the front door. Rabbi Huberband, a tall, thin man in his sixties with spectacles and a flowing grey beard, has entered. He's been encircled by the crowd and is being inundated with questions.

Father says, "Let us hope the Rabbi brings good news."

Rabbi Huberband holds up a hand for silence. When the crowd quiets down, he makes his way through them to the podium, a few feet from us.

"I have news from the German command and our Mayor, Werner Ventzki," the rabbi says.

The room quiets as we all wait for the rabbi's next words.

"It's not good. I was told there will be new restrictions on Jews, as well as Poles. The new rulings will be published and distributed within hours, but I was given a copy by Arthur Greiser, the Nazi representative who is in charge of the armed forces. He also told me in no uncertain terms that Hitler plans to rename Lodz and turn it into a German city."

My father and his friends exchange anxious murmurs.

"They also plan to transplant 40,000 Germans into Lodz, evicting Poles and Jews, but mostly Jews, from their homes, handing them over to the new arrivals. There will be no compensation whatsoever."

I exchange a worried look with my father as the crowd reacts angrily.

Rabbi adds, "There is no doubt we are in for a difficult and challenging time." He withdraws a large paper poster from his pocket. "I was given a list of Nazi Decrees that I was told will go into effect immediately. These new rulings will be posted everywhere in the city." Unfolding the sheet, he says, "The first decree states that all Jews over the age of ten are to wear an armband on their right arms. The armband is to be white with a blue Star of David."

"This is branding us like animals," Aaron states angrily as those around him murmur in agreement.

"It is what it is," Rabbi says. "There's more. There's another law that prohibits Jewish children and young adults from attending school. All Jewish schools are immediately shut down, and Jewish teachers are fired. This includes Jewish college professors."

An uproar fills the room.

My thoughts jump to my siblings, and the debilitating effects this will have on their scholastic dreams now turned to ash.

"It is not only we Jews who are being persecuted," Rabbi continues, "the Poles, too, have restrictions. They, like us, will no longer be allowed to go to the theatre, cinema, or museums. We will also be given instructions with designated hours when and where we can shop."

Boos erupt, reverberating through the hall.

"There's more. Jews will no longer be able to own businesses. And all Jews and Poles over the age of fourteen now must work for the Germans."

I grind my teeth. As I don't speak German, my plan to impersonate a Christian and secure a higher-paying job just disappeared.

"And this…" Rabbi continues. "Germans are allowed to beat Jews, and Poles too, and there is no one to whom they can complain about it."

Angry murmurs again fill the hall.

Rabbi raises his hand for silence. "Germans can also confiscate Jewish property without being offered any compensation whatsoever."

There is now stunned silence.

Father and I exchange nervous looks, knowing this could include our apartment.

"Evicted Jews are each allowed only one suitcase in which to carry all their possessions."

A voice from the back of the room shouts, "Who owns a suitcase?"

"Maybe the Nazis will pass them out in exchange for our homes," a tall man cynically wisecracks.

Rabbi continues, "Jews will no longer be allowed to stroll in parks, enter cafes, or ride in airplanes, trains, cars, or trams. But they are allowing us to ride bicycles."

More angry murmurings fill the hall.

"There's more. We are forbidden to walk on the sidewalks of our main streets. We must walk in the gutters."

"No! This is *farkakte*! Never!" voices rise in unity.

"And this is not the worst of it. Listen…" Rabbi hesitates while the crowd simmers down.

He folds the paper and pockets it. His face seems to have aged as he looks at the congregation, waiting until the last murmurs fade. "Starting next week, all Jews are required to work on the Sabbath. No exceptions for any reason."

Silence leads to bewildered faces.

Rabbi continues before the group can react vociferously, "And to ensure compliance, the last line on the poster states: Anyone, man, woman, or child, who refuses to follow these dictates will be executed."

Defiant murmurs surround me as the gravity of these decrees weighs upon us. The Nazis' orders are brutal and inhumane. They are ordering us to dig our own graves.

"Rabbi," Father says. "What can we do? We can't stand around waiting like farm animals to be slaughtered."

Ira says, "If we could get our hands on guns, we could at least give them a fight."

"The only way to get weapons is to kill the Germans," Aaron states.

"And how do we kill these soldiers?" Father asks.

"With hammers, shovels, knives, with my teeth if necessary."

"Suicide," Rabbi responds. "You would be committing suicide. There are thousands of them."

"There are thousands of us," Aaron counters.

"Yes," Father adds, "but how many of us have ever fired a gun? The SS are trained to shoot and kill."

Ira clenches his fists. "We must do something."

"I agree," Father says. "We have to organize, approach them as a united front, let the Nazis know we will not tolerate these abominable decrees."

"Who will lead us?" Aaron asks.

"Rabbi Huberband," I suggest, surprised to hear my voice.

The rabbi's eyes fix on me.

I ask, "Won't you, Rabbi?"

He scratches his beard and then shrugs. "I don't know what more I can do. I've tried to negotiate, and I've failed."

Now, feeling more a part of the conversation, I say, "They have a weakness we can exploit."

Rabbi's attention again centers on me.

I repeat my earlier words to the family, "They need us. They need our labor to work the textile mills and the coal mines. If we organize as a labor group, they'll have no recourse but to meet with us and, at the very least, rescind some of their edicts. We will first, of course, have to decide which of our freedoms to bargain for."

"Elias is right," Father says. "We continue to keep Lodz factories and the coal mines running. This is in our favor. It may be the only way we can survive. That said, we must organize." Father turns to Huberband, "Rabbi?"

The rabbi gazes at us for a long moment, then says, "I will try to speak with them again for the Jews of Lodz."

"How does one negotiate with madmen?" Ira asks.

Before Rabbi can respond, I notice the crowd's tone is no longer raucous but is now a low series of mumbles.

I turn to the front of the hall. "Tate," I say with a warning in my voice as I gesture to the entrance.

An officious-looking Gestapo officer wearing the uniform and hat with requisite death symbols has entered and stands, searching the crowd, as at least thirty machine gun-carrying SS soldiers file in behind him and fan out to either side of the doorway.

The crowd mutters with resentment and fear, but the deadly weapons the soldiers carry have a subduing effect.

The officer's eyes rack the room. They stop on Rabbi Huberband. The Gestapo officer marches toward the podium, Jews separating for him as if he were Moses parting the Red Sea. He stops before Rabbi. "You will dismiss this meeting immediately. Jews are no longer allowed to gather in groups larger than three. Starting tomorrow, there will be a curfew for Jews beginning at 7:00 p.m. and lasting until 5:00 a.m. Any person, man, woman, or child breaking curfew will be executed."

My heart freezes. Not because of the curfew but because I've just recognized Rottweiler-face. He is standing among the soldiers lining the front wall. His large head is moving, scanning the crowd.

I turn to the exit door on the right side of the hall, where a pair of soldiers are taking up guard positions.

I look to the exit on the left side of the hall. Two soldiers are positioning themselves at the door, blocking this avenue of escape.

Sweat breaks out on my brow.

Rottweiler's head turns toward me; black eyes zero in on me.

I am trapped.

Chapter 4

I feel the walls closing in. Then I remember the hallway behind the podium where I played as a child when I accompanied my father to his meetings. There's a back door, but it's always kept locked. There's a chance it may be open this morning because of the meeting.

I look to the front entrance. Rottweiler-face is coming toward me, pushing his way through the crowd. I mutter a quick "Shalom" to my father and his friends, and without waiting for a response, I hurry to the rear hallway, praying the back door is unlocked.

Running, passing a row of offices, I reach the door. I grab the handle and turn it—nothing. I stare at the two locks: one for a key, the other for a little twist knob. I turn the knob—the locking pin slides back. Again, I turn the handle—still locked. "*Gotteniul*," I mutter as sweat drips down my face.

I need a key, one I don't have, nor do I have time to search the offices.

Heart pounding, I say to myself, "Sorry, Rabbi."

I stand back—and kick. Wood splinters, the key lock mechanism breaks, and the door flies open.

I am outside in a heartbeat, almost tripping over a half dozen cats scrambling out of garbage cans, overturning them in a noisy clatter. Then, I am alone.

I run, heading up the alley. At the corner, I peer back over my shoulder.

No canine-faced soldier.

I take in a breath and stride hastily onto Jerzego Street. I head toward Bankowa Park and the path I will take home; I keep a wary eye out for Nazis. I pass shopfronts in this mostly Jewish neighborhood, and my antenna for danger rises as I come across soldiers, but they ignore me as they paste proclamations on walls and storefront windows. Coming upon one of the posters, I can hardly believe my eyes. It's a replica of the one Rabbi read at the synagogue. The heading announces, *"Obwieszczenie,"* which loosely translates to "Announcement and Order." What a sick joke.

I glance at the bottom of the notice. It reads, *"Punishment for disobeying is death,"* as the Rabbi had said only minutes ago. I wonder how the larger Jewish community of Lodz and the Poles, also targets, will react when they read these dictates? What can any of us do to fight back? I don't know the answers. The changes coming to my world are so difficult to fathom. Perhaps Father will have some answers when he returns home. One thing I do know is that the Jews of Lodz will suffer.

***

As I enter our apartment, Golda, my mother, and my siblings are in the kitchen area while Father paces the thread-bare Turkish carpet in the parlor.

He rushes over and hugs me in his strong arms. "Eli," he says, releasing me. "We were so worried. When you left the hall so quickly…"

To change the subject, so as not to alarm him that the German soldier I pelted with a snowball was coming after me and still might be searching for me, I say, "Just a few minutes ago, I saw soldiers pasting posters up all over shop windows and walls with those Nazi restrictions. Have you seen them?"

Tate makes a futile gesture with his hands. "Yes. There's nothing we can do about it."

"Eli, your face…" Mother says from the kitchen. "What happened to you?"

I exchange a quick look with Father, who subtly shakes his head, warning me to be discreet. I respond, "It's nothing. I fell when I was running through the park on the way home. I'm fine."

“Well,” Mother says, “you should be more careful with that pretty face of yours.”

A knock on the door makes my heart jump. Has Rottweiler-face somehow followed me? I shake my head; I can’t see how that is possible. Still, I am wary as I open the door.

Baruch Werstler, my sister Guena’s boyfriend, stands there. He is out of breath as if he has been running.

He nods to me, his eyes widening as he stares at my colorful blackening eye and cut lip. “Ouch! What happened to you?”

“I slipped on ice. It could have been worse.” I justify my little lie by recalling I did slip on ice, and my black eye *could* have been worse.

Then, looking past me, Baruch greets his soon-to-be father-in-law, “Mr. Feinzilberg.”

“Come in, come in,” Father says.

Baruch, a tall, skinny, blue-eyed young man with black curly hair, touches the Mezuzah, kisses his fingers, and enters as Guena, followed by Hanche and Reizl, comes from the kitchen.

Guena takes hold of her soon-to-be fiancé’s hand. They planned to marry next year after graduating college with dual business degrees. But now, who knows? Hanche and Reizl, until today, high school students, have schoolgirl crushes on Baruch. They smile at the handsome young man and exchange greetings.

Whenever I see Baruch, I think of his beautiful sister, Kajia. I used to be secretly in love with her. Maybe I still am. I never mentioned my feelings to her. The closest we ever came to spending time together was exchanging a few words now and then, along with lingering looks that always tugged at my heart. I’ve spent many hours dreaming of Kajia, but that was as far as I dared go. I was too aware of my financial position. I couldn’t offer her a future. All the earnings from my job went to help support my family. So, we drifted apart without ever really being together. I sometimes wonder, does Kajia know I cared for her? Does she ever think of me?

Baruch's voice interrupts my reverie.

"I've read the Nazi edicts," Baruch says. "Insanity! Pure hatred. We can't let them close our schools, fire our professors, and put an end to our education. Unacceptable crap, excuse my language Mr. Feinzilberg, but these German swine are trying to squeeze the life out of us. They're taking our freedoms away. They're actually telling us we can't walk on sidewalks—that we must use the gutters—can you believe that? Nor can we own our own shops. How do these Nazis expect us to make a living? Well, that's the point, isn't it! They want us dead. We can't let them get away with this."

Father nods wearily. "Baruch, we're the conquered. Unfortunately, the Nazi savages are in control. If we resist, they shoot us. At present, there is little we can do, if anything. That doesn't mean things can't change. We will organize. We will resist in every possible way. When they see we, Jews, are a necessary part of their economy, they will have to treat us better. If not, we will rebel. Better a quick death than slavery. Now, it's almost suppertime. You will join us, I hope."

"I don't wish to intrude."

"Yes, he does," Guena says. "Besides, with our college closing, we need to talk."

"It's not an intrusion," Father says. "You'll stay for supper."

"Thank you," Baruch replies.

I leave Baruch and my sister to have a somewhat private conversation.

***

As Guena's older brother, I am concerned for them. I like Baruch, and I am saddened that their future is now so uncertain. I am standing by the kitchen alcove, lost in thought when I overhear mother and father talking. I peek around the corner.

"How has it come to this, Yaakov?" Golda asks as she peels potatoes on the counter. "Why did the Polish army give up so easily?"

He shrugs. “It was never a fair contest. They weren’t organized to fight the Germans. The Nazi’s military strength and determination are incredible, perhaps unbeatable.”

“Where does that leave us?”

“We’ll have to wait and see. The Nazis aren’t going to make it easy on us. But we’ve lived with prejudice all our lives, even from some of our neighbors.”

“Yes, but not all Poles are like that. We have Polish friends whose company we enjoy. Our children, for the most part, socialize with their goyim companions. Yes, these are exceptions, Yaakov, but the Germans seem to be another species altogether. Mark my words. They’re going to try to eliminate us. From what we’ve heard, they’ve already started.”

“I know, Golda. I am as worried as you are. I’ll do everything in my God-given power to protect you and the children. I just wish I had done things differently so we could have money to emigrate.”

“Money isn’t always the answer. We have Polish friends who have offered to help us relocate. We can take them up on their offer.”

“That was before the invasion. Now that we’re occupied, they may not wish to endanger themselves by helping us.”

“And we probably shouldn’t ask. They have their own families to think of.” Golda stops peeling. “Hate is so destructive. It changes everything.”

“Always has. Always will.”

Mother resumes peeling. “I’ll pray for us, for a better world for Jews and Christians, too. Now, out of the kitchen and let me prepare supper. Hopefully, it won’t be our last.”

“Golda, be optimistic for the sake of the children.”

“Better to be honest for the sake of the children.”

Chapter 5

Early the following Friday morning, I enter the parlor and see my father by the door, putting on his dark blue overcoat.

"Good morning, Tate," I say, joining him and reaching for my coat.

"Good morning, Eli."

I take my overcoat off its peg.

"Wait," he says. He takes his overcoat off and hands it to me. "Let me have your coat. We're exchanging. You give me yours, and I'll give you mine."

"Why?"

"That soldier who hit you. There's more to this story than just staring, I'm thinking."

Tate is intuitive. I won't tell him a lie, but I don't wish to worry him either by burdening him with the truth. His blue eyes bore into mine for an uncomfortable moment. He throws his hands up. "I thought so. No need to explain. I'll worry less if I don't know, but to keep you safe, you'll wear my coat."

I understand his logic. There are not many grey overcoats as conspicuously shabby as mine.

Tate adds, "Quickly, we have to go."

"But—"

"No 'buts'."

Knowing my father has thought this through and knowing his reasoning may save my life, I hand him my overcoat and take his.

As we slip on our garments with their Jewish armbands, he adds, "Your cap, too."

We exchange caps. It's quite apparent my fifty-year-old father would never be mistaken for me with his iron-rimmed spectacles and salt-and-pepper beard. And I, too, look different in his dark blue overcoat and cap.

Satisfied with our transformation, I say, “Thank you, Tate.”

Walking out of our apartment, I breathe in the cold morning air. The snow has almost all melted, and the sun is an orange smudge on the horizon. Thankfully, there are no Germans in sight. Perhaps our neighborhood is too poor to be requisitioned by the army. I snuggle into Tate’s overcoat. It is warmer than mine, and I feel guilty even while knowing he would never trade back with me. Surreptitiously appreciating the warmth, I exhale and see my breath condense into a white fog.

Around us, dark figures move along the street like shadows, men on their way to work. There are no evacuees lugging their meager possessions, at least not so far.

A few trucks and cars pass, headlights still on. As the German soldiers have yet to make an appearance, I imagine them sleeping in their tents while Gestapo and SS officers reside comfortably in confiscated mansions and elegant homes. I think of the well-to-do Jews, mothers, fathers, and children who were evicted. Where did they sleep last night? Did they find shelter? Within me, anger, like a lump of burning coal, fuels a growing fire of resentment.

“This is where we part, Eli,” Tate says several minutes later as we come to a cross street. “Have a good day. And try to think positive thoughts. We will get through this.”

Have a good day? *Think positive*? *How is this possible*? I let out a long, frothy breath. Not quite able to smile, I nod. “Shalom, Tate.”

Father takes Dobra Street toward the huge manufacturing building that comprises Scheibler’s Textile Factory. On the far west side of Lodz, it stands out in the distance like a boxy mountain. It’s one of over fifty such factories, I’ve been told, that makes Lodz the Manchester of Europe.

It takes Father one hour to walk to work, where he is employed as a ‘stringer,’ loading thread onto spindles to feed dozens of textile machines. He has held this position for twenty years without a raise in promotion or pay raise. And now, with the Nazis' latest decree, Jews being forced to work on the Sabbath, will either of us get paid extra for this day? I doubt it.

I head down Kursy Street to the Jewish Home for Refugees, a thirty-minute walk where I am lucky to have a job as a secretary. My pay is 120 Zoltys a week, barely a subsistence wage for one person.

As I get nearer to my place of work, Lodz comes to life. People appear on sidewalks. Cars, trucks, bicycles, and horse-drawn wagons begin to fill the streets. I don't see any more evictions. But I imagine it's just a matter of time until the better homes are taken over by Nazi officers. Then, the enlisted soldiers will begin expulsions and confiscating apartments and smaller homes in my neighborhood. With Hitler's plan to transplant 40,000 Germans to live in our city, no Jewish properties will be spared.

SS appears with their armored vehicles and motorcycles with sidecars, followed by soldiers on patrol. It's almost beyond comprehension to think these invaders will now be a way of life in my city with their insidious regulations and barbarism. What's going to become of us? I don't know. I'm frightened.

***

As if in answer to my questions, a few days later, all Jewish businesses are closed by Nazi decree. The professional workers—real estate investors, bankers, stockbrokers, doctors, judges, and attorneys—will have to find work in the local coal mines or textile factories. These jobs, when available, are menial and barely pay enough to sustain a family.

Polish businesses, including bakeries and markets, can remain open, so there is still food available, but because of predatory SS soldiers who roam the streets looking for Jews to humiliate and abuse, it's dangerous to go shopping. Only yesterday, three of our neighbors, a mother and her two daughters were stopped on the street by Nazis who stripped their clothes off and degraded them. It has come to a point where Jews are afraid to leave their homes.

On this late afternoon, after we've returned from work, Tate and I venture out to search for an open market as we've run out of food. We plan to divide and shorten the time each of us will be vulnerable to passing SS patrols. I go toward Dornitz's Polish bakery two blocks away, and my father walks to a fish market three blocks in the opposite direction. We plan to meet back at the apartment.

This is where my 'Pole walk' comes in handy. It's a 'saunter' rather than the quick scurry many Jews have affected in their attempt to vacate the streets as quickly as possible. As I stride along in my father's dark blue overcoat and matching cap, my heart misses a beat—six burly SS soldiers have turned the corner directly in front of me and are walking my way. Without missing a beat, I circle them, offering, "Good day."

To my relief, they ignore me, and we pass each other without stopping.

Moments later, I am approaching Dornitz's Bakery, owned by a Polish Christian, Mr. Dornitz, who is an old family friend. The little bell attached to his front door jingles as I enter.

Mr. Dornitz looks up and gives me a friendly grin. "Elias, good to see you. I see you're wearing your father's coat and cap. What's with this?"

So much for my disguise, although I still feel the change of clothes will throw off the Germans. "He insisted to keep me warm."

"Ach, you're father's too good to you. How's your mother?"

"A little frazzled," I reply, inhaling the shop's heady aroma. "Too many Nazis around."

"My sentiments exactly." He notices my purple eye and cut lip. "What happened to you?"

"I ran into a low tree branch."

"You should watch where you're going. What will you be having today?"

I gaze at the shelves behind him with their variety of freshly baked loaves. The tops of the loaves have each been scored, denoting rye from wheat from challah. To the side of this display is a row of cookies and pastries. I stare for a moment, swallowing, knowing these are delicacies I can't afford. I say, "A loaf of challah."

The baker takes the bread from the shelf and hands it to me. It is still warm.

"Thank you." I pay him the posted 10 Zoltas, place the bread beneath my overcoat, and turn for the door.

"Elias."

I look back at Mr. Dornitz. He's holding out a small cinnamon cookie.

Saliva floods. I swallow as I take the little treasure. "Thank you, Mr. Dornitz. This is very kind of you."

"You're welcome. And this is for the family." He lifts a round apple tort covered with sliced nuts of some sort. It's just big enough to share with the family if Mother cuts thin slices.

He places the tort in a paper bag. "It's two days old. No need for thanks, Elias. And enjoy your little treat on the way home."

I smile broadly, knowing it's all the thanks he expects.

I leave, feeling there are still good people in this world. I have a lift in my step as I walk towards home, warily alert for Germans as I nibble my cookie, enjoying each delicious bite.

I finish my cookie and, still savoring its cinnamon flavor, I turn the corner onto Peltz Street and almost collide with our eighty-five-year-old family friends, Abraham and Ida Polanski. Crying, disheveled, and breathing heavily, Abraham is holding a handkerchief to his bleeding mouth.

Startled, I ask, "What's happened? Who did this to you?"

"Elias, thank God," Abraham exclaims. "Rudy Dankowski and his gang of thugs were harassing and beating us when your father came to our aid and helped us get away. But they're beating him now. You must help him! Hurry!"

I am running before Abraham finishes his last words. In my mind's eye, I picture Rudy Dankowski, the hulking, mean-spirited, anti-Semite, and his bunch of young bully Poles. I clutch the bakery bag as my feet pound the sidewalk.

Ahead of me now, I see Dankowski and his gang kicking my father, who lies on the sidewalk.

They'll kill him!

Knowing I am no match for these thugs, yet ignoring my fears and tossing my grocery bag aside, I pull the only possible weapon I have from my pocket, a fountain pen I use at work I pull off its cap and jump on Rudy Dankowski's broad back.

Rudy yells and spins around like an enraged bear. As he tries to dislodge me, I press the sharp, pointed nib against his neck.

I yell in his ear, "Stop, I have a knife! Stop them, or I'll cut your throat!"

Rudy freezes, as do his friends. All eyes are on us.

"Now, order your thugs to get away from my father. Now!" I yell, enclosing the phony weapon with my fist so as not to reveal its true identity. "If anyone touches my father again, I'll cut Rudy—from ear to ear!"

Rudy nods urgently. Recognizing me, he shouts, "Do as Elias says. This Jewish prick will kill me!"

The toughs back away from Tate, who, bloody-faced, manages to sit up. I notice his little beard has been shaved off—roughly—there are cuts on his chin.

He sees me and says, "I am fine, Eli. That one," pointing at Rudy, "he shaved my beard off with his jackknife, but you don't have to kill him for it. Maybe just cut off an ear."

"No!" Rudy yells, not recognizing my father's dark sense of humor. "Elias, take your father and get out of here."

Tate knows I could never kill a man or cut off an ear. But what am I to do? If I remove my faux knife from Rudy's throat, these mumzers will more than likely see it is a fountain pen and beat Father and me half to death or maybe even kill us. I remind myself there is no death penalty for killing Jews.

"Elias," Rudy urges. "Take the blade away. You and Yaakov can go. We won't touch you."

If only I can trust Rudy to keep his word, which I don't think I can. So, where does this leave me? I say, "On one condition. Give me your word of honor. You will let us go peacefully."

Rudy is silent, apparently gestating the offer that gives him a way out while at the same time showing his gang that their leader has honor. He finally nods, "You have my word. You will not be harmed. Now lower the knife."

I silently congratulate myself. Then, almost reluctantly, as I am enjoying this moment of power, I quickly pocket the fountain pen so no one can see it, release my hold on Rudy, and step over to Father. I help him to his feet as Rudy and his gang stand by, sulking like jackals who have just had their meal stolen.

"My groceries," Father says, gesturing to the sack on the sidewalk.

I pick up the grocery and bakery bags and take hold of my father's arm. Without another word, I lead Tate toward home, half expecting to be attacked, but after we turn down the street and walk another block, I hear Father let out a long breath.

"Eli, thank you, my son. You may have saved my life. At the least, you saved me serious injury. But I didn't know you owned a knife."

"This is my 'knife,' Tate." I take out the fountain pen and show it to him. I see black ink has stained my fingers as I replace its cap.

Father chuckles. "You did good, Eli. Yes, my boy, you did very good."

I grin, thinking, *Yes, I suppose I did.* Although I can feel the loaf of bread under my coat is now flat as a pancake.

***

"We're home," I announce as Father, and I touch the Mezuzah on the doorjamb and kiss our fingers, silently thanking God for our safe return.

"Yaakov!" Golda exclaims upon seeing Father's beard has been shaved off, leaving his chin blood-crusted. "What happened to you, *mein zeitgeist*?" she adds, rushing to him as we hang our overcoats on pegs.

I hold onto the squashed loaf of bread and grocery bags as Mother inspects Tate's bloodied chin.

"Golda, it's nothing," he protests. "A few scratches."

"What *ganefs* did this to you?"

"Eli saved me from that Dankowski brute and his gang. He pretended a fountain pen was a knife and held it to Rudy's throat, threatening to slice him from ear to ear."

I look at my siblings, expecting smiles and laughter, but they are unusually quiet. What has happened?

Mother, too, is reserved as she says, "You did well, Eli. Yaakov, why were they beating you?"

"I'm a Jew. That's all the reason those young hoodlums need."

"Speaking of thugs, come." Mother takes Father's arm and leads him toward the kitchen. "There is more sadness. Mrs. Ovitz is here. The SS shot and killed Daniel less than an hour ago."

I knew and liked Daniel, a good friend of our family and Mrs. Ovitz's husband.

"Oh, dear God," Father exclaims.

I follow Mother and Father into the kitchen, where Mrs. Ovitz, our neighbor, is sitting on a chair. Tears are streaming down her cheeks. I place the flat loaf of bread and bags on the table.

"Mrs. Ovitz," Father says, "I am so sad to hear—"

"They murdered my Daniel and kidnapped Elaina, my baby." She sobs. "What will become of her? I've heard so many horror stories… Please help me find Elaina and bring her home. She's only fifteen, like your daughter, Hanche."

My siblings crowd into the kitchen. The twins, Avi and Rivka, who are too young to absorb the gravity of the situation, peek into the grocery bags.

Mother places her arm around Mrs. Ovitz. "Yaakov, is there anything we can do?"

"I wish." Father sighs. "You know that since the invasion, we have few rights. We no longer have any legal authority to turn to. But I will see what I can do. I will try. Perhaps they will free her, but there is little hope, I'm afraid. We must pray Elaina survives."

I have never seen my family with such sad faces. It is now just hitting each of us how vulnerable and helpless we are.

Avi and Rachel, who have been inspecting our purchases, are sliding the tart out of the bakery bag. They ask in unison, "Eli, is this for us?"

"Later," I say, preoccupied with Mrs. Ovitz's grief. "Avi, why don't you take Rivka with you into the parlor?"

He nods, and as my two youngest siblings leave, I turn to our bereaved neighbor. Unable to adequately express the depths of my anger and sorrow, I simply murmur, "I am so sorry, Mrs. Ovitz. Is there something I can do? Anything at all."

"I don't know. I don't know what any of us can do. Thank you, Eli. Just being here with your family is helping me." But then, unable to stop herself, she repeats, "My Daniel is dead. And my Elaina, my darling angel, is gone… What will those monsters do to her?"

Mother nods to Tate and me. "Leave us alone for a few minutes."

Father and I go into the parlor, and he gestures to our overcoats. "We should talk." He nods to the door. "Outside."

The sun is setting behind a gloomy, overcast sky as I sit next to Tate on the front steps of our apartment. The snow has mostly melted away, but the temperature is dropping, and I am shivering.

As we breathe, our breaths turn to white wisps.

I glance up and down the street. It is unusually empty, with only a few passing vehicles. Not a German in sight. Despite the emotional lift of saving my father gave me, I am saddened by Mrs. Ovitz's loss of her husband and daughter. I knew them well. They were friends. With the arrival of the Nazis, we are now living in a brutal world, one that is getting crueler by the day.

Tate, too, looks downhearted. His eyes are closed behind his steel-rimmed glasses. His lips are moving. I believe he is praying.

I feel a sense of depression but also the fiery embers of defiance. I want the Nazis out of our lives and out of my city.

Tate opens his eyes. He turns to me, his blue eyes intense. "Eli, of all my children, I worry about you the most."

Startled, I think, *Why me*?

"You are my most rambunctious child. Ever since you were a youngster, you were always getting into situations beyond your capability, but that never stopped you. And, mostly, you prevailed well past your age level. You have never let defeat stop you."

I nod, accepting his praise as I wonder what he will say next.

"Eli, you have the heart and courage of a lion. And the brains to accomplish whatever you wish. And, when you've made mistakes, you've learned from them, seldom repeating the same one twice. As you've matured, you've outgrown most of your wildness, except for your pride… and your unwillingness to back down when confronted by an unjust situation, which is not such a bad thing unless you happen to be a Jew living in Nazi-occupied Poland."

Yes, I think. *Tate is right.*

I am proud and willing to fight for what I believe is fair and right. Aside from that, I like to think I am a 'free spirit,' one who enjoys helping an underdog whenever possible. I never pick fights, but I know one of my personality weaknesses is that I take offense too easily.

I have been working on that. For instance, in retrospect, I know throwing the snowball at the SS soldier was foolhardy, not to mention dangerous. I wouldn't do it again. Jumping on Rudy Dankowski's back and threatening to cut his throat when my only weapon was a fountain pen *was* a bit crazy—but to save my Father, I *would* do that again. And, reflecting on all of the foolish, sometimes dangerous things I have done in my life, I know Tate is right. I am overly sensitive and perhaps a bit too 'prideful.'

"I'm trying to be a better person," I respond.

"I worry that you won't learn in time." Father pauses for a moment, then adds, "You see, Eli, I love you so very much, and I don't want to lose you."

His eyes penetrate my being. My heart aches. "I love you, too, Tate. You won't lose me. I will control my temper."

"You have to do more than that."

I sigh, resigned to go along with whatever the man I love most in this world asks of me. "I'll do whatever you wish, Tate."

"It's not going to be easy for you, Eli." He takes my hand in his.

I cannot remember him ever doing this before.

"I want you to make me a promise."

Uneasy, I wait.

"I've never questioned your bravery. You possess that by the carload, sometimes a top-heavy carload. But what I am about to ask of you is going to take more than mere bravery. It's going to take courage that can only come from a man blessed by God, and I, for one, trust you are blessed. I know you can do anything you put your mind to. That's why I am asking you now, from this moment on, to ignore Nazi insults and anti-Semitic comments and be submissive in the face of danger."

My stomach tightens. "But Tate, that's not who I am."

"Yes, but it's who you must become if you are to survive."

"I…" is all I can manage.

"Eli, you must learn to turn away from evil. You can still feel what you feel, but these Nazis are cold-blooded killers, and they won't hesitate to murder you for the least provocation. Therefore, you must be strong and adjust your attitude."

"Father, I—"

"When you examine who you are," he interrupts, "who you really are, you'll find you possess wisdom and patience. These gifts come to you from God. Once you use these gifts, Eli, you'll discover they are stronger weapons than brawn, as they will allow you time to think. Using your brain is the only way for you or any of us to overcome the evils in this world. We Jews have used our intelligence for centuries against every imaginable foe, and we have survived."

I am listening now, hearing my father's words.

"This doesn't mean we won't fight, but we will fight on *our* terms. We will outlast the enemy and come back stronger than ever. This is the way it must be, the way it has always been, and this is how we have survived for centuries. And now I'm asking you to use the brains God gave you instead of your muscle. To do this, you must become the man I know you are: a man of wisdom, a man of patience, and a man of God. If you do this, all the might of the Third Reich cannot defeat you. Now, Eli, I want you to promise me you'll take a good look at who you are and whom you need to be. Then, and only then, you may find a path, albeit a rocky one, to survival."

I am speechless.

"It will take humility. Yes, I am aware it's not one of your strongest attributes, but it can become one. You'll become an actor, a performer who will outsmart your adversaries and save lives. From this day on, you will not antagonize Nazis. If you can do this, my son, you will have greater courage than any man I have ever known."

My face flushes. A part of me still yearns to protest, yet when I see my father's shining eyes, I see love, and any objections I might have argued dissipate as quickly as the white breaths we breathe. I understand Father's plea comes from the heart, from his love for me and his wish to keep me safe.

I take in a deep breath. It helps. It more than helps; I know now what I must do. It's going to go against the fiber of who I am, but yes, I can do it. I will learn to ignore insults, and I will do so only because it is a request from the one human being in my life whom I love more than any other.

Tate, realizing my mental angst, adds, "I am asking this of you because I want you to live, Eli. I want you to carry on the family; our Jewish heritage. I don't know what is going to become of us, but I fear… I fear…"

"I will do this," I say solemnly. "You have my promise."

Tears appear in Tate's blue eyes. My vision also blurs.

He embraces me. I am unsettled. I only hope to God I can live up to my promise to *survive*. I will try. *Dear God, I will try with all my heart.*

Chapter 6

I am at work at one of the few places where Jews are still allowed to be employed, the Jewish Home for Refugees. I am putting on my overcoat, attempting to ignore my new white armband with its blue Star of David. I dislike wearing this 'marker,' but since Tate spent hard-earned money to purchase it, I feel obligated to wear one.

I am heading for the door, leaving for the day, when I hear a loudspeaker blaring outside.

"Now what?" I mutter to my two workmates, Elka and Micha, a married couple in their mid-thirties.

"New edicts," Micha suggests. "What else?"

As I step out the front door accompanied by Elka and Micha, a dark green military truck with two loudspeakers mounted on top of the driver's cab is rolling by.

A German-accented voice announces, first in Polish, then in Yiddish, "All Jews must register name, place of work if employed, and home address within the next forty-eight hours at the nearest Nazi headquarters. You will be issued identity cards with the word "*Jude*" stamped on the front. Failure to carry this card with you at all times is punishable by death."

Death again? I think sarcastically.

Isn't there an alternative punishment, like fifty lashes? Or, on a friendlier note, a weekend in Siberia?

I shake my head with disgust. The broadcaster's voice drones on as the truck continues down the street.

Elka asks, "What more can they think of to humiliate us?"

"It's subjection they're after," Micha responds.

"It's more than that," I say. "It's a Nazi plan to squeeze the life out of every Jew in Poland until each and every one of us is a shriveled corpse."

I can't let this happen. Yet, I find it impossible to fight back physically as I am bound by the promise to my father to be a non-combatant. I must find another way to fight the Nazis.

A few hours later, I am walking down the street on my way home when I see a disturbance ahead. Two SS soldiers are harassing a young Hasidic couple and their two small children. The tallest of the soldiers grabs the young woman's tichel, rips it off her head, and uses the scarf to blow his nose. His hulking comrade laughs and knocks her husband's black hat into the street. When the Jewish man protests, the brute slams the butt of his rifle into his face, knocking him down. The children burst out crying and rush to embrace their mother.

I clench my fists. *Mumzers*!

The tallest soldier pushes the children roughly aside and grabs the front of their mother's overcoat. He yells in her face, "Filthy Jew!"

He slams her against a wall. She crumbles to the sidewalk.

The husband, blood running down his face from a possibly broken nose, screams angrily and staggers to his feet, demanding they be left alone.

"*Ja. Ja*," the hulking soldier beside him taunts, then kicks him in the stomach, knocking him back to the pavement.

The tall soldier grabs the terrified young woman, pulling her up roughly. He yanks open her overcoat. His eyes widen as he sees she is pregnant. "Ah, *schwanger*!"

He paws her figure roughly.

Tears stream down her face as she stands bravely in defiance. She cringes when his hand slides over her breasts and down her belly. He grabs a handful of flesh and squeezes. She cries out, pushing his hand away.

"*Jüdische hure*!" he snarls and slaps her face.

Quickly removing my Jewish armband and placing it in my pocket, I say loudly as I approach, "Heil Hitler!"

Startled, the soldiers spin around. They exchange looks of confusion as I stop abruptly before them.

I smile, and in a combination of Polish and Yiddish, I say, "*Dobry! Gut*!" which I hope translates to "Good! Good!"

I continue in Polish street slang, "I wish to join you, to kick these Jewish asses. I am Aari Poltervitz, a member of the Polish/German Christian Council."

I quickly make the sign of the cross, adding, "Im *namen des Vaters des sohnesund des Heiligen Geistes*," which I hope translates to "In the name of the Father, the Son, and the Holy Ghost."

When I see they understand the rudimentary German phrase I've picked up from Christian neighbors, I continue in Polish street slang, "We Christians are in solidarity with our German friends. We want all Jews out of Lodz. Completely out of our lives. We honor the Reich." I throw my arm up in a Nazi salute. "Heil Hitler!"

Obliged to return my gesture, they salute and repeat, "Heil Hitler."

It's a good thing they can't see the sweat trickling down my sides as I jab a finger at the young man in the street and yell, "Swine!"

I run to him and kick him. And then I kick him again and again.

I am pulling my kicks, hoping I am not hurting him more than he is already hurt. After I have made a good show of my 'beating,' I glance at the soldiers and congratulate them, "*Gut*! *Gut*! Bravo! We want all Jewish scum out of Lodz."

I grab the young Hasidic man's collar and pull him to his feet. His wife and children rush to him. I yell into their faces, "You vermin Jews, get out of my city! Go now! Move, or I'll help these good German soldiers beat you to a pulp. Go!"

I quickly whisper to the husband, "I am Jewish. Run!"

The young man's eyes widen. He grabs his wife's hand, pulls her and the children along with him, and they hurry away.

I return my attention to the soldiers, who seem confused as they look after the retreating couple. Before they decide to pursue them, I quickly add, "Very gut! I love our Fuhrer. Long live Adolf Hitler!" I shoot my arm out. "Heil Hitler!"

The soldiers respond, "Heil Hitler!"

For good measure, I shoot my arm out once more. "Heil Hitler!"

The two Germans are again compelled to follow my example and voice their less-than-enthusiastic responses.

"Heil Hitler!"

"Heil Hitler!"

Dare I salute once more? No, I decide, as the young family disappears around the corner. I grin at the two somewhat disgruntled soldiers and say, "*Auf wiedersehen.*"

The tall Soldier scowls. Then, in disgust, he waves me off and leads his comrade up the street.

Suddenly, I feel overwhelmed with a sense of accomplishment, of triumph. It's a new sensation. *Tate*, I say silently, *thank you for your wise words, for suggesting I use brains instead of brawn. From this day forward, I will become as wily and clever as a fox.*

I smile, and then a laugh escapes me. I believe I'm going to enjoy outsmarting Nazis. Yes, we Jews *will* survive.

Tate, it's just possible that one day, your son may become an actor or maybe even a politician.

Replacing my Jewish armband, I suddenly realize I am whistling as I head for home with a new jaunt in my step.

***

It's Friday, April 1940, my half-day off. On this chilly, overcast afternoon with the threat of rain, I am sitting on our apartment's front steps, listening to what sounds like distant gunshots. I assume the Nazis are practicing marksmanship.

There are very few pedestrians on the street. One of them, Jan Katzenel, the grey-haired writer for the Yiddish newspaper *Lodzer*

Naje Folkscagtung, tips his hat to me as he hurriedly approaches. "Shalom."

"Shalom, Mr. Katzenel. What's the latest news?"

"The world is *farkakte*!" Jan says, gasping for breath as he stops before me. "The Nazis shut us down. Thirty-five years, I wrote for my paper. And now, it's kaput. My job, my livelihood, all gone. The worst of it is I have updates on the war to report."

"What updates?"

He gestures with his hands as if I, his audience of one, is hardly worth his time. But then he shrugs and says, "The Wehrmacht has invaded, defeated, and occupied Belgium and the Netherlands, including Luxembourg, and now they're attacking France. One good piece of news: Britain has come to France's aid, sending troops, warships, fighter planes, and bombers. It's going to be one devil of a fight. We must pray to God, Elias, that these soulless *mumzers* are defeated."

He pulls a folded poster from the inside pocket of his overcoat. He opens it and shows it to me. "The Nazis have gone mad. Look at this morning's decree: Right here in our city, all 160,000 of us Jews have been ordered to evacuate our homes within the next 8 hours and move into the Lodz Ghetto, taking only the possessions they can carry. No pets allowed. Those who refuse to—"

"Eight hours?" I interrupt in shock.

"Yes. The deadline to enter the ghetto is eight o'clock tonight. Any Jew seen on the street after that will be executed. It's criminal, insane!"

My hackles rise. I gaze at the poster and see an area marked *'Ghetto'* encircled in black ink. It's in the low-rent industrial district, approximately five miles away. It appears to be one or two square miles in area. *How?* I ask myself. *Will 160,000 Jews ever find accommodations in this small section of city blocks? Can that many people, young and old, move from their homes in just eight hours? What of the disabled or those too sick to leave?*

This abominable situation is the result of Hitler's orders to relocate 40,000 Germans into Lodz.

"Elias, mark my words; this move is part of a larger Nazi plan: to get rid of Jews. They've already started burning our synagogues, murdering our rabbis, professors, Judges, and all of our political intellectuals. Regular Jews like us will be used for labor, and when we are no longer useful to them, we will be eliminated. Polish Christians from noble families are also being targeted, especially politicians and military officers.

"As I've long suspected, Adolf Hitler and his Russian accomplice, Josef Stalin, plan to annex Poland, dividing it between them. God help us all. Please, tell your father what I've said. You must leave Lodz today. I'm taking my family out of the city this very afternoon. Elias, you must save yourselves before it's too late. Shalom."

I freeze, staring after the figure of Jan hurrying down the sidewalk. My mind whirls. I am aware of the German conquests of Denmark and Norway from what I've heard at the Jewish Refugee Center, but I've heard nothing of those latest Nazi victories. And now the Wehrmacht is attacking France. What will happen if France falls? And is it true that Stalin is joining Germany in its fight against the European nations? I shudder to think what would happen to us if Adolf Hitler and Josef Stalin were ever to rule all of Europe.

I look up and down the street. A few vehicles and pedestrians are moving unhurriedly along as if nothing in the world has changed. But within a few short hours, life as we know it will never be the same.

I am about to go up to our apartment when I hear Tate call my name.

He is hurrying up the street, out of breath, disheveled, waving a poster in the air. As he stops before me, before he can speak, I say, "I've heard. Jan Katzenel told just me the news."

He nods. "Upstairs, come."

He is already hurrying past me to the door.

***

"Eight hours?" Mame asks, stepping into the parlor from the kitchen, holding a long spoon she had been using to stir a pot of soup.

Still in his overcoat, Father hastens past her, heading for their bedroom, "Yes, Golda. We must pack whatever we can and be out of the apartment before eight o'clock tonight."

"Eli," Mame says, turning to me. "When did this all happen?"

"Just minutes ago," I respond, taking off my overcoat and hanging it by the door. "It's the Nazi's latest ultimatum. We either move to the ghetto or we'll be executed."

"Feh!" Mame mutters in disgust, shaking her head at the absurdity of the decree.

Guena and my siblings gather around me.

Pearl asks, "Why are the Nazis doing this?"

"To make room for their soldiers and 40,000 German citizens, they're importing to take over our country. They're evicting us to make room for their countrymen."

"They can't do that!" Reizl declares. "This is our home."

"Golda, children, this is nothing we can fight," Tate says as he hurries out of his bedroom, stuffing his few personal belongings into an old satchel. "I am going on ahead to the ghetto to find us lodging before everything is taken. I only have 180 Zoltys, so whatever lodgings I find won't be as good as I would like, but I'll do my best."

He kisses Mame's forehead and moves for the front door.

"Wait," I say. I pull money from my pocket and hand him my last 45 Zoltys. "I wish it were more."

"It will help," Tate responds, taking the cash.

"Yaakov," Mame says, running into the kitchen. "I have 80 Zoltys."

"No, Golda, please." Tate raises his hand as Guena and my other siblings offer meager sums. "No. No. Save what you have. We will need it for food. I must go now. Golda, bring containers for water.

I don't know what conditions we will encounter, but we must be prepared for the worst."

He opens the door. "I must hurry. I will meet you there."

Tate closes the door behind him.

We all stare at one another.

"God in Heaven help us," Mame says, massaging her temples.

"What can I do, Mame?" I ask.

"Yes," Guena adds. "We'll all help."

Mame shakes her head. "We'll do what we must do. We're going to pack up and meet your father in the ghetto. Gather your belongings. I'll do the same. Keep in mind, I doubt we'll be coming back. I have sacks and a bucket in the kitchen that we can use to carry our essentials. Children, there is one advantage to being poor. It won't take us long to pack."

Rivka says, "I don't want to move."

"I don't either," Avi adds. "All my friends are here."

"They'll be moving too, Avi," Guena says.

Mame says, "There are times when we must do things none of us wish to do. This is one of those times. Now, no more complaining. Go to your rooms and pack up."

***

A short time later, surprisingly short, considering we all had an early quick supper of the vegetable soup mother had been preparing, I lead the family out the front door of our apartment and down the short flight of steps. We are each carrying our meager possessions in bundles, along with a few kitchen supplies.

SS soldiers line our street. They are armed with rifles, submachine guns, and truncheons they use to hurry people along.

"All Jews outside!" SS soldiers command. "March! Quickly! *Raus*! *Raus*! Faster!"

They strike out with the truncheons and rifle butts, right and left, without reason, their blows falling upon old men and women, children, and invalids alike.

Jews cry out, falling. They are struck again and again.

"Get up!"

"Get up!"

"Faster!" they yell.

"Move!"

"Lazy swine!"

Old couples and children are falling, crying, weeping.

As the houses empty, the street fills with people carrying their few possessions in suitcases and bundles. Sweat streams from faces and bodies.

Christian neighbors, friends we have known for years, stay in their homes, pushing curtains aside to peer out windows, watching but doing nothing. Old friends doing nothing… What can they do?

Mame walks with a set expression on her face, only talking to support us.

I look at my little brother and sisters. They watch with shock as the soldiers lash out with their clubs. They have never seen anything like the astonishment, tears, and fear on people's faces. A burning rage tempts me to lash out at these Nazis, but I know it would be suicide. I grit my teeth in frustration, promising there will be a time for payback.

"Faster! Faster! Lazy swine! *Raus*! *Raus*! *Schnell*!"

A fine rain tickles our faces as we draw our scarves around us and attempt to cover our sacks. I also lug a heavy metal bucket filled with soup bowls, eating utensils, a pot, a pan, and small containers of flour, salt, and sugar.

Guena covers her violin case with her woolen scarf to protect it from the mist. With the sidewalk becoming crowded, I lead us into the street, joining others who have already vacated their homes.

Our neighbors are dressed in overcoats, women wear tichel headscarves, and men have caps with, no doubt, yarmulkes beneath them. A few Hasidic families and several younger couples join our group, riding bicycles with possessions tied precariously to racks and handlebars. The older generation without children walks with us while others push small hand carts. In one of the carts, a single older woman pushes. I spot the nose of what appears to be a small white poodle half-covered by a shawl. Knowing pets are forbidden, I step out of my way and pull the shawl up, covering the dog.

"*Danke*," the old lady replies gratefully.

"You're welcome," I reply.

Two horse-drawn wagons and an automobile join our procession. With each passing block, more people funnel out of their doors.

A wind-swept mist swirls around us. I wipe moisture from my face and turn for one last look at our apartment house. My heart squeezes. As much as our rooms were small and crowded, it was still the only home I had ever known. The last time I had this feeling was two years ago when a girlfriend I knew moved away. It's not that I was in love with her or anything like that, but she was a close friend, and when she left, there was an emptiness in my life. Maybe I did love her. Did she love me? Ah, past history.

"Swine! Move!" soldiers interrupt my musing.

Five miles is not so far to walk, but today it seems like twenty.

I move the heavy metal pail from hand to hand as I fear the wire loop might cut through the skin on my fingers. My mother, little brother, and sisters aren't complaining, so complaining is the last thing *I* will do.

Gunshots!

Mame takes Rivka's hand. I take Avi's. The crowd ahead of us parts as two German soldiers run into view. They stop and raise their rifles, aiming... I see their target: a beautiful cream-colored Afghan hound is scrambling through the crowd. It must surely belong to one of the more affluent Jews in Lodz. The soldiers fire, barely missing the animal. Cursing, they take aim again… and fire.

The dog yelps and collapses to the pavement. Bleeding from its hindquarters but still able to move, it attempts to rise.

The soldiers hurry up to the wounded dog, congratulating each other on their marksmanship.

One of them hovers over the animal for a moment. He strikes the dog over its head with the butt of his rifle, knocking it back down. Then, grinning, he stomps on its neck—a sickening crack follows. "No pets allowed in the ghetto." the dog killer shouts.

The old lady with the white poodle holds her hand to her mouth in horror. She hurriedly picks up the bundle, holding her little dog, and runs off. What will become of her and her pet? God only knows. I wish her luck.

I hear a ruckus and see the soldiers have spotted another abandoned dog. A black and white terrier is scampering through the crowd. The soldiers race after it.

We move on. During the next couple of hours, turmoil rules. Displaced residents crowd the streets.

More soldiers appear. Handicapped people, easy targets for bullies, are harassed and prodded with rifle butts. Some are purposefully tripped, jeered at, and beaten when they struggle to rise. I am furious but keep my anger in check, remembering my promise to my father.

Neighbors, friends, and strangers, young and old, jostle each other as we follow along toward an uncertain future. We witness one household after another being taken over by eagerly waiting German soldiers.

Mame's face is drawn, and fear and uncertainty in her eyes. We are all in a state of shock. I tell myself we will survive this madness. I pray I am right. *God, let me be right.*

We turn the corner onto Marysinska Street and come upon barbed-wire enclosed city blocks with shabby buildings and medium-sized manufacturing plants. This is the Lodz Ghetto. Looking past the sea of bobbing heads, I spot an open gate encased in barbed wire. It is manned by four officers in black Gestapo uniforms who are accompanied by at least a dozen machine-gun-carrying SS soldiers hurrying people along, yelling, "*Schnell*! *Schnell*!"

Something like a wave of despair crashes into me. I cannot think clearly. I'm not registering what's before my eyes. I do not accept any part of what's happening. Nor do I wish to acknowledge what any of this means. But pushing reality aside lasts only until the arrow's shaft of sorrow, anger, and despair pierces my heart. I am surprised to find it in me. I've always assumed weapons so painful land only in the hearts of others.

"*Schnell*! *Schnell*!" the guards yell, directing us toward the gate.

Pushing ahead, my family funnels through the entrance. Spreading out, we attempt to slow our pace to absorb the surroundings, but we are prodded from behind.

"This way," I say.

I tighten my hold on Avi's hand and lead us from the crowded street to an area of sidewalk where we have space to stop and catch our breaths. It's been a while since I've visited this eastside of Lodz, and now I remember why. The street is lined with dingy one and two-story shops, most of which appear to be out of business. Stuck randomly between these structures are apartments with cracked and peeling paint. There are also small millinery workshops. It all reeks of extreme poverty, with discarded trash cans, refuse on the streets, and boarded-up windows.

Men and women moving past us have desperate faces. They must find lodging for their families, or they'll be left on the streets.

I recognize couples with children, shop owners, and friends from my neighborhood. They are dragging bags with their few possessions.

Guena stares at all of this with tears in her eyes.

Reizl looks miserable.

Pearl is humming, ignoring our surroundings.

Rachel wrinkles her nose. "This place smells."

"Rachel, please," Mame reprimands. "It won't be forever. We'll be just fine."

"There's Tate," I say, pointing across the street in front of a weather-beaten one-story building with a sign over its entrance that reads: 'JUDENRAT.' I know the sign identifies the Jewish Council.

Standing beside my father is a large white-haired man with glasses. He wears a fedora and a wrinkled brown suit. I recognize him as Chaim Rumkowski, one of my father's acquaintances from our old neighborhood.

Father sees us and waves.

Moments later, Tate is beside us. "I've found us a place. It's not much, but it's a roof over our heads until I can find something better."

"At this moment, anything will do," Mame says.

"Tate," I say. "Is Chaim connected to the Judenrat?"

"Yes, he's been put in charge by the Germans. He's been a big help. He and a few volunteers are setting up illegal daycare centers and schools for children whose parents are working in the mines and textile factories. He's also organizing food distribution, such as it is, and has assembled a group of doctors and nurses to help those in need. And he's found us a place to live. It's not much, as I said, but then there are no real choices. We're lucky to have anything. Come along, I want to take possession before someone grabs it out from under us." Tate takes Mame's bag from her and leads us up the sidewalk. "Chaim's also been appointed to represent us to the Germans and be head of the Jewish Police Force in the ghetto."

"We're going to have our own police?" I ask.

"Subject to rules laid down by the Nazis and our illustrious Mayor, Werner Ventzki."

Mame scoffs. "Everyone knows Ventzki is useless, a self-serving politician. At least Chaim is from the neighborhood. That may be worth something."

"Chaim's a wily fox," Tate says. "He'll help us if it's to his advantage. I'll find a way to work with him."

Tate leads us down Marysinski Street, one of three main thoroughfares that bisect the ghetto. A short walk later, we turn onto Wolska Street, and within a few minutes, he stops before a two-story ramshackle building.

I frown, biting my tongue. I realize how difficult it must have been for Tate to have found any lodging at all. The building I stare at is not what I would call an apartment house but a boxy structure with faded yellow paint and sagging front steps. The ground-level floor is a tailor's workshop.

The mist, following us all day, now turns to rain. It isn't a peaceful drizzle; it's a sad one. It weeps for us and our unsettled future. There's nothing I can do about it. I feel wretched and utterly hopeless.

"Inside everyone. We're upstairs," Tate announces.

Opening the building's ill-fitting front door, Tate leads us up a flight of rickety stairs to the second floor. He produces a key and opens the door to our new home. We crowd in. All I see is a rectangular room about the size of our former parlor. Mottled light shines in from two dirty windows overlooking the street. I look for doors leading to other rooms. There are none.

I didn't realize I had hopes for our new housing until my expectations crashed into my lungs, taking my breath away.

Mame and my siblings exchange looks.

Tate says apologetically, "It's temporary until I can find something better."

I scan our 'accommodations.' There are no electrical fixtures, plug outlets, cooking facilities, faucets for running water, or a toilet.

"It's all I could find," Tate says apologetically. "At least it's a roof over our heads. There's a communal toilet on the first floor. I will try again tomorrow. There are just too many people and not enough apartments."

Mame says, "I'll place the chamber pot in the corner and tack up a sheet for privacy."

Rivka and Pearl begin to cry.

Mame, too, has tears in her eyes. She steps close to Tate and takes his arm in hers. “We’ll get through this.”

He kisses her forehead.

I empty my bucket of eating utensils, soup bowls, a pot, and a pan and then place it by the window to catch the water drops dripping from the ceiling. Yes, we will have ‘running water’ whenever it rains. We won’t die of thirst. Food will shortly become our main concern. We’re going to have to make the best of a terrible situation. I say quietly to myself, “May God damn those damn Nazis.”

Chapter 7

During the next several days, we all try to adjust to apartment life in the ghetto. One thing we don't have to feel guilty about is being the cause of evicting former tenants; no families could have lived in this dirty and cramped space.

My sisters refer to our living quarters as 'the cell.' It's where nine hapless 'prisoners' attempt to survive.

The walls are so thin they provide only a slim barrier from wind and rain. And, as the days progress without employment for Tate and me, claustrophobia begins to affect us all, my sisters in particular. They are like enclosed cats, clawing the walls for their need to be outside, stretch their legs, and feel they are part of humanity. Mame, Tate, and I worry about their safety. We'd like to keep them inside, but we finally relent and let them out as long as Tate or I accompany them.

Everyone is aware of the dangers lurking in the ghetto. There are accounts of young women who have disappeared off the streets. These females, loved ones, are never seen again. Complaints to the Judenrat and to the Nazi command are ignored. We are told over and over that Jews have no rights.

As I walk the ghetto streets today, I keep my overcoat buttoned and my hands in my pockets to ward off the chill in the air.

People wander aimlessly about, appearing to be lost. Many are praying as there is no synagogue to go to, no place to meet.

Ahead, a crowd is gathering in front of the Judenrat building. Chaim Rumkowski, still in his brown wrinkled suit, is supervising unloading two fifty-gallon metal barrels from a German army truck while his assistants set up tables. As I draw closer, I watch as lids are pried off and brown soupy water is revealed. It's something the Nazis call 'stew.' I don't know where the brown comes from, but if I had to guess, I'd say the barrels weren't properly cleaned.

Chaim orders his assistants to ladle the thin gruel into small wooden bowls and distribute the rations to those now forming a long line. It's obvious from the start there isn't going to be enough food for everyone. The Nazis seem to be taunting us, offering just enough nourishment to tease us but not nearly enough to sustain 160,000 people.

I walk on, knowing that the soup will be gone by the time I stand in line and make it to the front of the serving table.

I pass pathetic-looking people who sit or lay about, too weak to get in line. Further on, I see Jews who have been unable to find lodging, huddling together for warmth in doorways of abandoned shops and small factories. Their faces are drawn and pasty. Hollow eyes follow me silently. I am reminded of pictures of destitute World War One refugees.

I can feel the coldness in their bones, their hunger, and their thirst. When was the last time they had something to eat or drink? Will they starve to death only yards away from an insufficient soup kitchen with its tantalizing aromas?

The Nazis, I'm coming to understand, always have a strategy. With the lack of food and water, they plan to starve us to death. What can I do to remedy the situation? It comes back to my basic need: I must find a job: something, anything to bring in money. If I have money, I can purchase food from the black market supplied by a few brave Jews who risk their lives to sneak in and out of the ghetto at night. I hear the echo of my father's words. *You must survive, Elias. You must survive.*

Yes, father, I am trying.

A sense of fear as real as the Nazi Swastika is taking its toll. What will happen to us? How long will the Germans keep us in this ghetto, this prison? It's obvious they won't return us to our homes. So again, I ask myself the nagging question, *What is their plan*?

No one knows.

Rumors of SS and Gestapo atrocities proliferate like a virus. I've heard that Jewish synagogues and temples are being looted and burned in the city. Many of these houses of worship are large, architecturally beautiful buildings with a long history of serving our Jewish community. And now, with the Nazis bent on destroying our culture, they will all soon be burned to the ground. I have often pondered why one religion believes that their God—whom they are willing to kill innocents for—is better than any other religion's God? Don't we all pray to the same God?

As I climb the flight to our apartment, my feet tread heavily upon the stairs.

When I enter, I find my parents and siblings sitting on the floor in silence. Mame and Tate's features are drawn, the strain of our situation aging them. I don't mention the inadequate soup kitchen that Chaim set up, but I repeat a mantra that has become my goal, "I am going out again later. I'll find a job."

My words fall flat. We all know the possibility of a Jew finding employment in this ghetto is close to zero.

"I will go with you," Tate says, breaking the silence. "We'll find a way to improve our situation."

"I've tried to take in sewing," Mame says with a helpless shrug.

"No one can afford to mend anything," Guena says.

I bite back words that form on the tip of my tongue. *We must escape! Leave this hell hole!*

I know my thoughts, if voiced, would be rude and hurtful, and that's the last thing I wish to do to my parents. We are aware that anyone attempting to escape the ghetto will be shot on sight. There is no place to run to, and even if it were possible, there's the ever-present problem of money—we have none.

Seeing the futility in my eyes, Tate says, "Patience, Eli. We will get through this."

I don't know where Tate gets his optimism, but real or fake, it reminds me of my promise. I say halfheartedly, "I don't doubt it for a moment."

***

After another uncomfortable night on the hardwood floor and an embarrassing use of the chamber pot, I slip on my overcoat and prepare to go out while everyone else lies in various stages of slumber.

My stomach grumbles. I eye a small portion of bread on the little table my father found and brought home a few days ago. I know it's our last portion of bread. It must be divided nine ways for breakfast, but I simply cannot take my share. I am out the door before anyone awakens.

Coming down the front steps, I am met by a sudden cacophony of horns and loud, festive German voices coming our way. An announcement *blares* from twin speakers mounted atop the first truck I see as it drives down the street, followed by other trucks, motorcycles with sidecars, and other military vehicles.

The announcer's voice proclaims in Polish and Yiddish, "Paris has fallen! France surrenders! Germany is victorious! Heil Hitler! Paris has fallen! Heil Hitler!"

I freeze. The words send chills through me. Paris has fallen? Is this really true?

Doors all along the street open, and people file out. I am transfixed as I recall: The Germans invaded France on May 10, 1940. Only six weeks later, the once-mighty French army with its highly touted 'Maginot Line' surrendered? It doesn't seem possible. Yet it must be true. The fall of France is a catastrophe that will resound around the world, and Jews are now in more jeopardy than ever before.

Tate, Mame, and my siblings open the windows above me and peer out. Their faces crumble when they hear the announcement. France, our great hope for defeating the Germans, has surrendered.

Days like this simply lay on me like stones. I sit on the steps and bury my head in my hands. I would cry, but I am beyond tears.

Suddenly, German Oompa music blares. I look up to see Nazi trucks arriving filled with boisterous beer-drinking soldiers. They are singing, cheering Adolf Hitler, and shooting guns. Our residents are frozen, too petrified to do anything but stare, but as it dawns on us all that the revelers are not shooting at us but rather celebrating their victory over the French, we start to relax.

I watch as the ghetto transforms. Additional trucks laden with food and drink arrive. Half-starved people rush forward and surround the vehicles, accepting handouts of boiled sausage, bread, and beer.

Loudspeakers continue to broadcast rhythmic, pounding German *volksmusik*. Soldiers grab Jewish women from the food lines and whirl them around, dancing and attempting to kiss them. Jewish men run over, attempting to free their women from the clutches of this drunken group of revelers. The Jews are knocked to the ground, but surprisingly, the soldiers do not beat or shoot them. These SS are in a festive, almost friendly mood as they release the struggling women and continue celebrating their victory over the French.

I am torn between being repulsed and being spellbound.

My trance is broken as my parents and siblings join me on the front steps. We all watch the celebrating Germans who are eating drinking, singing, and passing out food. It's quite an incredible sight.

"Wait here," I say. "I'll grab some food and drink before it's all gone."

"I'll come with you," Guena offers.

"Me, too," Reizl says.

"No," Father says. "This is not safe."

I now see what he sees. An SS soldier is dancing with one of our women on the far side of the street. He is pawing at her, laughing as he grabs her breasts. The woman struggles to get away, but it appears it is useless as the soldier takes further advantage.

"This isn't going to end well," I say, standing and moving toward the altercation. "Everyone stay where you are. I'll be back."

"Be careful, Eli," Mame warns.

I wave, acknowledging my mother's warning, and move through the crowd toward the struggling girl when, suddenly, the soldier releases her, laughing as she runs away. Changing direction, I move to the food line and join in the wait as the party circulates around me. I am offered a bottle of beer by a half-drunk soldier. I take it.

People who have been doled out food hurry back to their families to share their bounty. SS soldiers, privates, and officers alike are drinking heavily, enjoying their music as they continue to dance with a few of our women captured in their arms.

Jewish men watch from the sidelines with expressions of anger and fear while mothers begin to lead their daughters away from the festivities.

As the drinking and reveling escalates, the soldiers' intentions begin to change, and not for the better. I watch a Nazi officer struggling with a young Jewess as she tries to free herself. I am moving forward to intervene when she breaks free and runs off. I stop and shake my head, realizing my efforts to protect her would have been in vain, and I would probably have been beaten, possibly shot.

I'm finally at the front of the food line and given a few links of boiled sausage and a loaf of bread. Momentarily distracted, I take a few quick bites as I close my eyes. These are flavors I've almost forgotten.

My euphoria is broken by a gunshot.

Then Silence.

I turn to see a bearded young Jew lying on the ground. Above his eyes, which stare lifelessly, is a small hole encircled by a few drops of blood. The officer who shot him holds a Luger pistol in one hand while his other grips a young woman who must have been the dead man's girlfriend or family member. The shooter shrugs as if to say, *What did he expect?*

Then he drunkenly proclaims, "We are the soldiers of the Third Reich, the greatest fighting force on the face of the earth! You Jews are chattel, our slaves, for as long as you live. Heil Hitler!"

"Heil Hitler!" fills the air.

Oompa music resumes with increased volume.

The killer holsters his pistol and whirls the terrified young woman around in his arms. I cannot watch.

I make my way back to our apartment's front steps, where my family waits. Their faces reflect fear and loathing.

I give Mame the sausage links and bread and offer the bottle of beer to Tate.

He waves it off, refusing to take a drink. My anger must still be evident because my father gives me a look that says, *Good, Eli, good. You did good.*

I nod, accepting the acknowledgment of my self-control, but I am still annoyed at myself for *'doing good.'*

I take a long swig of the first beer I've tasted in over a year. It tastes as bitter as I feel. I glance at the young man's dead body surrounded by revelers, and the shooter's words bounce within the caverns of my mind: *We are the soldiers of the Third Reich, the greatest fighting force on the face of the earth! You Jews are chattel, our slaves, for as long as you live. Heil Hitler!*

***

Snow fell again last night. Three inches of powder covers the ground with a white blanket that shines in the morning sun, hiding debris and filth beneath its contours. It's July 1940, three months after the German victory over France and the distribution of sausages, bread, and beer. That was the last time the Germans distributed food. Our only nourishment now comes from the black market for those who can afford it and from the Judenrat, who pass out meager portions of carrots, cabbage, potatoes, and stale bread.

Starvation and dysentery are taking a toll as bodies pile up, left to rot. Rats feed on cadavers.

We suffer hunger and melt snow for drinking water in silence. Sanitation is abysmal, and outdoor latrines overflow. Typhus has broken out in the camp. Stench permeates the air.

I use a kerchief to cover my nose as I walk the streets to ward off the smell of decomposing bodies. I am more and more desperate. I must do something before my entire family dies of malnutrition or disease.

Tate and I talk to Chaim Rumkowski daily, seeking news of the war to take our minds off our situation. The reports we hear are of Wehrmacht victories across Europe and North Africa. The German war machine seems invincible. I pray for Adolf Hitler to die, to be assassinated, or for God to strike him with a bolt of lightning. God doesn't respond. I've noticed that a lot lately about my prayers asking for work, food, or for a way out of this ghetto. *God, I'm never going to give up on you. But I'll say this*: *if I were you and you were me, I would respond—especially with that bolt of lightning.*

Snow flurries begin. They swirl around me like a lacy curtain blown by an icy breeze that sweeps over the almost vacant streets. I pull my overcoat's collar up, wishing it reached my cold ears.

I trudge along, feather-light snowflakes whitening my cap and torso. I keep my hands in my pockets, attempting to warm them. Even though I wear a kerchief over my nose, I know it's pink with cold, and my toes, too, are numb. Why am I out in this frigid weather? To avoid staring at the walls in our apartment and because I am obsessed with finding work.

I avoid icy patches I could slip on. I pass 'lumps' I dare not explore. With the quiet snow falling softly, the ghetto reminds me of an abandoned cemetery, which it is becoming.

Breaking into my dark illusion are small pockets of life. A few fortunate people scurry about coming and going to work in small millinery factories where they have been hired to sew German uniforms and tents for the army. But, as I continue to learn, there are too many people and not enough jobs.

I turn a corner and discover a German truck with its driver waiting behind the steering wheel, parked in front of the Judenrat Office. A helmeted soldier stands in the open doorway with Chaim Rumkowski handing him a bundle of some sort. The German leaves, hurries into the waiting truck, and is driven off.

"Chaim," I call out, alerting the commander of the Jewish Council as he is about to carry his bundle inside and close the front door.

He sees me coming and waits. "Elias, what are you doing out in this weather?"

"Looking for a job. What else?"

"Come in out of the cold."

I follow him inside, immediately appreciating the warmth of his office, noisy as it is. Two rickety electric heaters are running, but no telephones. I don't question how he managed to have the building wired for electricity. But I remember Father telling me, 'Chaim is noted for making himself comfortable.'

As I look around, I am impressed to see six cramped desks crowded with people conducting ghetto business. At one desk, I overhear two women discussing the illegal daycare centers and schools for older children Chaim has set up for Jewish parents working in the textile mills. At another desk, a harried woman argues with two men over the impossible task of food distribution when there isn't enough food to distribute.

A man in a doctor's smock stands before a third desk beside me, pleading with a tired-looking woman for medicines and beds.

An older lady leans on a fourth desk, demanding the removal of two dead bodies from her apartment building. Voices rise and fall as I hear more demands for water, warm clothes, garbage removal, new latrines to be dug, repair services, etc.

Overwhelmed but encouraged, I think there must be a need for a young man like me to assist Judenrat's overworked employees. I turn to Chaim, who hands me the bundle he has carried inside, which I can now see are posters.

"More crap!" he exclaims.

Ignoring the bundle, I say, "Chaim, I need a job, and it looks like you need help."

"We do need help, Elias. But there's no money to pay you. All these people are volunteers. If you wish to work for future payments, we can—"

"I need money now. My family has to eat."

"I understand. Come back in a week, I'm hoping the Nazis will give me some cash. Now distribute those posters, and I'll pay you something when the money comes in. In the meantime, I'll put your name at the top of my 'to hire' list. That's all I can offer you."

Before I can say another word, Chaim's attention is drawn away by an irate woman demanding he send Judenrat policemen, another group he oversees, to arrest a pervert who peeps into her window every night, watching her undress.

Carrying my new burden, I walk out the door.

Outside, with snowflakes swirling around me, I look at the bundle's top poster. It is another Nazi decree dated August 23, 1940.

All Jews in Lodz, over the age of ten, are hereby ordered to wear a yellow badge in the shape of the Star of David. It is to be sewn onto the left side of your exterior clothing, both on the front and on the back. These emblems are to have the word "JUDE" written inside the star. The badges are to be 5 inches in diameter. These stars will take the place of the white armbands and must be applied within 10 days of this notice. Any Jew failing to wear the "JUDE" star will be shot.

General Fritz von Schmerling, Nazi Commandant.

My fingers shake, not from the cold but from anger. What more can these Nazis do to degrade us?

Paradoxically, a rather ingenious idea comes to me. I hurry down the street and begin passing out posters as I head for home.

***

Less than an hour later, I am in our apartment, having read the disturbing news to my parents and siblings. While they are still in shock, I say, "I have an idea to make the Star of David work for us."

My family looks at me like I'm *meshugah*—crazy.

I explain, "We find some yellow cloth and, with all of us working together, we cut and sew yellow stars for our fellow Jews. We should make a few Zoltys, don't you think?"

The circle of faces stares blankly.

"Well," I prod. "What do you think? Can we do this?"

"It's … possible," Tate responds hesitantly as he looks at Mame.

"Yes, it *is* possible," she agrees.

"Then we'll do it," Tate declares rather unexpectedly.

He grins for the first time in days. "Eli, excellent thinking. Now you must come with me to my friend, David Lachman's apartment. It's here in the ghetto. He used to buy and sell fabrics before the Nazis shut him down. Last time I was there, he had bolts of unsold fabric lying around. And if I remember correctly, I believe some of them are yellow. He owes me 75 Zoltys for work I did for him. I'll take the material in exchange. But we'd better pick the bolts up today before everyone realizes there's going to be a call for yellow fabric."

"Mame," I say. "Do you have sewing needles and thread?"

"One of the few things I do have are needles and thread."

"Good," Tate responds. "The Feinzilberg family is going to go into the sewing business, even though we hate that we must wear these stars."

My siblings approve.

"Yes," Mame confirms, warming to the idea as much as she can. "We'll cut out five-inch yellow Stars of David, sew the letters *JUDE* into the center of each, and then stitch them onto our neighbors' clothes. Everyone is going to need two, one for the front and one for the back."

"Won't we be working for nothing?" Reizl asks. "No one has any money."

"Some do, some don't," I explain. "We'll sell to those who do and give to those who don't. There are thousands of Jews in the ghetto. We can also barter for food."

"Eli," Tate says. "Your idea is a gift from God."

Really? I think feeling a touch of pride that my idea could help the family. And maybe it's just possible my thought *did* come from God. And if God's in a giving mood, it won't hurt to pray, so I silently say, *God, I'm still waiting for that bolt of lightning.*

Pearl, Hanche, and the twins, Avi and Rivka, all join in endorsing my plan.

Appreciating their support, I say, "We'll have to work fast. We won't be the only ones with this idea. I'm certain dozens of shops are going to be making these stars."

"Yaakov," Mame says. "How soon can you get the material?"

"I'm leaving now, and I'll be back in a couple of hours."

"Then we start today," Mame says. "The early bird gets the worm, does it not?"

Father and I grab our overcoats.

"I'm coming with you, Tate. You're going to need help carrying the material."

Walking out the door, I am feeling pleased, even though I realize that our enterprise will probably end in a few days, and we'll be right back where we started. But, in the short term, we'll have added a few Zoltys to our pockets and food to our stomachs. What happens after this is anyone's guess. One thing is certain; the Nazis will continue to harass us and make our lives miserable.

Chapter 8

It is so bitterly cold today that streams of fog trail after me as I exhale, walking along the gutter of the cobblestone street. I am sure this must be what living in Antarctica feels like, a place I never wish to go. And then, if I could jump back in time, I'd like to ask the first Jews who settled in Poland, Why didn't you pick the Greek Islands or the South of Spain, where it's sunny and warm most of the year?

A clump of snow falls from an eave and bounces off my head, bringing me back to reality.

By the time we run out of yellow material, the Feinzilberg sewing enterprise had been a minor success. We made 320 Zoltys and have had food to eat. We even have a few leftovers for the remainder of the week. But I worry, a now-constant habit, what will happen next? Keeping 160,000 Jews boxed up in this ghetto helps no one. I think the Nazis care *bupkes* about helping us, but still, it would be logical to have a productive plan. What are they waiting for?

Walking among my fellow Jews, who now wear the ubiquitous yellow Star of David on their chests and backs, I wonder how many were customers of my family?

As I look closer at the passersby, I notice some cutting and sewing do not measure up to the Feinzilberg standard of excellence. Then, I come across several individuals without stars. I assume they're Polish Christians, including Jahovah's Witnesses, Gypsies, or homosexual couples, who have run afoul of the Nazis. Gypsies are identified by wearing brown triangles, and homosexuals wear pink ones.

Stepping around a pile of refuse, I am reminded that as of the beginning of 1941, there is no longer a sanitary service to cart away growing heaps of garbage. One interesting, if morbid, observation is that the latrines are no longer frequented as often as they once were—starving people have less and less use for them.

A few steps later, I come upon a droopy-headed horse attached to a wooden wagon. Snowflakes coat the animal's backside and the shoulders of two Jewish men, huffing and puffing as they lift an emaciated corpse off the sidewalk and throw the body on top of other naked men, women, and children in the back of the wagon. I shudder as I walk past this horror, one which repeats itself time and again.

I promise I won't let my family starve and meet this fate. As the eldest child, I feel it is up to me to provide an escape from our misery. I mutter words that have become my mantra, "I must find a job."

My quest hounds me as I cross the street and again head for the one man in the ghetto with the contacts to help me.

I find Chaim in his office, as usual, dealing with a dozen things at the same time. He is called from desk to desk by assistants to settle disagreements and work with individuals active in securing food and medicines, as well as those involved with keeping our Jewish cultural life alive. These are busy workers, Jews organizing plays, concerts, and banned religious gatherings as there is no synagogue in the ghetto.

Chaim is talking to an attractive middle-aged woman who wears men's work pants and a shirt covered partly by a white apron. A jaunty red cap sits on her head. I see her hand him a thick packet that he quickly pockets.

I overhear her say, "Six, I'll have more by the end of the week."

She then asks for medicine for a new mother who gave birth last night and has had complications.

I catch Chaim's eye, and while conversing with the woman, he motions me over.

"Elias," he says by way of introduction. "Meet Stanislawa Leszcynska, our treasured midwife who delivers babies. Stanislawa, this is Elias Feinzilberg, son of one of my good friends."

She offers a weary smile. "Nice to meet you, Elias."

I nod, noticing she is not wearing a yellow star.

"How many so far, Stanislawa?" Chaim asks.

"As of last night, ninety-two healthy babies. And I really must leave now as ninety-three and ninety-four are due any minute." She starts, turning back to add, "I really need those medicines, Chaim."

"I'll get them for you if I have to raid the National Health Hospital myself. By tonight, I promise."

I believe Chaim will be good to his word as I've heard he has contacts at the pharmacy there and has a suite of rooms at the hospital where he lives in style with his family. He is a man of many talents.

Watching the midwife leave, I ask, "She's not Jewish?"

He shakes his head. "A Polish Christian. She's a nurse who's a miracle worker for dozens of our expectant mothers. She also brings my staff bits of food, clothing, and,"—he lowers his voice — "has supplied documents to several of our leading scientists, writers, and artists, who she then helps smuggle out of Poland. The woman is an angel from heaven."

"She forges passports?" I ask in a whisper.

He simply nods.

My mind races. "I need her services for my family."

Chaim looks at me with sad eyes and lowers his voice. "I like your father, Elias. And I would like to help you. But you have no money. Attempting to get passports made without Zoltys is a waste of time."

It's true, I have no money. The Zoltys, our family, made manufacturing the yellow Stars of David have been spent on food. But I am not about to give up. "And if I can find the money?"

"Then I will put you in touch with Stanislawa, and you two can work out the details."

Raising his voice to its normal level, he adds, "An opportunity for a paying job has come across my desk."

"For me?"

"For you and a large number of Jews."

I give him a skeptical look. "You said a *paying* job?"

"Yes."

My heart trips. Before I can question him further, he adds, "The Germans have requested 400 strong men to work building roads and railways. You certainly qualify. The first 200 will be leaving on October thirteen. I've added your name to the second group leaving October sixteen. The pay is minimal, but it's better than nothing. I think it best if I arrange to have your salary sent home to your parents."

A tremor passes through me. I want to sit down. No, I want to keep standing. I open my mouth to speak but can't articulate any words.

"Did you not hear what I said, Elias?"

I manage to nod and stammer, "I… I… I thank you, Chaim. This would be wonderful. Fantastic. Thank you so much. Thank you. Thank you. You have saved my family from starvation."

"I have to warn you," he says, waving a large finger, "it's going to be hard manual labor under very difficult conditions."

"I don't care if I have to break boulders with my fists. I'll be ready to leave on the sixteenth. Where will I be going?"

"Leibhof, Germany."

***

"Germany!" Mame exclaims with a worried frown.

"Eli," Tate says. "Germany isn't safe. They're murdering Jews, entire families."

"They need workers. They're not going to kill me."

"They will when they don't need you any longer."

"I'll leave before that happens."

"This job," Mame says with exasperation, "how long will you be gone?"

Frowning, I realize that's a question I forgot to ask. I respond, "As long as it takes. Probably a month, maybe two or three."

I can see their minds churning. They're worried about me, yet they know we need money to survive. I add, "Chaim said they'll be sending my paychecks to you here in the ghetto. This will put food on the table, and I'm hoping there'll be enough cash left over to save for my next idea."

Tate raises an eyebrow. "What are you thinking, Eli?"

"We leave the ghetto. Move to another country where we can live freely as Jews."

"And if we had wings," Tate responds, "we'd already be gone. Eli—"

"Before you say it's impossible or that we can't afford it, please listen to the rest of my idea. After I return, we'll use the money that's left over from the salary I've earned to leave Lodz. We'll travel fourth class, it's cheaper. If I make enough money, we can do this."

"You're forgetting identity cards," Mame says. "Jews are forbidden to use trains, or for that matter, any kind of transportation."

"I haven't forgotten. I met a woman a few hours ago at the Judenrat, a friend of Chaim's, whom I believe I can enlist to forge passports for us, giving us Christian names."

"I don't want a Christian name," Rivka states.

"Me neither," Avi affirms.

"It will only be temporary," I assure them. "It will be like playing a game."

This somewhat mollifies the twins. I add, "This woman, she's a midwife, by the way, has not only been delivering Jewish babies, almost a hundred of them to date, but she also helps Jews leave Poland."

"Where would we go?" Guena asks.

"Possibly Sweden."

"Why Sweden?"

"It's one of the few countries that doesn't persecute Jews. England and Portugal are other choices."

"I want to go to the United States and see the Statue of Liberty," Avi says.

"I vote for Australia," Pearl adds. "They have kangaroos."

"Or we could go to New Zealand," Hanche adds. "It's supposed to be beautiful."

"Eli," Mame says. "Why would this midwife help us?"

"It's what she does, is the simple answer. And Chaim said he would put me in touch with her when the time comes. I can't guarantee she will help us, but she's a friend of Chaim's, and I know he likes our family, so I believe he and I together can persuade her to help us."

"Who is this woman?" Tate asks.

I instinctively lower my voice to keep this information between me and my parents. "Her name is Stanislawa Leszcynska. She's been helping Jews escape from the ghetto."

"A Christian?"

"Yes."

"Why would a Christian help us?" Tate asks.

"Because she's a good woman."

Mame suggests. "She could be working with the Nazis and setting us up to be arrested or executed."

"If that were the case, Chaim would never be her friend. I believe that any woman who cares enough to be delivering Jewish babies is someone we can trust."

Mame and Tate exchange looks, and I realize my sudden influx of information must be overwhelming. Their oldest son has just said he will be leaving the family to work in Germany. They must be thinking I will never return. Yes, I admit, there is that possibility. But unless I take this opportunity, there is little chance any of us will leave the ghetto alive. And it was Tate himself who told me we must survive.

Tears appear in my parents' eyes. My siblings are unusually quiet. I gaze at the faces of my loved ones, and I am aware of a pang in my heart. I will be leaving the only people I have ever loved. I question my plans. *Can I walk away, possibly never to see them again*?

Mame embraces me, Tate joins us, as do my siblings.

Then I think of all the days, weeks, perhaps months without them. I can't breathe. It's like someone is stepping on my chest.

My sight blurs. Tears warm my cheeks. All of us are suddenly weeping. Hugging and crying. This is my family. I will leave the ghetto for them and for the promise I made to my father. The family line must survive.

***

My teeth chatter as I sit on the cattle wagon's cold floor, rocking back and forth with the constant clatter of wheels resounding over the rails. I can't snuggle far enough into my overcoat to warm myself. My head aches. Have I made the right choice, leaving my family? Will I ever see them again? If I die, will I simply disappear off the face of the earth without anyone ever knowing where I am buried?

The journey from Lodz, Poland, to Leibhof, Germany, usually takes a day at most, I was told, but because we have been sidetracked by high-priority trains transporting German troops and military equipment to the ever-expanding war front, we are now on our third day of travel without food, water, or sanitary facilities. Those of us who have handkerchiefs use them to cover our noses to avoid the stink.

Our boxcar is sealed shut. Anyone who attempts to break out by removing sideboards or flooring will be shot. The boxcar holds approximately eighty of us. It's one of three being used to transport workers. Four of our companions went to sleep last night and never woke up. They were stripped naked by those needing warmer clothes, and their bodies now lie exposed like discarded mannequins.

During our journey, I've become friends with over a dozen Jews from the ghetto who were complete strangers to me when we set out. By the second day, the three of us have become close. The oldest is Ezi, a skinny little man my father's age, a tailor. The next oldest, Dov, is an opinionated man in his thirties who is an accountant. The youngest is Adam, twenty-one years old. He's a tall, athletic fellow with movie-star good looks who used to play soccer for Poland's Maccabi Federation.

I must admit I didn't know anything about soccer until Adam explained the game to me and how the Maccabi Foundation sponsored Jewish players in sports all across Europe. Many of their players have become world-famous, to the chagrin of the Third Reich.

I've also learned several Jewish soccer players are led by men like Bela Gutmann and a fellow named Erno Erstein, who are famous in Poland, Vienna, Austria, Hungary, and across Europe. The Nazis shut down the Maccabi Federation in the late 1930s. Adam is certain that once the war is over and the Nazis are defeated, the Maccabi will be reestablished, and he hopes to play soccer for them again. There's a lot I don't know about Jews playing in international sports I hope to find out in the coming weeks.

Chapter 9

Allersdorf-Liebhof Labor/Concentration Camp
Camp #1 - November 2, 1940

I feel the train roll to a shuddering stop. The cattle wagon's door slides open. I blink, and my eyes take a few seconds to adjust to a thin ray of sunlight, a beacon that shines through a break in the overcast sky to highlight swirling snowflakes on this frigid morning. Usually, I would have been entranced by the otherworldly sight, but peering through the lightly falling snow, I see a score of German soldiers lined up on the arrival platform. Above them, on the façade of the yellow two-story building, a sign reads:

Dachau Railway Station

The soldiers, armed with sub-machine guns, have them aimed at us. An obese SS officer stands in front of them. Only the voluminous black uniform with its silvery skull-adorned collar and hat gives this round, florid-faced fellow any presence. *Countrybumpkin* comes to mind.

His small black eyes stare at us as he holds a truncheon in one hand and the leash to a large, ferocious-looking Doberman Pincer in his other.

The animal emits a low guttural rumble. Goosebumps prickle down my spine. The dog looks capable of tearing my throat out.

I struggle to my feet with limbs numb from the cold and lack of exercise. Adam, Dov, Ezi, and the others all rise unsteadily.

"Not the welcoming party I would have chosen," I remark.

Adam spits. "That dog looks about as friendly as a meat grinder."

I hold onto the side of the cattle wagon and peer out at our surroundings. To the east are open snow-covered fields with a cluster of small, scattered houses and buildings. To the west is a large flat area with at least forty or fifty structures enclosed by tall barbed wire fences with dozens of guard posts overlooking the grounds. Hundreds of men wearing blue striped pajamas offer little to protect themselves against the cold mill about aimlessly. This has to be the dreaded Dachau Concentration Camp. I've heard rumors of the savagery inside those barbed-wire fences.

To either side of what appears to be the main gate are two telephone poles with bundles attached to them. A shiver passes through me that has nothing to do with the cold. These 'bundles' are men. From what little movement I can see, they are alive. They have been strung up by their wrists with their hands bound behind their backs. Their shoulders are surely dislocated or broken and must be excruciatingly painful.

During the train ride from Lodz, I learned that we were being sent to the Allersdorf-Liebhof labor camp, one of Dachau's subcamps, where we will be living and working on building roads and making railway repairs for the Berlin-Pozman railways.

"*Raus*!" an SS officer orders. "*Raus*! *Mach schnell*!"

I step onto the icy slush covering the train platform, followed by Adam, Dov, Ezi, and my fellow Jews. The large Doberman lunges at us, to the amusement of the rotund SS officer holding his leash, but we keep our distance and are directed by a soldier to line up three abreast.

Behind us, Jewish workers from the other two cattle wagons also disembarked. Once the 200 workers, minus the men who died en route, have completed a line-up, the obese SS officer in command walks down the line with the Doberman.

He stops occasionally to place his truncheon beneath a man's chin and prod his face up. When he comes to Adam, who stands beside me, he stops to stare at him. "Coat off," he orders.

Adam seems about to resist but then sheds his coat, letting it fall to the snow. He is shivering as the SS officer steps close to him and prods the young man's lips with the end of his stick. "Open."

Adam swipes the truncheon aside. "Putz," he mutters.

The officer's eyes flare. He whips his stick up and smashes it across Adam's face—blood spurts from burst lips. Adam reels back, and I catch him in my arms. The SS officer lifts his truncheon to strike again, and I raise my arm protectively over Adam, who spits blood and shards of broken teeth.

Enraged, Adam shouts, "*Chaser*!" and lurches forward to attack the SS officer, but I hold him back.

"No," I plead. "Don't. He'll kill you!"

The SS officer strikes again before Adam can tear out of my arms, hitting him over the head. I cannot hold him as he collapses to the ground. Adam, his mouth a bloody mess, rolls over and, with a cry of fury, leaps to his feet and charges the SS officer.

"*Attackieren*!" the German screams, releasing the Doberman's leash.

The dog is on Adam in a millisecond, teeth flashing, biting, tearing.

Adam screams, falling backward. He attempts to kick the animal away, raising his arms to protect his face and neck. But the animal is now inside his legs, sharp teeth ripping flesh, arteries, stomach, and groin. It is over in seconds. With his muzzle dripping blood, the Doberman stands over Adam's dead body.

I am frozen in shock. It all happened so fast and with such viciousness that I could barely believe my eyes.

Dov and Ezi are speechless.

The Jews lined up on the platform mutter among themselves, equally shaken. I wonder if the reason the SS officer ordered Adam to shed his coat, making him more vulnerable to the dog's fangs, was not a deliberate plan. Is this fat, ugly man a sadistic killer? Why did he single Adam out? I can think of no answer that makes sense.

The SS officer grins, displaying a mouthful of crooked teeth. He approaches the dog, takes his leash in hand, and pets him. "*Guter hund. Guter hund.*" Turning, he stares at us as if we are sewage that has washed up on his doorstep.

We Jews are silent, subdued by the murderous action we've witnessed. All of us have seen that the Nazis are fierce and most, even brutal, but this! This is a return to barbarism.

I grind my teeth, restraining a surge of anger that has set my blood afire. Seething, I am about to attack this Nazi pig—when I hear an echo of my father's advice. *Be smart, live. You must not throw your life away. Eli, you must survive for yourself and for those that follow.*

When the silence becomes oppressive, the Officer speaks. His voice is high, feminine, "I am SS-Oberstrumbannfuhre Otto Steiner, sub-commander of the Alleresdorf-Leibhof work camp. Our camp Commandant is SS-Obersturmbannfuhrer Heinrich Palme. Remember this. Seal it in your skulls. As long as you are here, we are your masters. We are your Gods. We can have you starved, tortured, or executed; our decision, our choice. You Jews have been sent here to work. And work, you will. If you refuse to join the workforce, we will execute you or prolong your misery by sending you up the road to Dachau. Dachau is not a work camp. It is a death camp. The choice is yours. You either work or you die." He points his truncheon at Adam's body. "Consider this Jew a warning. We Nazis will not tolerate insults, insubordination, or any form of aggression. Now, you will be led to your barracks. You will wait there until you are given further orders."

He pulls a whistle from his pocket and blows it.

"*Schnell*! *Schnell*!" German soldiers yell repeatedly, prodding us with submachine guns, ushering us along the front of the train station, and pushing us away from my dead friend, who lies in a pool of blood.

I hesitate by Adam, reluctant to leave him. Once more, my mind churns as a battle rages between sorrow and fury. An urge to attack the fat SS officer compels me to move toward him, but I hesitate as I once again hear my father's voice … *Survive… You must survive…*

I feel my rage dissipate a bit. Reluctantly, I turn away, leaving my dead friend behind. I allow myself to be prodded by German soldiers as they lead us all to what surely is going to be hell on earth.

***

Snow falls in light swirls, propelled by an icy December breeze as we are transported, yet again, to the countryside, this time in open trucks.

I've lost track of time. So much has happened in the past seventy-two hours. I've left my parents and siblings in the ghetto for what I thought would be a fairly normal job, only to find myself in a work camp set up for slave labor. One would think if they wanted us to work, they would feed us.

My throat is dry and parched, and my stomach aches. It's been three days without a morsel to eat or a drink, except for what water we can squeeze from handfuls of snow. Almost 200 of us stand like ice-covered statues on this frozen landscape, awaiting orders to enter a block of buildings that appear as welcoming as our former boxcar.

Exhausted, swaying from side to side, I catch myself before I fall. Food deprivation and exhaustion are taking their toll. I question, how long has it been since we arrived in camp? I can't remember. I can no longer compute time as I stare at the bleak conglomeration of block housing.

Among these structures are prisoners digging holes while others carry rocks or sand in small pushcarts. None of them has as much as glanced at us. It's as if we didn't exist.

Aside from the dozen-odd guards standing by, ready to kill us if we break ranks, there are no German officers to give us orders on what barracks we are to occupy. With more time to think, my mind reverts to my unfortunate friend, Adam. Even though we didn't know each other for more than a few days, his optimistic personality and assurances that Germany was sure to be defeated were inspiring. If there's one thing I plan to do before I leave this place, it is to seek justice for Adam. I don't know how I will accomplish this feat and keep my promise to my father, or even if it's possible, but if it is, that fat SS officer Otto Steiner will have his comeuppance.

"Will this *farkakte* waiting never end?" Dov, my accountant friend, asks. "I can't stand here much longer."

"Nor I," Ezi says, on the verge of collapsing.

Another spell of waiting.

I close my eyes, half-sleeping as I stand on the icy ground, my legs turning to stone. I dream of Lodz ghetto, my mother, father, and siblings. I hope to make enough money to pay for my family to escape Poland. Is this all a fool's dream?

Ezi collapses onto the snow.

I grab his arm. "Ezi, up. You must get up."

Before he can respond, a soldier steps over to us. "Rise! Rise Jew!"

Ezi lets out a long breath and struggles to his feet, but not before the German uses the butt of his rifle to hit him in the ribs. Ezi falls back, groaning in pain.

"No!" I yell, forgetting to be afraid. "No. Leave him alone. Leave us."

The soldier glares, ready to strike me.

A murmur from Jews standing close by, changes his mind. Saving face, he yells once more at Ezi, "Up! Get up!'

I help Ezi to his feet. The soldier moves off, casting a dirty look in my direction.

"Thank you, Elias," Ezi says, brushing snow from his overcoat. "For a moment there, I was saying my Kaddish."

SS Officer Otto Steiner, his Doberman on its leash at his side, steps from a building across the courtyard. Beside him, a Nazi ensign flutters in the frigid breeze atop a flagpole.

Two soldiers and a man in civilian clothes wearing a blue Star of David armband and holding a truncheon accompany Steiner and his subordinates as they approach. Steiner is short of breath, huffing and puffing, as they stop almost in front of me. The Jewish civilian is a strong-looking man in his mid-thirties with a thin esthetic face.

"Jews," Steiner says. "This is your block supervisor, Kapo Falk. He will oversee your work gang while you are our guests. You will obey him as you would me. He will now take you prisoners to be showered and then assign you to your barracks."

"We are not prisoners," Dov speaks up loudly. "We are workers. Paid volunteers from Lodz. We will shower after our first day's labor."

SS Officer Steiner glares at him, then says, "Correct, you are not prisoners…yet. But I demand cleanliness in this camp. You are fortunate I am not having you deloused and all your hair shaved off. Now, you will follow Kapo Falk to the showers."

Kapo Falk slaps his truncheon against his thigh. "Workers, follow me."

He leads us off, followed closely by guards, to the center of the camp, where we stop before a row of a dozen outdoor showers.

"Strip off your clothes," Falk orders. "Strip now."

As we begin taking off our overcoats, Kapo Falk adds, "You will take turns showering. You are limited to one minute each. This includes washing your filthy rags. Bars of soap are on the trays beside the showerheads. Begin."

"If we wash our clothes, how do we dry them?" a voice from the workers asks as we strip.

"This is not my problem."

Angry murmurs emanate from the crowd.

Kapo Falk slaps his truncheon loudly on the palm of his hand. He threatens, "I don't want to hear any complaining!"

The murmurs quickly fade to silence.

"Excellent. You now have fifty seconds to wash. Move!"

***

Later, shivering and miserable, carrying our overcoats, shoes, and still dripping clothes, Kapo Falk and his SS guards lead us to stand before a row of four barrack blocks. He orders, "Divide yourselves into groups, approximately fifty Jews, to a building. The first building is for intellectuals and educated individuals. All of you skilled workers step forward."

After a moment of indecision, approximately forty men move up.

I turn to Dov, who has stayed beside me. "You'd better join them."

"They're separating us to shoot us. Nazis hate Jews with brains."

"Maybe not. They may need someone to add and subtract. If you don't go now and they find out you're an accountant, they *will* shoot you."

Dov lets out a breath and steps forward.

"Intellectuals and skilled workers go to the first barracks now," Kapo Falk orders. "The remaining three groups take the other barracks. You will share your bunks, three men to a bed. You are to go to sleep immediately. You will be served soup and bread at six in the morning and be given job assignments at 6:30. All of you, go. Now!"

With my stomach protesting its lack of food, I follow the others trudging through ankle-deep snow to the next barracks. I think about Kapo Falk. How can a fellow Jew work for the Nazis? Maybe his mother dropped him on his head when he was a baby. I grin. *That's possible.*

Or, on a more serious note, if a prisoner is asked to be a Kapo, it's not a request one turns down—if one wants to live.

"*Raus*!"

"*Mach Schnell*!"

"*Schnell*!" The guards prod us along with their ever-present truncheons.

As we approach our barracks, we see a medium-sized hill of three-tiered beds spread outside the building covered with snow. We are told these are our beds and to clean them off and bring them inside.

Half an hour later, our fingers stiff and blue with cold, we lug our sleeping pallets inside a dark, gloomy rectangular room with just small windows at either end. As my eyes adjust to the darkness, I see the floor is dirt—muddy dirt.

We arrange our wet-planked beds and, of course, see there are no mattresses, covers, or pillows. But I am thankful to have my overcoat, even though it's damp and will be uncomfortable. I can't stop shivering as I feel like I'm on a peak of the Carpathian Mountains. Is it possible the barracks are colder inside than out? It seems so to me.

I take the first bottom bunk I come to and plop down on hard boards. I roll up my overcoat to use it as a pillow. As soon as my clothes dry, I will unfold my coat, and it will be my blanket.

A middle-aged stranger stops by and gives me a look as if to say, 'May I?'

I nod, and he squeezes in next to me. He, too, uses his overcoat as a pillow.

"Just like home," I mutter sarcastically as another prisoner slides in beside us.

At least there's a roof over my head.

Before I can think about much more, I fall asleep.

***

"Outside! Everyone out!" SS Otto Steiner yells from inside the doorway, holding his Doberman Pincer on its leash. "Out! *Raus*! *Raus*!"

I'm half-awake and bleary-eyed from a miserable, restless night. Too tired for conversation, I exchange grunts with my bedmates and roll off the cot.

I am relieved to find my clothes are dry. I slip on my overcoat, and we trudge out of the barracks.

Outside in the slush and cold, a thick blanket of grey clouds covers the camp. Summer and fall have passed us by like windswept leaves. Will the sun ever shine again?

SS guards yell orders, and we march around the corner of our barracks. My spirits pick up as I spot a table with streaming caldrons of soup.

Small wooden bowls with half-filled watery broth are handed out. In addition, each person receives a piece of brown bread. It's stale, but nonetheless, I salivate. There are no spoons, not that I would take time to swallow a spoonful at a time.

We step a few paces away and, seeing the nearby benches covered with snow, we sip from our bowls, standing up. The soup is meatless with unfamiliar vegetables. Despite the mysterious ingredients, it is edible. I dip stale crust into the liquid and chew slowly, valuing each bite.

Gazing over the camp, I see groupings similar to ours. I assume they, too, are workers as they have the yellow Star of David sewn onto their civilian clothes.

Otto Steiner approaches with his Doberman and Kapo Falk at his side. He suddenly stops to stare at an able-bodied young man slurping breakfast from his bowl. Steiner stares at him for a long time.

The young man nervously does his best to ignore him.

Suddenly, and without provocation, Steiner lashes out with his truncheon, knocking the bowl from the young man's hand.

"Schmuck!" the youth retorts.

Steiner's truncheon whips savagely across the young man's face, knocking him to the icy slush. The Doberman lunges, but Steiner holds the snarling dog back, inches from the terrified young man's face.

Steiner stares at the bloodied youth, grinning, enjoying himself. He finally nods to Kapo Falk, who gestures for the man's companions to pick their friend up.

As the battered, semi-conscious young man is pulled to his feet, Steiner says with satisfaction, "*Gut*! *Gut*. Jews, let this be a lesson to you. Name-calling is not tolerated. Not tolerated! If you disrespect a German, any German, you will be beaten." He glances at the bloodied youth. "Perhaps next time, even killed."

He gestures to Falk. "This man is your kapo. You will obey him at all times, or you will meet the same fate. Falk, take over."

Otto Steiner walks off with the Doberman at his side as our kapo stands staring at us. "Five minutes," he says. "You have five minutes to finish your meal, then you go to work."

The man standing next to me responds quietly, "Too handsome. That's the reason that Putz_hit that young man's face, attempting to disfigure him. Steiner's a sick man. Add to that he's fat and ugly and can't stand seeing anyone who's attractive and physically fit. He's known for having good-looking Jews beaten."

I am reminded of Adam. He was a strong, handsome Jew. If that's all the reason Steiner needs to murder or have one of us killed, he's a dangerous psychopath, one that will make working at Liebhof a challenge.

A half-hour later, our groups of Jews are divided into work parties. Four submachine gun-carrying guards accompany our crew of fifteen as we trudge through ankle-deep snow. This leaves me to question if we are volunteer workers or prisoners. There doesn't seem to be much difference in the minds of the Germans.

The snow-covered road we have been following abruptly ends. Nearby are piles of sand, rocks, a tar mixture, and horse-driven carts that appear to be used for construction. From what I've heard, other groups from the Lodz ghetto will be working on roads similar to this one as well as repairing railroad tracks.

We are given instructions on road building. It's grunt work, mostly hard manual labor. We are ordered to take shovels from a nearby pile of tools, and we begin clearing snow away and leveling the earth along a straight path that has been laid out with red-flagged sticks. It's a long, long track, but I don't mind. As long as I am fed and paid with the money going to my parents, I will help with this road. Although, I do have a twinge of guilt as I ask myself, am I helping the German war effort? But I proceed with the work at hand.

As far as me repairing the actual railroad tracks, well then, if that time comes, I will have to reevaluate my decision to work—or be shot.

Chapter 10

Months go by, and scant news of the war reaches us. From what little information new workers bring to camp, it seems Germany is winning battles on all fronts. Denmark and southern Norway have fallen, along with the Netherlands, Belgium, and Luxembourg.

As far as our progress on the road, it is growing, slowly, painfully, engineered by the labor, sweat, and grit of our Jewish crew under the ever-watchful eyes of SS Steiner, a new Kapo by the name of Dvorak, and our guards, all of whom are quick to beat those who seem to be slacking off or are too exhausted to keep up with the other men.

I witness the killing of prisoners, but there is no one to complain to and no place to seek justice. Jews have no one to turn to for protection. It's become common knowledge among us that we are expendable in the eyes of the Third Reich.

One thing I must be thankful for is the warmth that comes with spring. For a while, I thought winter would never end. We no longer wear overcoats as we pull weeds, shovel dirt, and level the naked earth.

All in all, road building with limited tools is a back-breaking job. To make our lives more miserable, the SS guards are constantly on us. One guard shot a man in the stomach yesterday after he sat down, too exhausted to continue working. The wounded man was hung with his arms tied behind his back from one of the poles by the front gate. He will stay there until he dies. It reminds me of the two men I witnessed under the same conditions when we arrived all those months ago.

Aside from the ever-present fear of punishment and death, we are always hungry. I've come to believe the Nazis have a plan for us;

sustain us with just enough food and water to stay alive and work but not enough to grow strong and become a threat.

In the evenings, when we return to camp for our meager supper, I'm often able to sit with Dov and Ezi. Recently, Dov was called to work as an accountant in SS Headquarters under the watch of the camp's commandant, SS-Strumbannfuhrer Heinrich Palme.

While working in his office, Dov communicates only with Polish-speaking Germans. He has kept secret his ability to read and speak Nazis. Playing dumb has given him access to high-level conversations, short-wave messages, and teletype correspondence with news of the war. Through this snooping, Dov also keeps us abreast of developments in territories where Jews are being persecuted, as well as world events.

I sip my soup slowly, listening to Dov's latest information.

"...and here's what's happening in the outside world. The latest communications inform us that Germany, Italy, and Japan signed an alliance called *Axis.* From what I can piece together, I believe their plan is to conquer the world and divide it among the three countries. I don't envy Hitler's partners; he won't be one to share power."

I agree with Dov's assessment. But aside from the war, what concerns me most are my parents and siblings. "What have you heard from Lodz?"

"Nothing. Nothing at all. I'm worried, too. My family wasn't in good shape when I left."

"Dov," I say. "During your accounting grind, have you come across any correspondence indicating that our paychecks are being transferred to our families?"

"No, nothing. And I've been scouring the books looking for those transfers."

Ezi spits. "Either Rumkowski was lied to, and the Nazis had no intention of paying us, or he steals the money, which is also possible."

Either way, I think, if Ezi is correct, there is no reason for any of us to stay here. But I doubt the Nazis will just let us walk out of this 'work camp.' We are guarded day and night, and we've been told there is no way to leave without proper papers.

Obtaining permission from the Germans is a pipe dream. As far as escaping, there is one major impediment in our way. We know we're in Germany, but we have no idea how to find our way back to Lodz. And to make escape feasible, to search for a way home, we will have to travel, and travel takes money. Money we don't have.

And there's another problem. A fellow worker, starving and desperate, might report any of us who attempt to escape to the SS for an extra ration of food. I put that problem aside momentarily, and my thoughts turn to SS Otto Steiner. I am still haunted by visions of Adam's murder. The Nazi needs comeuppance. I must do something. But what?

Then, a thought occurs to me, one that makes me grin. *Yes*, I think. *It just might work.*

I am distracted as Dov adds, "I have another piece of news. Since November, over 500,000 Polish Jews have been rounded up by the Nazis and sealed in a ghetto in Warsaw. They have no food, medicine, or any of the necessities to sustain life. From what I've overheard, there's no country with guts enough to come to their aid. Our people may all be slaughtered."

"Five hundred thousand men, women, and children," I respond. "Not even the Nazis are that insane. The entire world will rise up and condemn them."

"I wouldn't bet on that. Besides, Hitler doesn't give a damn what the world thinks. In fact, last March, the 'great Fuhrer' appointed an obviously malicious anti-Semite, Adolf Eichmann, to head of the department for Jewish affairs of the Reich Security Main Office, also known as Gestapo."

"The Gestapo is brutal to begin with. Now they'll turn their attention toward the Jews," Ezi says.

Images of my parents and siblings flash before me. "Dov, in your office, is there a way I can get a message to my family in Lodz? Maybe through Chaim Rumkowski?"

"I wish there were," Dov responds, shaking his head. "I don't even know what's happened to my own family."

"Hitler's gone crazy," Ezi says. "He's wasting time and money rounding up Jews while he's attacking Yugoslavia and Greece at the same time."

"It's true," Dov confirms. "And that's not all. From the office correspondence I've read, he's preparing to invade the Soviet Union next."

This doesn't seem feasible to me. I say, "Russia is an ally of Germany. Aren't Hitler and Stalin friends?"

"Hitler has no friends," Dov responds. "Right now, the German army is moving troops and armaments toward the Soviet border."

"I hope Hitler does invade Russia," Ezi says. "And meets the same fate as Napoleon."

"What's with the United States?" I ask. One of my hopes is that the USA will enter the war and stop Germany's aggression.

"They're being isolationists," Dov answers. "Their politicians are keeping them out of the war. The people don't want to get involved."

"Dinner is over!" A loud voice rings out. "Return to your barracks immediately."

"This isn't a work camp," Ezi remarks with disgust. "It's a *farkakte* concentration camp."

"Dov," I say as we rise from the table. "How difficult would it be for you to add a line or two to one of the communiques that arrive from Nazi Headquarters in Berlin?"

"It's doable," he responds, then frowns. "Why?"

"It's just something I've been thinking about." Knowing the precarious position I'm asking Dov to place himself, I add, "Of course, if you think it's too dangerous…"

"Make it short," he responds without hesitation. "In the meantime, I'll try to dig deeper, find something about our work payments."

"Be careful."

"Always."

***

During the next few days, a late summer storm descends on our camp with blustery winds and heavy rains, making work on the road impossible. As torrents pound the roof, my roommates and I are huddled together, sitting or lounging as best we can on the hard boards of our cots.

I am listening to prisoners discussing our next assignment that begins as soon as the storm lets up. We will be repairing railroad ties and replacing rails that have been damaged along the line that parallels the camp. While contemplating this next assignment, I again begin thinking of SS Otto Steiner. The man is an anathema to the human race and to us Jews in particular. How to deal with such an individual before he is responsible for more murders… I am not one to ever condone violence, but there may be a way…

Dov enters, interrupting my thoughts.

"I was worried about you," I say as we meet and find a quiet spot to talk. "Any word from Lodz?"

"Nothing about payments to our families. But I do have something interesting. Germany invaded the Soviet Union on June 22."

While I'm disappointed Dov was unable to discover an update on our families, I say, "Hitler's going down the same road as Napoleon."

"I agree," Dov concurs. "The German high command is rushing troops to the Russian front that they could use elsewhere to better effect."

I ponder this new development for a moment, and then the notion I've been thinking about for the past few hours crystalizes. "Do you have a piece of paper and a pencil?"

"I'm an accountant, aren't I?" He hands me a pencil and a scrap of paper.

I write out the line that just came to me and hand him my note and the pencil. "I'd like you to add this to one of the next incoming German teletypes."

Dov glances at the paper and laughs. "This is good, Elias. I love it. And very, very timely. Can't wait to see this happen."

***

Early the next morning, during roll call, I notice a tall, thin man standing on the headquarters' porch beside SS-Oberstrumbannfuhre Otto Steiner and Kapo Dvorak. This stranger wears a smartly tailored blue uniform as he leans on a cane. From the two winged bird pins on either side of his be-ribboned chest, I assume he's Luftwaffe, Air Force. An Iron Cross hangs from a ribbon around his neck.

As he studies us with the keen eyes of an aviator, I wonder what has brought him to Liebhof.

After a few moments, the pilot nods to Otto Steiner and points to me and four other prisoners. I frown as I see Kapo Dvorak apparently writing down our numbers. What do these Nazis have in store for us? I wager it's not good.

Later, after our meager breakfast, Kapo Dvorak strides up to me. "You, come with me."

I rise, apprehensive. Dvorak leads me to where the other four prisoners the pilot has selected have been gathered. He motions for us to follow him. Exchanging nervous glances, we trail after the kapo to the front gate, where, to our surprise, we are ordered into the rear of a military truck. Two SS guards follow us and take seats as the rear panel is slammed shut.

Kapo Dvorak steps up to look over the transom. "You five are very lucky. You have been selected to work for four days at a hotel overlooking the Donau River. I was there once. Pretty spot. I recommend an invigorating swim every evening before supper."

Funny man, I think, as the truck pulls away. But the idea of visiting a hotel on a river is something to look forward to. Anything is better than staring at barbed wire fences, guard posts, and SS soldiers with torment in their eyes.

An hour and a half later, the truck pulls to a stop beneath a hotel's colonnaded overhang or *porte-cochere,* as I've heard these things called. The two soldiers guarding us drop the truck's rear panel and leap to the ground.

"*Raus. Raus*," they order in unison, motioning for us to evacuate.

Leaping to the cobblestones, I see a marquee,

Hotel Von Donau

The wide entrance area is dominated by an elaborate set of beveled glass double doors where half a dozen hotel employees in blue and gold uniforms stand by. They openly stare at us with expressions akin to nausea as they ogle our tattered striped pajamas.

I stare back at them. I give them a wink.

No reaction. These male and female employees are a combination of the very young and the very old. There is not an able-bodied person among them. This answers the question I have had on my mind. Why have we been transported here? We are desperation hires, sent here to work.

Curious to take a look at the exterior of the building, I move a few steps to the side of the overhang. I catch my breath. This structure is as elegant, or more so, than any of the hotels or office buildings I've seen in Lodz city center. The construction is a solid stone with artisan-worked panels and figurines adorning its façade. Below its domed metal roof are five stories, each with its own set of floor-to-ceiling leaded glass windows that glimmer in the afternoon sun. Its location, on a park-like slope overlooking the river, takes my breath away. I've never seen a more beautiful setting.

The truck's rear panel slams shut, interrupting my reverie. I turn to see the vehicle driving off with the two guards staring out after us. As I walk back to my companions, a feeling of freedom suddenly comes over me. All I have to do is wander away. This fantasy evaporates as the leaded glass front door opens, and the Luftwaffe officer who selected the five of us in Liebhof walks out with the aid of his cane.

"Welcome to Hotel Von Donau," the officer says congenially. "I am Generaloberst Manfred von Reinhardt. I have brought you here for a period of four days to help my overworked employees bring this hotel back up to its former elegance and to chop wood for our many fireplaces."

It takes me a moment to realize Manfred von Reinhardt is speaking Yiddish. And he speaks it flawlessly. I look at this man with renewed interest. How is it possible that he speaks like a Jew?

He must have caught my look of surprise because he adds, "Yes, I speak your language, as well as my own, along with Polish, English, and French. Speaking multi-languages is a necessity for hotel owners. You will now speak your name out loud, and I will connect your name to your face." He looks directly at me. "Begin."

I clear my throat and reply, "Elias Feinzilberg."

Manfred stares at me a moment, then says, "Next."

My four companions announce their given names, and then Manfred von Reinhardt says, "Elias, you will come with me to the fifth floor."

He gestures to a young man standing nearby with a group of employees who have been quietly waiting. "Jans, have the last two men taken to the forest behind the hotel. They are to chop wood until the woodshed is replenished. I believe that should take four days. The two remaining prisoners will start cleaning the bedroom suites on the bottom floors and work their way up. I want them spotless. You are to instruct them on how to thoroughly clean each room."

Jans responds, "*Ja, mein Herr*."

"Elias, you will follow me."

I follow Manfred across the hotel's marble floor, a bit relieved not to be on the wood-chopping detail. We stop before a gilded wrought iron enclosed cage, the hotel's elevator. A man, appearing to be in his nineties, rises from a nearby chair and slides back the metal gate for us to enter.

The old man follows us inside, pulling the collapsible gate closed.

"Felix, fifth floor," Manfred orders.

The old man moves a lever. The lift begins to rise, and as it does, I hold my breath. We ascend slowly, floor by floor, with the cage swaying and squeaking. This is a new and somewhat frightening experience.

I glance up and see that long, thin cables are all that are holding us up. A disconcerting thought. Will we fall to our deaths? I say a little prayer.

Stopping abruptly on the fifth landing, Felix slides the gate open. Manfred steps out and motions with his cane for me to follow. I quickly scamper out, happy to be on solid flooring.

I follow the hotel owner down a wide hallway. As we approach a set of tall, brass-adorned double doors, Felix, who has been following us, scurries ahead to open them.

We enter the room, and I stop short. The last time I saw anything close to being this grand, even with white sheets covering most of the furniture, was in a movie when my friends and I went to the cinema in Lodz, and then I thought those rooms were all make-believe. This is real.

I look up at the ceiling and stare. It is at least fifteen feet high. It is painted sky-blue with puffy white clouds. These puffs are being used as sofas by naked male and female angels. There's a huge marble fireplace, and over it, a painting of partially nude women. Statues are everywhere.

There are bookcases with leather-covered volumes and artifacts. The floor is covered with thick, colorful carpets. Even the walls are carpeted with panels of woven cloth depicting strange animals in park-like settings, as well as rivers and waterfalls.

"Ah…" Manfred says, looking momentarily at a loss. "I forgot your name."

"Elias Feinzilberg."

"Elias, the rooms on this floor are our finest suites, and you will spend your four days here cleaning, scrubbing, and polishing."

I am still gaping at the surroundings when Manfred adds, "I can see you appreciate fine things."

All I can do is nod.

"These suites are special, as is this hotel to me. This is the very place I learned to be a responsible young man."

My curiosity is piqued. I wait for him to continue, and he does.

"My grandfather's best friend, a man by the name of Itzhak Altman, formerly one of Germany's wealthiest Jews, was in the hotel business with my family. My father insisted I go to work for Itzhak in this very hotel to learn the trade. It was an interesting relationship, to say the least. I was a spoiled, wild young man, and he was a tough old taskmaster. We clashed many, many times, but in the end, I not only learned to speak Yiddish, as it was the primary language of Hotel Von Donau's clientele, but Itzhak taught me almost everything I know about being a hotelier and about people. When the war started, the Nazis confiscated this hotel, and I joined the Luftwaffe. I was flying Messerschmitt's until I was shot down and lost the use of my left leg. While convalescing, I discovered the Von Donau had been abandoned. I immediately began negotiating with the Nazis to purchase it."

His face darkens. "Dealing with Nazis is half selling one's soul to the devil. At best, it's never easy." He glances at the old man who stands by, waiting for instructions. "Felix, go to the master suite and begin removing the dust protectors. Elias will be along shortly to assist you."

The old man nods and leaves us alone.

Manfred lowers voice, "Elias, between you and me, I personally find the Nazis and their ilk reprehensible. But I have to deal with them. The hotel became mine at a high personal cost, and I'm not talking about German marks. I know you don't have the slightest idea what I'm saying, Elias. But you will soon find out. And when you do, you will end up hating me."

End up hating Manfred? I don't have any reason to hate the man or even dislike him. I remain silent, at a loss as to what he is referring.

"I leave you with Felix. He will be back shortly and give you instructions on where you are to begin."

Bewildered, I watch him leave. What could he have possibly meant? I will end up hating him?

***

At the end of my four days, ones I have enjoyed, I am finishing my assigned work, polishing floors, when I suddenly realize there are others in the room. I turn to see Manfred and a middle-aged man in the black uniform of the Gestapo standing before the open double doors. They have been watching me work.

"Don't stop, Elias," Manfred says. "I am just showing SS Gruppenfuhrer Heinrich Muller our rooms."

I continue laboring on the floors when the Gestapo officer remarks, "Who is he?"

"A Jew from Allersdorf-Liebhof labor camp," Manfred replies. "I borrowed five of them to help refurbish the hotel."

"This one is not Jewish," I hear the Gestapo officer say adamantly.

I can now understand enough German to discern the meaning of his words. I turn around to see the officer staring at me, shaking his head. "No. Jews do not work this hard. I know."

Manfred and I exchange a subtle look, and then I go back to my polishing. Manfred responds something close to, "He may have me fooled."

"Ja. Definitely not Jewish. They are lazy dogs. Maybe Romanian, although they, too, are lazy."

There's a commotion at the open door. I turn to see a group of Gestapo officers leading in several young female prisoners.

Gruppenfuhrer Heinrich Muller grins. As the females are led inside, I am spellbound. Even in their tattered striped pajamas, these are some of the most beautiful young women I have ever seen. I imagine their ages range from fifteen to early twenties.

SS Heinrich Muller strides up to them and touches the women inappropriately, pointing out their physical attributes as the girls suffer, some with teary eyes, others with defiance.

Now I understand why Manfred said I would hate him.

These young women, girls really, will certainly become prostitutes for men like SS Heinrich Muller and his Gestapo officers.

There are ten girls. I imagine one for each bedroom on this floor. I immediately think of my sisters, how vulnerable they are, and our neighbor in Lodz, Mrs. Ovitz, whose fifteen-year-old daughter was kidnapped and disappeared. So many young Jewish women have simply vanished. Was this their fate?

I feel sick. I have been refurbishing rooms so they can be used to accommodate the rape and abuse of women. Yes, these rooms on von Donau's fifth floor will become a high-end bordello. While there are literally hundreds of such establishments in Poland and Germany, I am still shocked to be in a place where this will happen.

I have heard stories that orders, supposedly from Adolf Hitler himself, stipulate that only Christian women are to service German soldiers. Aryan blood must never be polluted by non-Christian or Jewish blood. Despite this law, I wonder if Jewish women, especially the prettiest ones who have disappeared off the streets, have been furtively forced into bordellos. It's a possibility, but not one I linger over as I don't wish to think of it.

I've also heard that the females in these houses of ill-repute 'accommodate' a soldier every twenty minutes for ten hours daily. Perhaps even hundreds a week. How many of these girls will commit suicide or be murdered if they become pregnant? It is a common occurrence.

I pick up my equipment, and without a word or even a glance at Manfred, I walk out of the room.

Chapter 11

It's a week later, and the rains are gone, and it's a clear, sunny morning. My crew and I are being escorted by four SS guards toward our new assignment: repairing railway lines.

We are walking parallel to the tracks approaching Dachau Railroad Station's yellow building when a black Mercedes pulls up to the loading platform where a train is waiting. Black smoke from the coal-fired locomotive rises, darkening the blue sky.

SS Otto Steiner steps from the Mercedes, followed by his driver, who hurries after him, struggling with two large suitcases. Steiner glances in our direction and his face twists into its customary scowl.

I wave at him and say cheerfully, "*Auf Wiedersehen.*"

The scowl turns into a snarl. Steiner proceeds to the train and boards as his aide hands the suitcases to a porter.

I see Steiner has taken a window seat as we come abreast of the train. He glares at us as we march past.

A few moments later, the train moves, rolling forward.

"Let's give Otto an image to remember us," I suggest as the locomotive's loud whistle drowns out the rest of my words.

As the engine catches up to us, we stop beside the tracks and turn our backs to the passing windows. I'm looking over my shoulder now.

When I see Otto Steiner's face, I say, "Now!"

Fifteen members of our repair crew drop their pants—flashing bare buttocks.

Steiner's eyes protrude, his face flushing—and then he is gone.

"Bravo!" I say as we all cheer.

Our guards, no admirers of Steiner, are unusually quiet. Two of them are actually smiling.

Pulling up our pants, I notice Kapo Dvorak as he walks out of the railway station, where he has obviously been watching Otto Steiner's departure. He wears a wide grin as he turns and walks back toward camp.

Ezi looks from Dvorak's departing figure to me. "Our Kapo approves."

"I believe so. But we have Dov to thank. He added a sentence I wrote to a dispatch that came in from Berlin Headquarters. It read:

SS Oberstrumbannfuhrer Otto Steiner is hereby ordered to deploy immediately to the 12th Infantry Division on the Russian Front to take part in Germany's assault on Leningrad. Signed, Field Marshall Wilhelm Ritter von Leeb.' Apparently, no one dared to question my little addition.

Ezi laughs out loud. Gathering himself, he says, "Bravo! If that piece of drek only knew he was following your orders."

I can't help but smile.

***

Months go by. My crew and I are repairing rail lines. The weather is turning cold, below freezing on some days. So much for Autumn. The steel rails have become frozen again and stick to the palms of our hands, our flesh tears when we pull free, making our lives more miserable. I am off by myself, lugging gravel to the rail bed, troubled by thoughts of my parents. I haven't heard anything about them from Dov. How are my brother and sisters managing? Are they getting enough to eat? Is Guena practicing her violin?

My thoughts are interrupted as Dov enters our work area, which is a first for him. Something must have happened.

"I have news," Dov says. "But first, about our pay that was supposed to be sent to our families. That's not happening."

"The lying dogs," I say as my suspicions are confirmed.

Dov adds, "The odds were never high Germans would pay Jews a single zolty for our labors. But that aside, here's the latest that just came in over the teletype. The Japanese attacked Pearl Harbor on December seventh."

It takes me a moment to realize we are now in a second World War. After the lessons of the Great War, no sane person would ever have thought this would happen again. But then it's insane that we have no control over who brought us to this terrifying event. Thinking of the latest enemy attack, I ask, "Pearl Harbor? Where's that?"

"Hawaiian Islands, they're in the Pacific. The Japanese caught the United States Navy fleet completely by surprise. Dozens of ships have been hit, several were sunk. And get this: one day later, the United States declared war on Japan. Germany then declared war on the US, and now the US is at war with both countries."

I feel like cheering, shouting, and jumping up and down, but I restrain myself as I digest this news. The United States is the one country in the world that has a chance of defeating the Axis powers.

"What's Germany's reaction?"

"At the moment, the teletype is very quiet. But it won't be for long. Hitler is going to have to do something, especially if the United States and Britain get together, which they are bound to do."

"Maybe Hitler can be defeated after all."

"There's more."

More? I think. *What could possibly top this awesome news*?

"You and I will be parting company. You and your crew are being transferred to Wittenberge concentration camp first thing in the morning."

My stomach churns. I've heard rumors of Wittenberge's concentration camp. None of them are good. "Tell me what you know."

"From what I can make of the latest communique I've read, they're short of labor. It's their own fault. They've been murdering Jews instead of putting us to work. Now, someone in command has wised up, and they've started using more of us for labor. So, as long as you and your crew keep out of trouble, you should be safe, hopefully, for as long as it takes the Allies to whip Hitler's tushes. But as you know, Elias, things can change overnight. No one knows what these mumzers are up to next."

"Thanks for the update. You're a good man, Dov."

"You have your moments too. I still get a chuckle whenever I think of your addition to the German high command's teletype. Brilliant."

I smile at the thought of Otto Steiner arriving at the German-Russian front line. "I hope he's enjoying the experience."

"Couldn't happen to a nicer fellow. Well, my friend, I've got to get back. Shalom. Stay alive."

"I'll try. Shalom."

***

Eyelids drooping, I am almost asleep, lulled by the rocking of the boxcar as the train takes us on our way to Wittenberge concentration camp. The hours roll by to the sound of wheels clattering. It seems never-ending, but then a foreign sound—a high-pitched whine—intrudes, and my eyes widen. I sit up straight.

My friends, Ezi, David, and Avram, sitting close to me, exchange anxious looks. We've all heard this unmistakable sound—an aircraft approaching. I'm intent now, listening. Decibels rise, and this high-pitched drone draws closer and closer...

RAT, TAT, TAT, TAT.

Small circular holes burst through the ceiling of our boxcar. Arcs of light shine into the dim interior where eighty men huddle. Cries. Moans. Men topple over, bloody and torn. The shooting stops, and the engine fades.

Ezi, David, Avram, and I exchange looks.

"Are you hit?" I ask, shaken by the cries of the wounded.

"No, we're good," Avram says after glancing at Ezi and David.

Aware one pass may not suffice, especially since the pilot may have recognized Panzer tanks and military equipment being transported on the train's flatcars, I say a quick prayer, "God, protect us."

We sit in silence, waiting…

I turn my head toward a faint whine. Its volume is increasing…

"He's coming again," I say quietly.

My friends and the other occupants in the boxcar sit still. There's nothing else we can do. We're in God's hands.

The high-pitched whine grows in volume…

I swallow nervously and press my forehead against the side of the boxcar. I peer out through thin openings between the wooden slats.

A single fighter plane flashes in the sun. It's coming at us. I blink as I recognize the circular insignias on its wings—British!

"No! Stop!" I stupidly shout as if the pilot could hear me. "We're Polish! Polish Jews! We're Jews!"

My words are lost as a rain of bullets tear through the car, slamming into flesh, wounding, killing. The fighter plane shrieks away, its engine whine fading.

Silence…except for moans and cries from the wounded.

Then, just as I begin to hope the plane is gone, the high-pitched drone is approaching again.

David and Avram stay silent, huddled close by. Ezi and I press against the side of the car for what little protection it affords. My parents and siblings flash through my mind. Will I ever see them again? If I'm killed in the next few seconds, I will be buried in an unmarked grave, and Mother and Father will never know what happened to me. How ironic to lose my life to friendly fire. *God,* I pray silently, *help us live through this. I need to see my family again. I need to—*

RAT, TAT, TAT, TAT.

Wood shatters…splinters fly…additional holes…eerie arcs of light beam through the darkness. I hear the cries and groans of those who have been hit.

We wait…

Moments later, I realize the plane is gone.

Surrounded by anguished outcries, the shuddering car, and the steady rotation of wheels, Ezi and I exchange looks, our faces dappled by arcs of lights coming from holes in the bullet-ridden roof. Thankful to be alive. I whisper, “Thank you, God. Thank you.”

Ezi, sitting close to David and Avram, suddenly realizes they are still—too still. He calls their names.

Nothing.

And then we see the blood—the gaping head wounds. Our two friends are dead. My heart clutches. A deep and mournful pain takes hold. I silently curse this senseless war. I pray, asking Almighty God, “Why? Why do such good men have to die?”

Ezi’s eyes well with tears. I say nothing. There is nothing to say. I carry my agony like a cradled nightmare in silence.

***

September 1942.

Bone-weary, Ezi, our work team, and I traipse into the barracks after a barely edible supper and a backbreaking day of work. A new prisoner lies in the bunk across from me. He’s taken over the space of a Jew murdered this morning for the unforgivable act of staring at a guard. Had he been staring? Or was he just in a dazed state of fatigue? I’ll never know.

I plop down on my cot and wince as the hard planks dig into me. Is my skin getting thinner like the rest of me? I close my eyes and attempt to sleep, fighting off memories of the senseless killing.

“I’m Alan Goldman,” a voice across from me says quietly, “from Lodz.”

Interested, I raise my head to get a better look at this prisoner. He’s a medium-sized fellow, bald-headed, and so skinny his pajamas appear to belong to a much larger man. I say, “I’m also from Lodz. I’m Elias Feinzilberg.” Eager for an update from home, I ask, “Were you in the ghetto?

"Yes. My family and I..." There's a catch in his throat choking off his words, but then he continues, "They're all gone. I'm the only one left."

It's an all too familiar story, but what happened to his family?

"The worst part," Alan adds before I can put my question into words, "they took my children. My three little angels, Maja, Zofia, and Julia. They were our babies. So young. So loving, so…"

I prop myself up on my elbow, waiting for him to continue.

"My wife and I couldn't believe it when we heard Chaim Rumkowski tell us the Nazis' latest proclamation. It ordered all Jews, under threat of immediate death, to give up the best we possess—our children and our elderly."

A stab of fear pierces my heart. "What do you mean, give up children and the elderly?"

"The edict stated that 20,000 Jews had to be removed from the ghetto and sent to concentration camps. Those expelled were to be the elderly, the infirm, and the very young children below the age of ten."

Below the age of ten? A sense of relief passes through me as I realize the youngest of my siblings, my brother Avi, is now eleven years old.

"Before we could even digest this horror," Alan continues, "it started to happen… Children and newborns, still at their mother's breasts, were torn from their parents' arms. Everyone was frantic. The cries, screams, and struggles of mothers, fathers, and children were indescribable. My dearest wife, Ruth, who suffered so much misfortune and whose life has been one long sacrifice, was kicked and beaten to death as we tried to hold onto our girls." Alan emitted a deep moan. "I was hit over the head, knocked out. When I regained consciousness, my wife was dead, and my children, my dearest little girls, were gone. Why did they kill my Ruth and not me? Why? My girls…what's going to happen to them? I fear they will be murdered."

Tears stream down Alan's cheeks as he weeps.

Tears are streaming down mine as well.

I give no thought to attempting to console him. It's impossible. There are no words that can soothe this kind of anguish. I know this as I think of my family and how I would feel if this tragedy were to happen to them. This brings my thoughts to Mame, Tate, Avi, and my sisters. I pray they are safe. Thank God I've been able to have my salary sent to them. It will help them to survive.

I am still feeling Alan's pain. I don't know how we'll all survive these Nazi atrocities—but I will try. I will try with every fiber of my being.

Chapter 12

Wittenberge Concentration Camp
Camp # 2 - January 1943

Our train rattles to a screeching stop, awakening me from a nightmare-filled slumber. *Where am I*?

Yes, now I remember. We were being transported to Wittenberge concentration camp. Peering through the cattle car's slats, I see only darkness. Opposite me, on the other side of the car, lights filter through the sideboards. Outside, I hear harsh German voices.

The door scrapes open. Squinting, I raise my hand to fend off a battery of floodlights. I discern the outline of a brown one-story wood-framed building with a wide loading platform manned by four black-coated SS officers and at least thirty armed soldiers.

My eyes are drawn to the snarling snouts of three German shepherds. These dogs tug against their restraints as if eager to tear us apart. I wonder, *Have the Nazis trained dogs to identify the yellow stars we wear*? How else can they tell we're Jews to be attacked by a single command?

"*Raus*! *Raus*!" SS Officer's yell. "*Schnell*!"

Our wounded begin to limp and stumble out of our cattle car. Others are carried. Hesitating by the side of the door, I wonder if Ezi and I should carry out David and Avram's bodies. Before I can give it another thought, soldiers move in and begin jostling us, prodding us out with their weapons.

"*Schnell*! *Schnell*!"

"*Raus*!"

On the platform, joining the able-bodied, I turn to see David and Avram's corpses being dragged out of the car by their feet, streaking the floor with trails of blood.

It crosses my mind that I don't know David and Avram's last names. Like me, they came from Lodz and had family there, but without knowing their surnames, I won't be able to locate their parents out of 160,000 displaced Jews. I won't be able to inform their mother and father that their sons were killed by friendly fire on a boxcar somewhere near Wittenberge.

"*Raus*! *Raus*!" SS officers continue to yell.

Excited by all the commotion and the smell of blood, the dogs bare their teeth, growling. Those of us who can walk are herded to one side of the platform. The living watch as more corpses are dragged from the car, but for the grace of God, I could have been among them. *Why*, I silently ask. *Why am I still living*?

I don't know. But I do know my will to survive will never leave me.

The worn and emaciated bodies being dragged by us will soon be buried in unmarked graves as if they never existed. A familiar question haunts me. Is there life after death? I believe so, but I don't know for sure. No one does. It is a little unsettling, but one must have faith. I push these thoughts aside.

"*Schnell*! *Schnell*!" soldiers shout, prodding us with truncheons and guns.

The German language has become so ugly to me. Its harsh sounds seem ingrown with the belligerence of the SS.

We begin tramping off the platform toward a sea of darkness.

I hear a gunshot.

Then another.

And one more.

I flinch with each *bang*, knowing they represent the executions of my fellow Jews, who are wounded or simply too wasted to continue on.

With my world deteriorating, I feel pain flowing through me as we march away from the train station. In the darkness, we stumble, we fall, but we help each other. We are a moving mass of humanity struggling to live.

Finally, we enter Wittenberge's concentration encampment. It is a small camp surrounded by barbed wire. In its center is a factory. In these eerily quiet hours before dawn, we are led to a barrack. It's one of several raw wooden single-story blockhouses.

Our SS escort orders us inside. The guards remain outside. Once we have all filed in, the door is locked behind us.

A lone lightbulb dangles from an electrical wire in the center of the ceiling, giving off just enough luminance to identify two rows of double-decker beds, perhaps forty cots in all. Surprisingly, each has a pillow and a blanket.

We fall onto the first beds we come to and lie there, mentally and physically exhausted.

I am thankful to be alive. Tomorrow, there will be unknown challenges, none that favor Jews. The uncertainty is unsettling. I close my eyes and attempt to sleep. The more I tell myself to go to sleep, the more slumber eludes me.

I think of my parents. Then, the plight of Jews. I think of one madman, Adolf Hitler, who wants to remove us from the face of the earth. I think of mankind. What makes a person decent or immoral? I am sure most men are decent. But, if so, how has Hitler managed to alter the entire conscience of a whole country? Maybe he has simply empowered those who were immoral already? But are there really that many wicked people in this world? I find this hard to believe, yet when I see these Nazis in action and watch their heartless tortures and murders, I have to believe there is real wickedness in them. Where did this wickedness come from? Is evil inherent in Man? I can't find answers that satisfy me. And I can't stop thinking.

***

The door bursts open, slamming against the wall. Awakened, I sit up groggy-eyed, having slept at most two or three hours. Standing in the open doorway is a tall SS Officer. He is slim, in his mid-thirties, and wearing a holstered pistol. He grips a truncheon in his right hand. His uniform is slightly different from the ones I've seen before.

He slams his stick against the doorframe.

"*Steh auf*! *Schnell*!"

I roll off my cot, as does Ezi, and we join the workers outside. It must have rained overnight as the ground is muddy. I pull my striped shirt close around me to help ward off the morning damp.

Two SS officers direct us to one of several tables nearby. We are fed a breakfast of lukewarm soup and hard bread. There is no coffee.

Twenty minutes later, we are led to the factory in the middle of the camp.

The SS officer who led us out of the barracks is waiting inside. The interior of the building is dim as the sun has yet to fully rise, and the few overhead lights do little to illuminate the large barn-like space. All around us are open vats of dark, steaming liquid and workstations where men are measuring and mixing a white powder into dozens of five-foot-tall, twelve feet in diameter, circular vats. Each tub has a ramp over it where workers are perched as they measure the powder and pour it into the viscous liquid. They then stir the mixture with long spoon-like poles. The emaciated men at work are red-faced, sweating, and seem to be on the edge of exhaustion.

Breathing in, I whisper to Ezi, "This place smells like rotten eggs."

Ezi grunts. "My throat isn't happy."

The SS officer slaps his truncheon on the palm of his hand. "My name is Wilhelm Dreimann. Welcome," he adds insincerely, then continues, "You are now part of one of our Reich's tire-making factories. We, and others like us, keep the wheels of the German Army rolling. Your efforts here are of vital importance and will be treated as such. You will be working twelve-hour shifts seven days a week, turning cellulose into rayon. This rayon will, in turn, be made into tires. Wittenberge, as you may have noticed, is on the Elbe River.

We are also a reprovisioning port for our navy. Consequently, there will be breaks in your work when ships arrive in port. You will then be sent to the docks to load and unload cargos. You will also be required to clean and do general maintenance on the ships. When those assignments are completed, you will be escorted back here to continue your work."

Ezi and I exchange glances. Working on ships will at least afford us a chance to get out of this stinking warehouse.

"Pray for a ship to arrive," I whisper.

"A dozen or more," Ezi remarks.

"Work begins immediately," SS Dreimann orders, "and you do not stop until I tell you."

He leads us to various workstations in the dimly lit room, and as my eyes adjust, my heart sinks. The workers here are in the worst physical condition I have yet seen. One of them is assigned to show me what I am to do. The man takes me to a station, and I quickly learn my job. I am to divide a granular white powder that has been delivered in barrels and transfer this substance into measured beakers.

When I lift the lid on the first barrel, a strong chemical odor makes my eyes water. "What is this?" I ask the emaciated worker next to me as I notice red burns on his hands and arms.

Throwing a cautionary glance at SS Dreimann to see he is not watching us, he whispers, "It's lye. Don't let it touch your skin if you can help it. It burns like the devil. My advice to you if you want to last around here: Do what Dreimann tells you. He's a living horror and won't hesitate to—"

A blood-curdling scream!

We turn to see one of the workers has fallen into a vat of the dark, steaming liquid. The other men run to him and try to help, offering a long pole to grab onto.

SS Dreimann hurries over and knocks the pole aside with his truncheon. "*Nein*! Stand back! You may not help." He stares at the flailing, screaming man. "Let us see if he can get out by himself or if he burns first."

Ezi and I watch the poor devil splashing wildly, screaming, attempting to crawl, to climb out. I gasp as he falls back, his eyes and mouth streaming dark, viscous liquid.

"All stand back!" Dreimann orders. He wears a tight grin as if he's watching an inanimate vertebra thrashing about, not a human being in the throes of excruciating pain. He remarks, "Lye is a curious chemical. We will let this experience run its course."

I can't believe this is happening. That Dreimann is allowing it to happen.

After a few minutes, the thrashing man stops moving and rolls belly up. His clothes are steaming tatters, his body chemically burnt, flesh eaten away in patches. His eyes are black holes. He is dead.

In stunned silence, SS Dreimann, still wearing a tight grin, begins to clap his hands. It's as if he is applauding a performance and not the death of a human being.

***

A few mornings later, four army-green trucks with canvas-covered beds pull into the camp and park. Soldiers hurry to open the rear drop-down panels.

"Ukrainians," the man beside me identifies. "These guards are Ukrainian. If you think Wilhelm Dreimann is evil, you haven't seen cruelty. These mumzers live to mete out punishment."

"Thanks. I'll make it a point not to step on their toes," I respond, wondering why Ukrainians are helping Nazis. How could they be worse than Dreimann?

"Onto trucks!" the tall SS officer orders. "Twenty men to each. *Schnell*! *Schnell*!"

Two hours later, Ezi and I and our companions, glad for the fresh air, are still riding in our assigned truck. The other three trucks left us a while ago.

Our vehicle turns onto a side road, and when I raise a portion of the canvas covering us, I see a river busy with boats and barges of all sizes and shapes.

We enter a pair of gates fronting an industrial harbor. A sign identifies it as *Elba River*.

Our truck parks in front of a barrack-type building paralleling a long dock where two barges and a formidable German military cruiser, bristling with armaments, are secured to the pier. Navy personnel scramble about maintaining their warship while men in striped prisoner uniforms load and unload supplies on the barges.

After we disembark and are assigned our barracks, our group is lined up on the dock under the watchful eyes of an SS Officer and two armed guards. I almost laugh. *Do they actually think we might attack them and try to escape*?

The officer in command yells, "Attention! Stand at attention!"

When we straighten up, he adds, "You Jews are here to work. And work, you will. Those of you who do not perform satisfactorily will be shot. If I approve of your labors, I will see to it that you are given full rations of soup and bread. Your jobs will be to clean, maintain, load, and unload barges, as well as clean toilets, pump bilges, scrub kitchen equipment, and mop floors. You will work from sunup to sundown. The first ten of you will go to the barge at the end of the pier and begin work. The second ten will take the barge behind that one. Work begins now."

Now? I think with a tired sigh as I look out over the river at passing ships.

Most of them are barges, tenders, and military vessels, but then I spot a luxurious-looking yacht, maybe 100 feet in length, the type I've only seen in pictures. I wonder at the disparity between the lives of those aboard and those of us on the dock. *God, where are you in all of this? Why do some people live like royalty while we Jews live like slaves*?

A truncheon whacks my arm, stinging me back to reality, if one can call it reality.

"*Raus*! *Raus*!"

I give the Ukrainian who hit me a hard look that earns me another whack, and we move down the dock to our assigned barge.

"It could be worse," Ezi says. "We could be dead."

"That's debatable. If we were dead, we might be in Heaven. Instead, here we are in another hellhole."

"Elias, you're putting nails in my coffin. I count on you to keep me from depression. Please…"

"It's these Nazis, they're wearing on me." I rub my sore arm, thinking, we need some good news. Are the Brits and the United States winning or losing? I don't know.

Suddenly, I think of SS officer Otto Steiner. I imagine seeing the rotund Nazi arriving on the front line in Stalingrad, where I've heard that the German mortality rate is nearly 90%. While I wish no one's death, I would like him to experience the constant fear of death he instilled in us. Yes, it would be Providential. Feeling a bit more optimistic, I say, "Ezi, I just had a comforting thought."

"Hold onto it, Elias. Good thoughts are a rarity nowadays."

***

Watched day and night, we are put to work loading and unloading vessels containing munitions, replacement parts for armored cars and tanks, and food, beer, and wine. It is hard, torturous labor with no days off and few rest periods. The food we are given is no better than the slop we've been eating for months. It particularly vexes me to see fishing boats tied up at the docks with their holds brimming with freshly caught fish, knowing we'll never have a chance to eat a morsel.

Today, a German warship ties up at the end of the longest pier. I learn that ships in the navy are given female pronouns, and this 'she' ship is named *HANS LODY*. She is 390 feet long with an armament of five large-bore cannons, a dozen anti-aircraft batteries, eight above-water torpedo tubes, and ten depth charges. Her crew consists of ten officers and 315 enlisted men. She's in port for three days to reprovision food and fuel supplies.

I soon discover *Hans Lody's* crew is loath to perform certain lowly tasks. So, taking advantage of forced labor, the German Captain requests Jews for the job. Ezi and I are ordered to clean her bilge tanks at the bottom of the hull beneath the engine room.

Now, as Ezi and I are splashing around in ankle-deep water at the very bottom of the hull, bumping our heads on steel plates that support the four huge diesel engines above us, Ezi says, "This is the dirtiest, foulest-smelling job I've ever had."

"Yes," I agree. "My eyes are running, and my throat is raw from the damn fumes."

The young sailor guarding us, watching us from a nearby perch, grins as we drain and swab out bilge wells with mops that we then squeeze into buckets and empty topside by throwing the contaminated water into the sea.

Ezi says, "The Germans must piss and shit in this water."

"Work, no talking," the sailor orders.

Surprised to hear my native language, I ask, "Polish?"

He shrugs. "Half. Mother is a Pole. Father, German."

"I'm Elias. And this is my friend, Ezi."

"I am Olaf. You Jews are good workers."

I suddenly double over, my stomach cramping painfully.

Ezi drops a mop and hurries to my side. "What is it? What's the matter?"

"I … I don't know. I ... I feel sick, really sick."

"You're pale and sweating like a—"

I cough, interrupting him, and then I continue to cough. I can't stop myself.

He touches my forehead. It's hot. I have a fever. I take out a kerchief and hold it to my mouth to suppress my coughing. Finally stopping, gasping for breath, I glance at the cloth—blood.

***

"How long have you been coughing up blood?" the young Nazi Doctor asks as he moves away from where I sit on the edge of his examining table. He stands behind a utilitarian office desk. The only decoration in the room is a picture of Adolf Hitler hanging on the wall.

"It just started suddenly," I respond, barely getting the words out before I start coughing again.

The doctor pulls a handkerchief from a pocket to cover his nose and mouth. "The coughing and fever?"

"That too," I answer, unsettled by his questions. "I've been healthy as an ox."

"Not anymore. I'm sorry to inform you. You have tuberculosis."

My muscles jump. "How can I have tuberculosis when I felt healthy yesterday?"

"You weren't feeling healthy when your friend brought you in a short time ago. Sickness, fevers, and coughing up blood are not healthy signs. You have TB."

"You have to be mistaken." I cough once more. "I tell you, I'm healthy."

"No, you are far from being healthy. And, to make matters worse, you are contagious. Tuberculosis is a very infectious disease. I must report this to my superiors."

A death sentence. He's giving me a death sentence. I can almost feel the bullet plowing into the back of my skull. "They'll execute me. You know this, don't you?"

The doctor stares at me for a long moment and finally says, "I'm sorry, but there's no alternative. Besides, you're going to die in a short time anyway."

I grasp for an idea, anything. I cough again and finally stammer, "Allow me a few days to go home to see my parents, my brother, and sisters. I'll keep my distance. I won't touch anyone. I just want to say goodbye. That's all I'm asking."

He shakes his head. "I can't do that."

"Yes, you can. Give me a pass to leave this afternoon. I promise you I'll be back, and then you can do with me as you see fit."

"I can't let you leave." He reaches for the telephone on his desk. "I am calling for a car to take you to a place outside the camp where you will be dealt with."

He dials a number and speaks rapidly in German.

Somewhere in the caverns of my mind, I hear my father's voice. *Survive, Elias. You must survive.*

A short while later, I am handcuffed in the back of a green army truck with two SS soldiers in the cab and driven out of camp. Sitting on my haunches amidst a pile of tools, I can see we are descending a tree-lined mountainous road. I can imagine what the Nazis have in store for me—a bullet to the head. This is not how I want my life to end.

Oddly, considering I'm about to be executed, I begin to take notice of the forest we are passing through. There are so many species of trees that someone like me, who grew up in the city, cannot hope to identify more than one or two. But I've heard names that ring familiar: spruce, pine, beech, and oak. So, I imagine these are the trees I'm passing in this wilderness of greenery.

I cough again as flashes of water appear, to be revealed as a small trickling stream. I spot a herd of deer grazing and birds, lots of birds. As we bounce around the curvy dirt road, I shift my tush on the metal floor to get comfortable. I almost cry out. Something sharp is sticking me. I reach down and find the culprit: a nail. I see it's part of an open packet of 1-inch nails. My imagination leaps.

A short time later, the right rear back end of the truck begins to list to the side, followed shortly after that by the *thump, thump, thump* of a flat tire.

The driver brakes to a stop at the top of a hill. The doors open, and the two soldiers jump out and walk to the back of the vehicle.

"*Verdammt*!" the driver exclaims, staring at a flat tire on the rear passenger side of his vehicle.

I nod with satisfaction. Opening the packet of nails and dropping them one and two at a time over the side of a moving truck offered no guarantee of puncturing the tire. But one of the last nails caught the tread and did its job.

The driver retrieves a black metal tire jack from beneath the truck's bed and throws it at me. He points to the flat tire, where I can plainly see a flat nail head sticking out of the tread. He barks some gibberish in German.

I imagine he's ordering me to change the flat. I hold up my manacled hands. He and his partner exchange exasperated looks.

The driver reaches into his pocket, removes a key, and approaches me. He unlocks my cuffs, and following his directions, I jump to the ground. The driver points to a spare tire under the back section of the truck. He speaks to me again in German as if I might understand him this time. While it's still gibberish, I do understand his intent. He's ordering me to change the tire.

I remove the spare tire from the rack, hold it in place beneath the truck, roll it up against the front fender, and then pick up the jack. I squat in front of the flat. Although I've never changed a tire, I've seen them change it often enough. It seems fairly self-evident.

I play around with the jack for a few moments, then set it up beneath the rear axle and pump it up and down using a little bar attached to its upright pole. The flat tire rises, almost off the road, but then I stop when an inch of the tread still rests on dirt. Next, I pick up what looks like a crowbar with a hollow globule on its end. I fit the hollow end over one of six bolts attached to the circular plate affixed to the axel. I then twist the bar around and around, unscrewing the bolt. Placing it on the ground, I begin repeating the motions on the other bolts.

The two soldiers pull out cigarettes, light them, and walk several paces away. They speak their German gibberish, all the while keeping an eye on me. I finally remove all the bolts and muscle the flat tire off, grunting as it's quite heavy.

The driver nods his approval. I stand and grab onto the spare tire, leaning against the front fender. I am about to roll it to the rear of the truck when I glance at the steep hill below me. A thought presents itself. I look back. The soldiers are ignoring me.

I give the tire a push. It begins to roll down the incline.

I yell.

The soldiers turn to look at me.

I gesture to the tire rolling away.

Cigarettes fall from their lips. They start shouting gibberish, gesturing for me to retrieve the rolling tire.

I am off and running after the tire as fast as I can.

My heart jumps when, moments later, the tire is edging to the side of the road. Then it careens off and hits a tree, coming to a stop a few moments before I—run right past it.

Behind me, I hear angry yells.

Although I am feverish, I run now as fast as my legs will take me.

A small dirt path appears on my left. I trip and almost fall, catching myself, and turn onto the path. A split-second later, shots whistle past me.

Feet pounding, I enter a thick forest. Birds and small animals scatter before me. I keep running. A stitch in my side makes me falter, and a coughing fit bursts from me. I have to grab onto a tree trunk to keep from falling.

Now, except for my panting breath, all is quiet.

Moments pass. Birds tweet again and jump from branch to branch. Small animals scurry through the underbrush.

There is no sign of pursuit.

It takes me a moment to realize I am free. I say quietly, "A *brokhe*! Mazel Tov to me!"

Yes, I am blessed.

Then, remembering Him, I add, "Thank you, God! Mazel Tov! Elias Feinzilberg thanks you."

A sudden coughing spell reminds me of my limited future. All I want to do is to see my parents and siblings once more before I die. With a focused sense of determination, I leave the dirt path and begin walking cross-country, heading northwest as I believe Lodz lies in this direction.

Again, coughing grabs me. After it passes, I walk on. I have a plan now. I am confident I will come across a road if I keep going in my current direction. And, using evasive tactics to avoid Nazis, my journey could take three or four days. It all depends upon how much time and effort the German command thinks I'm worth to organize a pursuit. Hopefully, not much.

I think the two soldiers I left behind will just report they shot me and avoid the embarrassment of saying I escaped.

A tickle in my throat, and I start coughing. I can't stop. Finally, I'm able to breathe without hacking. I look at the handkerchief I've held to my mouth—more blood.

Dear God, please allow me to see my family before I die…

***

"The cough is bad."

Coming out of my latest hacking spell that leaves my chest aching, I roll over to see the end of a double-barrel shotgun pointing at me. It is held by an old man standing several feet from the barn stall where I slept last night. Before I can respond, another cough escapes me. Catching my breath, I finally reply, "Yes. I believe it is."

Then, I realize the man is speaking Polish, and I ask, "Can you tell me where I am?"

"In a barn, on my farm."

"And where is this farm located?"

"Outside of Sierdz. Where are you from?"

Sierdz, I remember, is a town about forty miles from home. "Originally, from Lodz. I am Elias Feinzilberg."

He nods noncommittedly, then glances at the yellow star on my overcoat. He steps a bit closer. "*Juden, ja*?"

"Yes. But please keep back. I am very sick." I add, "Tuberculosis."

Assaulted by another series of coughs, I taste blood and think I'm either going to be shot by a grandfather or turned over to the Nazis and then shot. One way or the other, my future seems to be limited.

My family floats into my thoughts. I close my eyes, thinking, *Tate, this surviving thing isn't getting any easier. Maybe Avi, when he grows up, is the one to continue the family line. I don't think I'm going to make it. Sorry, Tate. I tried.*

This grey-haired man steps closer and kneels beside me, laying the shotgun down. His pale grey eyes peer into mine. He then lays his palm across my forehead.

"I have tuberculosis," I warn.

He grunts and then gestures to my mouth. "Open."

I follow his command reluctantly, thinking he's an old fool.

"Tongue," he commands.

I stick out my tongue.

He grunts once more and begins to open my jacket. "I must check."

He proceeds to unbutton my shirt and inspect my chest. He explains, "I was a medic in The Great War."

Medic or not, he's pretty foolish if he's not frightened by tuberculosis. Before I can say anything further, he picks up his shotgun and then picks me up in his arms. This old man is stronger than he looks. I weigh 140 pounds, or at least I did before the Germans invaded Poland.

We start for the door, with me feeling as helpless as a babe in arms.

He lays me on a couch in his parlor. Milosz Bajor, whom I've come to learn is the old man's name, hovers over me.

Having just heard him pronounce his prognosis, I ask, "Are you certain?"

"Yes," Milosz confirms. "You do not have tuberculosis. You have bronchitis. An acute case, but nonetheless, it is bronchitis."

"I'm coughing up blood."

"It happens. With the pills I've given you, the blood will stop. Your bronchitis will go away in a few days."

I'm dubious, and it must show on my face as he adds, "After the war, I became a veterinarian. People and animals are much the same."

I'm not sure Milosz knows what he's talking about, but if he's correct in his diagnosis, I am hopeful. My thoughts shift to the young Nazi doctor who diagnosed me. Considering his youthfulness, I wonder if he graduated from medical school and the Germans, short of accredited doctors, had conscripted him for the sole purpose of treating Jews. The latter is very likely. That *farkakte* doctor was going to have me shot all because he diagnosed me incorrectly. Now that I realize I may not be at death's door, I need a bit of reassurance. "I'm not going to die?"

"No, Elias, unless you run into Nazis, and they choose to use that star on your overcoat for marksmanship practice."

I sit up and look at my benefactor. He is risking his life simply by taking me into his home. I don't know what to say. How do you thank someone for such bravery and kindness?

"I have a stew cooking," Milosz announces. "You will eat some, yes?"

As much as I'm tempted to accept, I shake my head. "You've done too much already. Having me in your home is very dangerous. Nazis execute people for harboring Jews." I button up my shirt. "I thank you for your hospitality, Milosz, and for letting me know I'm going to live for at least a while."

I start to rise, only to have Milosz put his hand on my shoulder and push me back down.

"No. You are not leaving. You need rest and more pills."

My curiosity piques, and I ask, "There are pills for bronchitis?"

"I have a new antibiotic my cousin in Denmark sent me. It is called penicillin. It helps cure bronchial diseases like pneumonia. I believe it will help acute bronchitis."

It sounds promising. "I'll take the medicine, but I can't stay here. It's much too dangerous."

"I will worry about the danger. You are staying here until you feel well enough to travel. No argument."

I study his determined face. Finally, I say, "I will stay one day. Then I must leave."

"We will see."

I must ask this question, "Why are you, a German, risking your life to help me?"

"My mother was Polish, my father German. Why, you ask, am I helping you?" He shrugs. "It is the Christian thing to do, to help our fellow man," Milosz says, then adds with a wink, "Even if our fellow man happens to be a Jew. Elias, I have an interesting thought on this subject. Since Jesus was Jewish, why then aren't we all considered to be Jews?"

A good question, I think, looking into his grey eyes. I've had the same thought myself.

"Perhaps," Milosz adds, "all those years ago, it had something to do with politics. Don't you think?"

"Yes," I respond with a grin. "Politics. That sounds about right."

I spend the rest of the day with this exceptional man. I am given vitamins, penicillin pills, and a wholesome dinner and supper. I learn Milosz has a son in the army in Africa and that his wife died six months ago from an ear infection. It was the ear infection that had prompted Milosz to write to his cousin in Denmark regarding the new antibiotic, penicillin, asking him to send him the pills in hopes of saving his wife. But the pills arrived too late to save Hanna. Subsequently, the penicillin pills have cured pneumonia in two of Milosz's neighbors. And now, I can already feel they are curing my bronchitis.

I go to bed feeling better. Despite a lingering cough, I realize today has been one of the most gratifying days I've spent since I was last with my family. I am feeling rejuvenated and anxious to be on my way to Lodz. Tomorrow morning, I am determined to leave.

***

The next morning, Milosz checks my vitals and insists I remain with him for two more days. I compromise and agree to stay one extra day. Consequently, as I am now leaving a day later than I had planned, I am feeling better, with only an occasional cough to remind me of how ill I have been.

It's a brisk morning with white puffy clouds floating across a blue sky that reaches as far as the eye can see. Milosz and I walk to a pickup truck parked beside the farmhouse. He has insisted upon giving me two hard-boiled eggs, a packet of bread, and a small bit of cheese.

After we sit in his truck, he hands me a small bottle of pills and starts the engine. "Take one every day until they are gone."

"Thank you, Milosz," I respond, pocketing the bottle, "for all you have done for me. I'll never forget your kindness."

"God's gift."

We drive off. I'm on my way to the ghetto to see my family.

Chapter 13

LODZ GHETTO
January 1944

"This is good," I say when we are two blocks from the entrance to the ghetto.

Milosz pulls the pickup truck over to the curb.

He offers his hand. "God be with you."

I clasp his palm and shake. "With all of us."

I step from the pickup and close the door behind me.

And now, I am walking toward the front gate, feeling excited at the thought of seeing Tate, Mame, Avi, and my sisters. I am aware my breathing is easier now, and the bronchitis is mostly gone, thanks to Milosz's pills.

As I approach the barbed-wire enclosed ghetto, I notice how few people are on the streets. Two SS guards armed with sub-machine guns step from the guardhouse. Their eyes narrow upon seeing the yellow star on my chest. They exchange looks, seemingly confused. I know I must be a rarity, a Jew who wants to enter the ghetto instead of escape.

"Halt," a guard orders. "Your business?"

"I want to go home."

I am searched, and a few minutes later, I am hurrying down Marysinski Street. My heartbeat increases with excitement up until I begin to pass thin, emaciated men, women, and children, along with scattered bodies. These people have been stripped of clothing and lay uncollected.

Garbage is everywhere. Rats scurry. I pass Wehrmacht Headquarters, where my good friend, Dov Cohn, was working two years ago when I left. *Is he still there*? I will check on him later.

I continue on, passing the Judenrat Office where Chaim Rumkowski, the Jewish opportunist, officiates. I have an urge to confront him regarding my paychecks that he said would be sent to my parents for my work in Wittenberge. I will see him later.

I turn the corner onto Wolska Street. Reaching our building, I stop before the sagging front steps.

I am home.

I hear Guena playing her violin and smile as my heart fills with joy.

I dash up the short flight of stairs and enter. I continue up a longer stairway, and I am at our front door. I try the handle. It's open. I touch the Mezuzah and kiss my fingers as I enter, announcing, "Tate, Mame, I'm home."

I stop short. The room is empty.

Crestfallen, I take a few steps into the small room. I see discarded objects on the floor. There are scraps of familiar clothes on pegs. Next to my feet is Avi's little wooden train, the one he pushed around the floor as he pretended the family was traveling safely to Switzerland, Portugal, or England. It's broken. I pick up a few of the pieces. Holding them in my hands, I blink tears away.

"You should have this."

I turn to see our old neighbor, Mrs. Ficowski, and her daughter, Lila, standing in the doorway. They are Roma Christians, and while the Nazis consider Roma's enemies of the Third Reich, it appears they have so far been spared Hitler's wrath in Lodz. I notice Lila is holding Guena's cherished violin.

Unable to respond, I gaze at the beautiful stringed instrument, and suddenly, Lila becomes Guena in my mind's eye. I imagine seeing my sister play.

She looks at me. She smiles. My whole family is with me now. I watch as Guena's fingers and the bow move gracefully across the violin's strings. I can almost hear her music filling the room. My eyes blur once more. *Oh God*, I pray, *let my family be safe.*

I wipe my cheeks and take in a ragged breath.

"Mrs. Ficowski," I say. "What happened? Where's my family?"

"Gone," is all she manages to say.

Lila adds, "The Nazis took them away."

Dread leadens my heart. I swallow, momentarily speechless. This can only mean one thing.

Lila holds up the violin. "Guena said I should have this as the Germans wouldn't let your family take their possessions." She holds it out. "You should have it."

My mind is reeling. I shake my head, knowing Guena often let Lila practice on her violin, as Lila's was an inferior instrument. "No, please, you keep it," I manage to say. "At least until I locate Guena and my family."

May God protect them, I pray.

"I'm sure Guena will share it with you when I find them and bring them home. Mrs. Ficowski, did you hear where they were being taken?"

"No. No one knows. The Nazis took so many. Even though I am Christian, I've heard they may come after us… Roma's next. I'm afraid, Elias. We must all be careful; the walls have eyes and ears. And I fear there's no end to this 'relocation.'"

"I'm worried, too. I'll be careful. God be with you."

My mind is stricken with frightening possibilities. Leaving the violin is a little thing, but on top of other little things, it breaks something inside me as fear for my family's safety grows.

I must find them. These poor neighbors can't help me. There's only one person I know of who can answer my questions. One of my least favorite people.

***

"Chaim, where is my family?" I demand, standing in front of Rumkowski, still the Nazi-appointed frontman of the Judenrat, as he sits behind his large desk.

Behind me, two of the ghetto's Jewish policemen hurry in, ready to grab me and throw me out at Rumkowski's command. These policemen are Jews who work for the Germans, turncoats, in my opinion.

I scowl as I order, "Tell these goons to get out."

Rumkowski sighs and waves them away. As they leave, he says, "Sit down, Elias."

I hesitate.

"Please," he insists. "There are things you need to know."

I sit in the chair in front of his desk.

"First of all, Elias, it was stupid of you to return. This place is death waiting to happen."

Before I can respond, he adds, "There's no easy way for me to say this. I am afraid your entire family is dead."

"What did you say?" I ask shakily, not willing to believe his words.

"I'm sorry, Elias. Your family is dead."

I stare at Chaim, but I'm not seeing him. Flashes of Tate, Mame, and my siblings arise in my mind during happy times, tearful times, and silly times, the last moments we spent together when we all sang 'Chiribim, chiribom' and danced.

This cannot be true! Dear God, don't let it be so, that my parents are dead, my beloved Tate and Mame, my loving sisters, Reizl, Hanche, Pearl, Rivka, Rachel, and my dear little Avi are gone. My Tate, the kindest, gentlest man I have ever known, is now just a memory. I did not get a chance to say goodbye.

My dearest Mame. I will miss her every day of my life. When I was young, all I wanted to do was be with her in the kitchen as she spoiled me with special treats. I will never see her smile again.

The thought of never being with my family again closes my throat and chokes me. Are they really gone, victims of Nazi hatred, stolen from me, murdered?

My head falls into my hands. *I won't cry*, I tell myself, *I won't. Not in front of this putz*.

I look up. "How do you know they are dead? How did they die?"

"Your father starved to death at the end of 1941."

"Starved?" I open my mouth to question what must be a lie, but no words come forth.

"He refused to eat. He gave any food he had to your mother and siblings so they could live."

Bitterness, sadness, and anger come into me. I turn away, attempting to suppress the flood of tears. It's impossible. A painful moan escapes me as if my heart is being ripped from my chest, the heart that loves the dearest man in the world.

I catch my breath. I must not fall apart. I wipe my face. I won't let Chaim and his secretaries see me collapsing. Then it hits me again. *My Tate is dead.*

A sob escapes. I shake my head in denial, a denial I know is useless. My dear, loving Tate sacrificed himself so Mame and the children could survive, yet for what? Oh God, if only I had been here. Somehow, I would have helped save him and my family.

Then I notice Chaim's corpulent figure. He certainly hasn't starved. He looks like a well-fed pig in a feedlot. I wipe my cheeks and glare at him. "It's obvious you haven't suffered for lack of food while those around you starved. Why didn't you help my father? He was one of your oldest friends."

"Believe me, I would have had it been possible, but my situation is overwhelming. No one knows the problems I have. There are far too many Jews, thousands and thousands, for me to help one man, no matter how dear a friend. There was nothing I could do."

I know Chaim was never Tate's closest friend, but still, they were friends. "My mother, brother, and sisters, did they also starve to death?"

"No." He exhales. "There's been a pogrom going on in the ghetto. Over the last several months, more than 55,000 Jews have been rounded up on orders from Nazi Headquarters and taken to the extermination camp at Chelmno. Your mother and siblings were among them. Believe me when I say this, Elias, there was nothing I could do to save them. No one survives Chelmno."

My thoughts are spinning. My family has been gassed … cremated? I wipe my tearing eyes. I imagine seeing their beautiful faces and torsos turned to ash and deposited in unmarked graves. I'm living in an insane asylum. Nightmares have become reality. I can barely breathe. My heart sinks to what feels like a bottomless cavern within my body.

I finally realize Chaim is talking as his words reach the abyss I have descended into, "…this is all part of Hitler's master plan. Only last month, three hundred thousand Jews were deported to Treblinka to be 'dealt with.' It's going to continue until every Jew is murdered. In our ghetto, the bastards have been going after children, the elderly, and the incapacitated. Last month, the SS raided our hospital, where babies and youngsters were taken from their beds and put into trucks, never to return. One SS soldier even threw a baby from a third-story window."

Tremors run through me. It's too much…too much to conceive. It's unimaginable.

Rumkowski lifts a piece of paper from his desk and throws it at me. "This came in an hour ago. The Germans are demanding our ghetto police, Jews, mind you, participate in rounding up 13,000 children and 11,000 elderly. All to be transported to Chelmno, where they will certainly be exterminated."

"Hitler's gone completely mad!" I cry out. "The world will never tolerate this annihilation."

"The Allies know it, and they *are* tolerating it, looking the other way. No one, not one politician, not one country, not even the Vatican, the bastion of Christianity, is offering to help us, to fight for us. Elias, the murders of your mother, your siblings, and the starvation of your father are the result of the Nazis' ever-present hatred for us Jews.

The camps are a living hell. Young women are given to officers until they tire of them, then they are executed and replaced by new ones. There are rumors of medical experiments at Auschwitz—horrendous tortures—performed on living Jews of all ages, children even. These 'experiments' are too repulsive to describe, not to mention all the regular atrocities. Only God and their butchers know what happens to these poor souls before life is wrung out of them, their bodies burned to leave no trace."

I feel my chest caving in. I can't define my horror and rage. I take in a deep breath. Finally, not willing to overlook Chaim's culpability, I say, "And you sat there and did nothing to save my family?"

"I said there was nothing I could do," he replies heatedly. "There was no possible way I could save them or, for that matter, any of the other Jews once the Nazis chose for them to be eliminated."

"I don't believe you!" I yell. "My family and you were friends. You could have hidden them or warned them to go to another location, helped them get to the countryside, anywhere else. There's always something someone can do. And for doing nothing to help them, Chaim, I'll never forgive you. Never."

I rise and stride out of the office and the Judenrat building.

I am walking along the sidewalk. Wherever I look along the sidewalk, there is nothing but drab despair around me, and I have a soul to match, all mangled and torn. My broken heart bleeds as my thoughts flash to so many memories.

I see my mother. *Mame*, I silently say. *I am so sorry that I never had the chance to tell you how much I love you. Oh, how that bothers me now. If I could just have you at my side one more time, I could let you know how very much you mean to me.*

I'll never forget your love for me. When I did foolish things, you corrected me but always let me know you still loved me with one of your great big hugs. Those hugs!

And Tate, how I wish I could tell you how proud I am of you, how I love you. I am so sorry for all the times in my life I must have disappointed you. I know I must have been a cross to bear. But you always forgave me for my foolish actions.

I long to tell you now how much this means to me, how much I admire and love you. And Avi and my sisters, how I regret I wasn't a better brother. Forgive me for all of our little misunderstandings. I love you all so very much.

If I could only hug you one more time. Oh God, I should never have left you. I should have stayed in Lodz. It's possible I could have saved you. I would never have let you starve to death, Tate! If only ... if only...

"Elias!"

I turn to see a familiar man striding toward me, wearing a big smile. It's Dov Cohn. I quickly wipe my cheeks.

"Dov," I respond, aware my eyes are red from weeping.

"I am so happy to see you!" he exclaims. He gives me a bear hug and then pulls back, his brow furrowing as his eyes bore into mine. "Elias, what is it? What has happened?" And then a shadow of gloom shrouds him as he adds, "Ah, the family…?"

"Yes," I acknowledge. "I'm too late. My father starved to death. My mother, brother, and sisters were taken to Chelmno and murdered."

"Oh, dear God…" He shakes his head in sympathy. "I am so sorry. Really sorry. Such a wonderful family. Such an anguishing loss."

His appearance helps to soothe my inner turmoil a bit. He looks much the same as he did two years ago, only fifteen to twenty pounds thinner, as I must look to him.

"Is there anything I can do?" Dov asks.

"No. There's nothing anyone can do."

My memory flashes to our collaboration when we had SS Otto Steiner transferred to the Soviet front lines. The thought gives me a little lift. "What are you doing here?"

"My superiors were transferred. I go where they go. Elias, we must talk. I would invite you to my office for a cup of tea, but as you might guess, it's inside Wehrmacht's Headquarters."

"You're still fooling them then?"

"Yes, they've never caught on that I can read and write German. I'm just the numbers Jew. Please, let's sit over there on the bench. I have a few minutes before I'm expected back." He gestures to a settee on a nearby patch of gravel where grass once grew.

As we sit, we attempt to ignore emaciated people dressed in rags who pass by without so much as a look in our direction.

"Dov, it's good to see a friendly face."

"And how are our pals?"

I let out a long breath, recalling their deaths. "David and Avram were killed by friendly fire when a British plane strafed our convoy."

"Damn shame." He shakes his head. "And your friend, Ezi? Where is he?"

"We had to part company in Wittenberge. But he's his old self, ready to singlehandedly attack a division of Nazis with a spoon or a fork or anything he gets his hands on."

"Yes, I miss him. Tell me, what are you doing here?"

"The short version: I was diagnosed with tuberculosis by a hack doctor in Wittenberge, and—"

Dov's brow wrinkles. "You have tuberculosis?"

"A false diagnosis."

I quickly explain my escape from the SS soldiers who were about to execute me and how I met up with the kind doctor, turned veterinarian, who took me into his home. I add, "This old man examined me and explained I had Bronchitis and not TB. And after giving me some new medicine, he drove me to the ghetto. And here I am. I'm just sorry things went down so fast that I couldn't take Ezi with me."

"Good to know you're healthy."

"What's the latest news at SS Headquarters?"

"This liquidation of Jews that's been going on was planned years ago. But it really started in earnest in March of '41 when Hitler appointed Adolf Eichmann, that *farkakte* anti-Semite, as head of the SS. Then Hermann Goring, another putz, appointed Reinhard Heydrich to commence with what they call the 'final solution.' Since '42, extermination camps have been set up, and Himmler ordered the liquidation of ghettos in Poland and the Soviet Union. Lodz was temporarily spared because of our textile mills and the labor we supply. But the Nazis are still at it. The Belzec concentration camp started executions in March, and so far, they've murdered 600,000 Jews. The numbers are horrific. And now, here in this ghetto, it continues. The SS, with the help of the ghetto police, are at this very moment rounding up thousands of Jews to be sent to Chelmno."

"Yes, I just heard the news from Chaim Rumkowski at the Judenrat. What is to become of us?"

Dov shakes his head at my unanswerable question. "It's a horror movie. No sane person could possibly believe this is real, that this is happening." Dov pauses and seems to reflect. "I think part of the reason is because Hitler's 'invincible' 6th Army surrendered at Stalingrad in January of '43. This must have pushed the great Fuhrer over the edge. I believe he's gone completely bat-shit insane. Even the Generals in my office are talking about his lack of judgment, wasting valuable military assets on rounding up and exterminating Jews. So, Elias, here we are in a ghetto that from what I hear, is also about to be liquidated."

A feeling of helplessness reminds me of how out of touch I've been over the past two years. I finally ask, "Have the odds of the Allies coming to our aid gotten any better?"

"Not a bit. Jews are not a priority for Roosevelt, Churchill, or Stalin. Winning the war is. In the meantime, Elias, I'm planning to get out of this hellhole before it's too late. I have contacts with a partisan group that I've become a part of. Come with me. Help us kill these bastard Nazis to avenge every man, woman, and child they've tortured and slaughtered."

This is something that now more than ever appeals to me. I can't stand by and do nothing, especially if I'm offered a chance to help in the fight against the Third Reich. "Count me in," I respond. "Except … killing … it's not something I can do."

"Not a problem. We need supply chain support. You won't have to fight. Just help supply us with food and medicines. It's an important job. Without supplies, we're dead in the water." He glances at his wristwatch. "I must be going, but we'll keep in touch. Now, where are you staying?"

"My family's apartment."

"Good." He takes off his overcoat and pushes it at me. "Here, take this." Before I can argue, he adds, "I have another one at the office. You need something to keep you from catching pneumonia."

I hesitantly take the coat. It is old but quite heavy and will be a welcome addition to my striped pajamas. "Thank you, Dov. I don't—"

"Please, it's nothing." He waves away any protests I may have and adds, "Now, here's what I want you to do. Go to Wizenberg Textiles, it's on Bracht Street. Tell Kaz Wizenberg, he's the manager; I said to give you a job. While you're here, you have to look busy. Otherwise, you'll draw attention to yourself. It will only be for five days. We're leaving to join up with our partisan group Sunday night."

"Why will this Kaz fellow help me?"

"He's part of us." Dov glances again at his watch and stands. "I must go. I'll be in touch."

"Thanks, Dov," I say as he hurries off. "Thanks for everything."

I slip on the overcoat and immediately feel its warmth.

Sunday, I anticipate, will be an eventful day. Escaping from this well-guarded ghetto won't be an easy task. But Dov is as smart as they come, so I'm not as anxious as I might be if I were partnering with a stranger.

***

Kaz, the skinny, barely five-foot-tall manager, looks me over, sizing me up. He shakes his head dubiously. "I don't know if you'll be able to handle the work here."

"I can handle just about anything," I insist.

"Perhaps. See those bins over there against the wall?" He points to several large containers. "Go over and take a look inside one of them."

Curious, I walk over to the boxes and see they are closed. The writing on the side of the box reads:

CHELMNO.

My hand is shaking as I hesitantly lift the top off the closest bin.

Oh God. I'm staring at bundles of hair—human hair!

A surge of bile sours the back of my tongue. I swallow it back as a tremor passes through me. I want to lash out at the devils responsible for this abomination. *Oh, dear God, this hair could have come from my mother, my siblings. It certainly came from the heads of Jews.*

I feel sick as I turn to Kaz. "Why did you want me to see this?"

"I want you to know what this factory manufactures before you come to work here."

Disgusted, I ask, "What can you possibly make with human hair?"

"The Nazis have come up with a way to process hair, turning it into thread. They ordered the owners of this factory, under threat of death, to use this thread to manufacture fabric. This cloth is then used in various ways. When felted, it is made into seat cushions and upholstery. The yarn itself we spin into socks and underwear. We make entire German uniforms and greatcoats from human hair." He adds sarcastically, "Ingenious these Nazis, don't you think?"

"Obscene."

"I completely agree."

"I can't work here."

"That's exactly what I said a year ago."

"How can you do this, this abomination?"

"It's the only way I know how to stay alive and fight back. As Dov must have mentioned, a group of us are part of a partisan group. This job, which I suffer through daily, has been a means to an end. It enables me to plot and work against the Nazis, and with Dov's leadership to help organize us, we're going to be making some big moves in the coming days."

"Sorry. It's just not something I could ever… I would rather die first than work with…" The words get stuck in my throat.

"Fine. Go out in the street, and when you see some SS soldiers yell, 'God damn Adolph Hitler!' and your wish will come true." He adds, "Or if you can put aside your revulsions and come work with us. Then, in a few days, you'll be part of our partisan group and help us eliminate these Nazis."

I stare at him, thinking, *Do I have the stomach to work here*?

If I leave now and I'm caught wandering the streets, I'll likely be arrested and placed in a death camp. Or if I take this job, I'll become a part of Dov's partisans, which is also a problem for me. I say, "I'll stay on two conditions."

"Oh, you're making demands now. You are an interesting fellow, Elias. What are your conditions?"

"First, I won't work with human hair. Second, if we make it out of here and join the partisans, as I told Dov, I won't; I'm not able to…kill anyone."

Kaz lets out a breath. "Your first condition, I can meet. There's plenty of work around here besides hair processing. Your second condition, I have no control over."

He gazes at me for a long moment, then asks, “Can you cook?”

I think back to my attempts at cooking. They weren’t too successful, but I can’t tell Kaz that. “A little,” I say.

“Good. That’s better than most of us. You’re now a partisan. Congratulations.”

Chapter 14

It is late as I climb the stairs to my family's one-room apartment. Despite all its memories or actually because of them, I have decided to sleep here until I leave with Dov on Sunday night. This room, small as it is, holds so many emotions; it's the last time my family and I were all together under one roof.

I close the door behind me.

As there is nothing but the floor to sleep on, I take off my newly acquired overcoat and lay it down on my old sleeping spot. I settle on top of it and pull the sides over me. It's cold, and I'm hungry, but it's nothing I am not used to. Besides, now that I have a job, I am sure Kaz will have some food for his employees. At least, I hope so.

While I can't shake feelings of depression, I find a smattering of solace in the presence of these four walls. I close my eyes. I imagine myself in the midst of my family once more. I can almost hear their voices, laughter, the melodies from Guena's violin, and the little squabbles between my siblings as they banter back and forth. We had fun together. We were happy.

I weep as the weight of their deaths presses upon me. But then, suddenly, I am grinning as if a rainbow just entered the room. In my mind's eye are Tate and Mame holding hands, and then they steal a kiss, thinking we children aren't looking.

***

I hear pattering against the windows; it's raining outside. Dawn is lighting the sky. I must have slept for hours, an unusual happening.

Rapid knocking on the door.

My pulse jumps. *Nazis*?

I roll out of bed and jam my arms into my overcoat. There is nowhere to hide. I am trapped.

"Elias, Elias," Mrs. Ficowski's voice calls from the opposite side of the door.

Letting out a sigh, I rush to open it. My neighbor and her daughter, Lila, each hold a small bundle and stand before me, worry creasing their features. Lila carries Guena's violin case.

Before I can say a word, Mrs. Ficowski says, "They're coming for us at this very moment. My neighbors warned me just minutes ago. It's all over the radio. This time, it's not only Jews being rounded up but us Latter Day Saints, too. We're leaving immediately before it's too late. You must go, Elias. Run, run while you still can. Goodbye, and good luck to you." With those last words, my neighbor and her daughter dash down the hallway to the stairs.

Run? *Run where*? I think of Kaz. *Yes, I will head there.*

A sudden burst of yelling and screaming draws me to the window. Pushing aside the curtain, I look to the street below.

Two large horse-drawn wagons have arrived. A group of police, obviously from Rumkowski's Judenrat and identified by their distinctive black Star of David armbands, are participating in the roundup. I watch, frozen in place, as dozens of men, women, and children are forced onto the vehicles.

Mrs. Ficowski and Lila are struggling with two officers, attempting to free themselves. Lila swings her violin case at an offending policeman and has the case ripped from her hands. He throws it into the street.

I catch my breath as a passing truck runs over it, smashing the case and the delicate instrument inside to pieces.

"Guena!" I cry out silently with memories of Guena playing the violin.

I feel as if the officer has stomped on my heart. I am impotent as anger seethes. Mrs. Ficowski, Lila, and so many others are dragged onto the horse-drawn wagons.

Suddenly, the downstairs door slams open. Adrenaline spikes. *What to do*?

There is only one stairway in the building. There is no other way out. Then I remember the utility ladder in the janitor's closet at the end of the hall. It leads to the roof. I dash out of the apartment and race down the corridor with the sounds of heavy boots tramping up the stairway.

I yank open the utility room door, squeeze inside, and pull it shut behind me. It's so dark I can't see my hands in front of my face. I feel for the rungs of the ladder, grasp them, and scamper up as fast as I can until my head bumps into the little door at the top. Praying it isn't locked, I push. It opens, and I am quickly outside. I pull the ladder up behind me, close the lid, duck, and crawl to the edge of the roof.

Below me, the street is pure chaos. Jews and others are being evicted and loaded onto horse-drawn wagons.

Half an hour passes. The military trucks have left with their cargo of Jews.

A horse-drawn wagon, only half full of captives, still lingers. I have noticed one thing about the Judenrat's police: they are less violent toward us. Good for them.

The horse-drawn wagon now starts off. It is time for me to leave. I plan to find my way back to Kaz's and stay there until Sunday night when Dov and our little group of partisans will be leaving the ghetto. My only concern is whether Kaz has been arrested.

Minutes later, I am walking toward Wizenberg Textiles when a middle-aged, rather attractive woman suddenly appears in my path.

"Halt! You are under arrest."

Surprised, I stop in my tracks as this woman, who wears the black armband of the Jewish police, has a pistol pointed at me and seems capable of using it.

She orders, "Walk ahead of me to the next corner, turn right, and you will see our wagon. You are being transported to another camp. Move."

"Can we talk about this?" I suggest, as the thought of being in another concentration camp is unacceptable.

"No. Start walking."

Reluctantly, I follow her orders. After a few paces, I say, "If I run away, would you shoot me?"

"Yes."

"You and I are the same, Jews. Why would you shoot me?"

"Stop talking."

"But if you hear my story, I think you may let me go."

"If you continue to talk, I will shoot you in the arm."

This threat is enough to keep me quiet until we turn the corner, and I see a large horse-drawn wagon similar to the one that was taking part in the earlier eviction of Jews. This wagon is so filled with people that the driver, a kindly-looking man in his sixties, gives the woman who captured me a pained look. "We're full, Tisha."

Tisha studies the wagon crammed shoulder to shoulder with displaced Jews for a moment, then suggests, "This one can sit up on the bench between you and me."

The older man shrugs.

Tisha orders, "Up you go."

I balk. I believe being transported to a concentration camp will be the end of me.

"Go," Tisha orders.

Reluctantly, seeing I have no choice in this matter, I climb up the side of the wagon and take my place next to the driver. Tisha sits next to me.

The driver slaps his reins on the rumps of the two horses, and we start rolling up the street.

After a few minutes, with desperate thoughts circulating, I ask this Jewish policewoman, "Can we change places?"

"No."

Hmm. I try again, this time using her name in hopes of finding a grain of sympathy between fellow Jews. "Tisha, I am scared to death of going into another concentration camp. I've been in camps before, and I almost died. I can't go into another camp where I will surely be executed."

"I understand. I do not wish to be sent to a camp myself. So please, do not ask me to let you jump off this wagon and escape." Before I can respond, she adds, "If you look over your shoulder, you'll see a German military truck full of SS soldiers has driven up behind us. These soldiers will happily shoot you if they see you attempting to escape."

Tisha's right about that.

It starts to rain, and with it, I see hope. With raindrops dripping off the tip of my nose, I think this rainfall is a gift from God. One I must act upon. "Tisha," I say. "When we round the next corner, the Germans will momentarily lose sight of us. It's then I will be leaving this wagon."

"Are you forgetting something?"

I glance at the pistol she holds on her lap, its barrel pointing at me.

"No. I'm just hoping you'll pretend you never saw me, that I don't exist. One way or another, I will be jumping off this wagon when we turn the corner."

Tisha's eyes bore into mine. She says nothing.

A bit unsettled, I ask, "You wouldn't really shoot me, would you?"

"I would, and I will."

The driver guides the wagon around the corner, momentarily blocking us from the military truck.

My heart pounding, I wipe the rain from my face.

Tisha's dark eyes continue to stare at me, obviously judging my intent.

I flash her my friendliest smile and say, "I don't believe you'll shoot me. I can tell you're a good person."

"I'm not."

Rounding the corner, I know it's now or never. Without another word, I vault over Tisha and land on the muddy ground, expecting a bullet to smack into me. Realizing Tisha hasn't pulled the trigger and is letting me go, I am off and running as fast as my feet will take me. Within seconds, I disappear in the rain, dashing down a side alley.

Ah, I think as my feet splash through puddles. *I've made it*!

This rain pelting my face feels like the most wonderful shower I've ever had. *Thank you, God. And thank you, too, Tisha, my Jewish angel*!

An hour later, I arrive at the factory and drag my soaking self through Kaz's front door.

"You're late," Kaz says. "Look at you, dripping all over my floor. Get a mop."

I begin to laugh. It's a laugh of relief, a laugh of happiness. I am alive!

***

Two days go by, and by the grace of God, I am still free. The Germans have stopped their roundups and evacuations, at least for now.

Kaz and I are sitting on boxes in his small office, having a cup of watered-down tea from his diminishing stash of leaves. His illegal radio is on, updating us with news of the war.

As I listen to the English announcer reporting, Kaz translates for me. "Despite Nazi Germany's early victories, the tide of war is turning against Germany and Italy. Last summer, with Germany, bogged down in a battle of attrition with Russia, Allied forces began bombing Italy. The United States 82nd Airborne Division and British X Corps under the command of General Mark Clark have invaded Salerno. The Italian forces are now in full retreat, leaving the German army to defend Italy. As the battle rages, Germany is retreating, and surrender is anticipated within the week. This is the BBC bringing you the latest up-to-date news—"

Kaz turns the volume down and raises his teacup. "To the Allies and a quick victory."

I raise my cup. "The quicker, the better." But I'm worried it won't be quick enough.

Kaz has assigned me the job of making, of all things, earmuffs for the German military after, of course, I've made sure the material I am using comes from pure lamb's wool. And, as I can find no sensible way to make these muffs defective, I simply go ahead and sew them to their designated pattern. It's easy labor, and my fellow workers, a dozen men and women, Jews of all ages, have accepted me as one of them. Kaz has turned out to be a *mensch*.

After a meager lunch, Kaz and I are talking. Actually, I'm listening; he's talking, telling me about his lack of a love life. I've come to learn it's a favorite lament of his.

Draining my cup, I am distracted as I hear more news announced on the radio. I dial up the volume as Kaz translates.

"As of the first week of September, Reichsfuhrer Heinrich Himmler, Nazi Minister of the Interior, ordered General Arthur Greiser to ready a mass relocation of labor from the Lodz Ghetto to the Nazi concentration camps of Majdanek and Auschwitz-Birkenau."

"Bastards, not again," Kaz exclaims, turning the radio off. Like many of his employees, he has a habit of cursing and swearing. "Those mumzers keep killing us off, then order replacements and work us to death. It's insane. It never ends." He hides the radio beneath a floorboard by his desk. "Tomorrow night can't come soon enough."

"Dov's going to meet us at 10:00 p.m.," I say, then jerk my head around at the sound of fast-moving vehicles approaching.

I glance out the window.

My body freezes.

A long line of military trucks carrying armed soldiers approaches rapidly and begins to park at intervals along the street.

"Damn! They're at it again." I seldom use this explicative, but now it fits like a glove. "Kaz, take a look."

Kaz comes up to peer over my shoulder. We watch in silence as German drivers scramble out of cabs, dash to the rear of their trucks, and release tailgates that clang noisily to cobblestones. Soldiers jump down and form lines as German Shepherds are uncaged and placed on leashes.

"*Zoff*!" Kaz exclaims. "So much for tonight's plans."

We watch out the window as SS officers shout orders. Whistles are blown. Soldiers disburse, fanning out.

These criminals, for that's what they are, begin breaking down doors and entering businesses, apartments, and homes.

The evacuation of the ghetto has suddenly become a serious business for the Nazis.

They systematically, heartlessly, root out Jews—young and old bear bloody marks of truncheons. The entire population on the east side of the ghetto, over 20,000 Jews, dressed and half-dressed, are being marched or dragged out of their homes and offices with the assistance of menacing dogs.

Yelling, shouting, tears, and screaming are non-stop as some Jews, malnourished and unsteady on their feet, fall and are shot on the spot.

Kaz and I watch these horrors unfold in stunned silence, our anger boiling as we exchange furtive looks.

We are trapped in Kaz's office. There is no place to run. We wait for the inevitable.

It doesn't take long.

The front door is kicked open, rifles aimed at us.

"*Raus*!"

"*Macht Schnell*!"

I stand my ground, glaring, as a surge of adrenalin enflames every muscle in my body.

Kaz lays a hand on my arm and says something I can barely hear, but it is enough to remind me: *survive*.

I let out a pent-up breath, and I follow Kaz out the door into the hands of our captors.

Men, women with babies, and young children are herded like animals, worse than animals, as we are prodded, whipped, clubbed, and kicked along the cobblestone streets. Other Jews, who have yet to be rounded up, watch from windows and partially open doors. The fear in their eyes reflects the grim knowledge that their time is coming.

We reach the main gate with its armed guards, and I can see the Radegast railway station that services Lodz, a short walk beyond. Black smoke billows into the blue sky from a train's locomotive engine as its conductor and crew wait to open the throttle, shift gears, and pull its cargo of Jews to a meeting with their Creator—there is no other end.

After passing through the gate, we are led toward the line of over a dozen boxcars, animal carriages, and our transportation to either Majdanek or Auschwitz-Birkenau. It matters not to me which one we end up in.

I've been searching for Dov among the milling mass of humanity. I know that being an accountant for the Germans will not save him for long. But he is nowhere to be seen. I hope he's safe at his office, waiting for another day with more favorable conditions to escape. Perhaps he'll still leave tonight as planned and join up with any partisans who are still around. I wish him luck.

Thousands of us are herded toward the train by SS guards while the ever-present German Shepherds bark and snarl. It's bedlam as we pass cattle wagons with people crawling through open side doors while others, already inside, offer hands, helping them up.

The guards motion for us to load.

Kaz, who is shoulder-to-shoulder with me, asks, "Which car?"

"The one with a bar, catered meals, and feather beds."

"I believe that's the next one ahead. I've read it has a four-star rating."

"Can't wait."

"Mind if I join you?" a familiar voice asks.

I turn to see Dov Cohn almost on top of us as he's being escorted by two SS soldiers who stop and push him roughly into the crowd.

"Danke," he says, smiling at his grim-faced escorts who watch after us as we reach our 'four-star' cattle wagon.

"What are you doing here?" I ask.

"I couldn't stand to see you boys leave without me." He gestures to the open door where people are pushing past us, climbing into the dark interior. "After you."

The three of us crawl up into the container. It is packed shoulder to shoulder with frazzled-looking men and women, frightened young children, and crying babies.

We find a small space to stand just as the door is slammed shut, encasing us in semi-darkness with slivers of light filtering in from cracks in the siding. Another arc of light filters in from a tiny, barred window in the upper corner of the boxcar.

"Tell us, Dov," I say. "How do you happen to be gracing us with your presence?"

Kaz adds, "With an armed escort to boot."

"Let's just say I was caught with my pants down."

"But they already knew you were Jewish," Kaz remarks.

The three of us chuckle—a welcome moment.

Clink, the sound of boxcar couplings. We lurch forward, and as the train begins to move, we sway against each other. There's literally no place to fall.

"Here's my sad story," Dov says. "I went to my office early this morning to work on forging our papers for tonight's escape. I am the only one there, with the exception of a guard stationed at the front desk, whom I've become friendly with over the last several weeks. Normally, he leaves me alone, and I do my accounting. This morning, while I was engrossed in doctoring our papers, he brought me a cup of tea. This was a first. He's never brought me a cup of tea.

"Well, anyway, he was looking over my shoulder, and before I knew it, and, well … I was caught red-handed forging our 'official' German passes. Since he liked me, he gave me a choice: he could either shoot me right then and there or he could let me join this going away party. So here I am."

***

Three days after our journey had been side-tracked for hours upon hours by military transports commandeering the rails, our train pulls to a shuddering stop at a train station. The air in our cattle wagon is rancid with smells of sweat, urine, and feces. Most of the children have collapsed around the feet of their parents. On the verge of death, men, women, and children stare at nothing.

A mother holds her dead infant to her breast only a few feet from me. We've had nothing to eat or drink since we boarded.

Thirst tortures our throats. Our tongues are swollen, and our bellies cramp with hunger pains. Our toilet, one bucket in a cramped corner for eighty people, has overflowed and sits in a reeking puddle.

Dov, Kaz, and I are leaning against the wall of the car as the wooden door slides back.

Chapter 15

Concentration Camp #3 -March 27, 1944

A gust of cold air wafts into the cattle car. I inhale gratefully and gaze out at a railway platform where I read the sign:

AUSCHWITZ-BIRKENAU

I notice six men in striped pajamas who seem to have been waiting for us. They are wearing armbands with the stenciled word *SONDERKOMMANDO.* Standing behind them are a dozen SS officers in their spotless black uniforms and several German shepherds on leashes.

"Who are these Sonderkommandos?" I ask Dov as we struggle to rise with our legs stiff from lack of movement.

"They're prisoners like us. They work for the Nazis under threat of death, doing all sorts of crappy jobs in return for cigarettes, better lodging, and a few extra scraps of food."

One of the Sonderkommandos, a rare heavyset individual, orders, "Out! All out! Move!"

I limp forward with Dov and Kaz, following the mass of humanity. I watch old men, young men, boys, young girls, women with and without children, some with babies, and a few cripples who can barely walk, crowding out of cattle cars and onto the wide platform.

I see now that our train is parked at a huge railway yard fed by tracks crisscrossing in many directions. This must be a major hub for the German military.

In the distance ahead is a long brick building with an archway at its center that I think must be the entrance to Auschwitz.

The camp, I can see, is enclosed by a double row of thirteen-foot-tall, barbed wire fence and has dozens of two-story guard posts hovering over housing, spread out as far as the eye can see.

Hundreds, thousands of us, are prodded and crowded along the platform while other cattle wagons continue to unload their human cargo. All of us are desperate for water and food.

The stout Sonderkommando who first spoke now raises his voice above the noise of prisoners swarming the platform. "Attention! Attention! I need silence!"

After the crush of humanity settles down, he adds, "I have a warning for you, one you must pay attention to if you wish to live. We have had instances of prisoners smuggling money and jewels, specifically diamonds, into camp. This is forbidden. Anyone caught harboring valuables will be executed, no exceptions. I strongly suggest you deposit paper and coin money, gold rings, necklaces, and any items such as bread that can hide contraband into a basket at the bottom of the stairs leading down from this platform."

I immediately think of a small bread roll I've tucked beneath my waistband. I've been saving it to share with Dov and Kaz when we get to camp, as there is no telling when we'll next be fed. Now, my immediate problem is how to reach the little roll and stuff it into my mouth without being seen. Since Dov, Kaz, and I are at the head of the line in plain view of the Sonderkommandos and Nazis, I realize I will probably be shot before I savor the first bite.

"Those of you at the head of the line," the Sonderkommando barks, "follow me. We are proceeding to your new home."

The Sonderkommando, along with his associates and armed SS soldiers, leads us off, a worn out, stiff-legged group of Jews barely able to stand, let alone walk anywhere. Starting down the flight of steps, I withdraw the small, crushed round of bread from my waistband and toss it into the basket at the bottom of the stairs. Feeling gloomy, I chastise myself that I should have eaten it yesterday. What a sorry waste.

We pass a group of soldiers stopping prisoners at random, stripping them on the spot, and searching them. An older woman who has had her undergarments taken off is having the hem of her camisole searched. The soldier rips out the hem's stitching and withdraws a string of pearls. He pockets the necklace, raises his rifle at the now-crying woman, and shoots her in the head.

We march on.

Two more gunshots ring out. I cringe with each report, knowing if I had held onto my round of bread, I, too, could have been executed.

"Look," Kaz says, pointing to a large black Mercedes escorted by four motorcycles with sidecars as it drives out of Auschwitz's main entrance.

Small Nazi flags flutter above its front fenders as the vehicles turn into a lot beside the main gate and park beside a small group of tables beneath an awning. Soldiers hurry to open the Mercedes's rear doors.

Two high-ranking Nazi officers exit the car. They stand for a moment, preening. They are armed with the usual pistols and truncheons. As soon as their 'Praetorian guard' encircles them, they proceed to the tables and wait, staring at us as we approach, like we're a load of cattle being brought to slaughter.

"Ahh," Dov remarks as we are led toward the new arrivals. "See that younger officer?"

My attention focuses on the thinner of the two Nazis. "Yes."

"That's Doctor Josef Mengele. I've seen his photo. He's one of Auschwitz's chief physicians, and, from the rumors I've heard at my former office, he's a psychopath—and a virulent anti-Semite."

"None of the rumors do him justice," Kaz adds. "He's as sick as they come."

I take a closer look. The doctor is in his mid-thirties, of average height, with no characteristics I can see that would make him stand out in a crowd except for a gap between his two front teeth that shows as he chats with his compatriots. It interests me how a mentally deranged individual can appear so normal.

"One of his specialties," Dov adds, "is performing 'experimental' operations. He has a special affinity for twins, dwarfs, and individuals with deformities, all supposedly for the sake of science and improving the Aryan race."

"Vile," is all I manage to say, as I still feel so deeply the horror of my family's deaths.

Dr. Josef Mengele and his subordinates stand, coldly staring at us, from beneath an awning where two Kapos are seated at a table, notepads in hand.

"Prisoners," the Sonderkommando in charge barks as he leads us over to Dr. Mengele. "Line up before the tables. Men take your overcoats and shirts off. Women, remove your overcoats and line up before the table for a physical inspection. One at a time, you will present yourselves before Dr. Mengele."

I watch with trepidation as we men take our coats and shirts off while the women remove their overcoats. It seems an eternity since leaving the ghetto. Everyone is exhausted. Toddlers and babies are crying. Older men and women can barely stand. How much longer will this torture continue?

Feeling a cold breeze on my bare chest, I'm aware I have lost considerable weight. I'm quite skinny.

The first prisoner in our long line steps up before Mengele. The doctor glances at the man's emaciated figure; he's skin and bones.

He flicks his gloves to his left. An SS soldier grabs the man's arm and leads him to what quickly becomes one of two groups.

During the next several minutes, I see a pattern emerge: the young and healthy are placed in one group, and the old, the infirm, and all the women, including their children, are designated to a second group. It doesn't take much imagination to figure out that the fate of the second group is not good.

As the prisoners watch Dr. Mengele's gloves flick to the left (death) and to the right (life), we are all beginning to catch on to the significance of his gestures. Anxious murmurs grow as the line inches forward. My fate, and that of my friends, lies in the hands of one despicable man.

My muscles tingle and jump as I witness the outcome of those ahead of me. No man should have this power of life and death. I fantasize about dashing up to Mengele, yanking the Luger from his holster, and shooting him. It's a fantasy. I would be shot before I pulled his pistol halfway free, and I promised my father I would survive. As difficult as it is becoming, I will try to honor that promise.

Only minutes later, I am standing before Doctor Mengele. I stare into his black eyes. If this soulless human being can feel anything, he must sense my hatred.

The Doctor stares at me. A moment passes, then his gaze moves to appraise my bony figure—too skinny? Muscles tighten in my stomach. His eyes dart back to mine—my spine aches. The moment drags...

Black gloves flick to the right.

Relief floods through me, and I almost thank him. I regain my senses, silently cursing my momentary weakness, and I move on.

I turn to watch Dov move up and stand before Mengele. The men eye each other. Mengele looks Dov over—and flicks his gloves to the right.

I let out my breath as Dov joins me.

Kaz steps before the doctor. He looks rail thin as he stands as tall as I've ever seen him, arching every centimeter of his five feet in height.

Without a moment's hesitation, the gloves flick to the left.

"No," I cry. "No…"

Dov grips my arm tightly. "Elias, there's nothing you can do except get yourself killed."

Kaz looks over his shoulder at us as he is being led to the condemned group. He puts on a brave face as if to say, 'Goodbye, friends, don't worry about me.'

My mind is in turmoil. I can barely see my surroundings. I turn away, unable to look anymore.

A while later, after Kaz and his group have been led away, Dov and I, along with sixty or more men who have passed the physical test, are led away toward the camp's main gate.

As we approach, there is a two-story brick building to the left of a tall, curving wrought iron gate. My eyes focus on an iron banner welded to the top of its arch. It bears lettering that reads,

ARBEIT MACHT FREI

Dov answers my silent question. He translates, "Work Sets You Free."

"That's nice to know. We should be out of here in no time at all."

"Dreamer."

Before we actually enter, we are halted. Milling around, cold and exhausted, I notice our Sonderkommandos are replaced by SS guards who now lead us away from the camp. We march across a set of railroad tracks and continue over an open field toward another camp in the distance. I am barely able to drag myself along, with my feet feeling like two clumps of cement.

Trudging over the rocky ground for what seems like a dozen miles, but in reality, it is probably only a couple of miles, I hear Dov mutter, "Birkenau."

"What?"

"That beautiful hunk of brick ahead."

The appearance of Birkenau's main building is far from beautiful. It's a long single-story structure with a three-story tower in its center. Beneath the tower is an open archway with train tracks running through it into the camp.

There is another, shorter gated archway to its right. Then, paradoxically, I see small splashes of yellow among the nooks and edges of buildings—flowers! Scraggily, fragile blooms. These flowers are much like us Jews, surviving where they can, struggling tenaciously to hang onto life against all odds.

Yes, if there is hope, we will find it. Hope and God. As surely as there is Spring, our faith will carry us through these darkest of days. I recall my promise to survive and reaffirm it. *Tate, I will try.*

I see smudges of black smoke curling above its double thirteen-foot-tall barbwire fences and buildings. A premonition of fear grips me, and I ask, "What do you know about it?"

"Only what I've heard while working at my office. None of it is good. It's been called hell on earth. It's the sister camp to Auschwitz Birkenau and is the larger of the two camps. It's used almost exclusively for exterminations. The specialty here is gassing Jews and other prisoners with Zyklon B. It's a poison gas insecticide used for killing rats and insects. I've been told it's an agonizing death. Nice, huh?"

I try to grasp the horror of Dov's words.

"It's a very efficient and a cheap way to kill large numbers of people. The cost to gas a person, adult or child, is one penny."

I shake my head at the barbarity. "Then why does Mengele bother with the 'right' 'left' selections when everyone who comes here is executed?"

"No idea. But I guess they must need laborers to dig foundations and build barracks. See those chimneys?"

How can I miss them, I think as I follow his gaze to two tall brick smokestacks spewing black smoke.

"After the gassings, the bodies are burned. That's the smell in the air—burning bodies."

Breathing the foul odor, I am nauseated.

"From what I've heard, Auschwitz has one crematoria, and Birkenau has four, each with about fifty ovens. These operate twenty hours a day, every week, and every month of the year. I'm an accountant, and let me tell you, that's a lot of dead Jews. They bury the ashes or toss them in the nearest river or pits, and poof—we never existed."

I picture the gassings and the flames in the crematoria—devouring my flesh and bones—and I can't help but think of the agony my family must have suffered at the Chelmno extermination camp—I imagine seeing Mame, my little brother, Avi, my sisters, Guena, Reizl, Pearl, Hanche, and Rivka as they are pushed naked into a boxy windowless room with scores of other Jews. First the gassing and then the burning. *No*! *No*.

I must not imagine any details of my family as they face death. I can't bear the pain! My sweet, God-loving family who would never hurt another human being. I blink away tears as a moan escapes me, reaching from the bottom of my soul. Then I am in the present again, hyperventilating and shaking.

"Elias?" Dov asks with a worried frown. "Are you all right?"

Catching my breath, I respond, "I'm better off than those poor souls." I nod to the billowing smoke as I attempt to quiet my tormented soul. "Why is God letting this happen?"

"That's a question for rabbis," Dov replies with a shrug. "I don't know if even they can answer it."

"I don't understand," I say, at a loss, with anguish still simmering.

Unable to contain my grief, I fall back upon my faith. I erupt, "God is always with us. He will be the one to stop this evil."

The guards press us along. To my eye, we resemble a hoard of nomads, which is what we are. Homeless Jews. History is repeating itself as it often does without humanity having learned from the past. I often wonder if mankind will ever become compassionate. Ah, foolish me, hoping and praying for miracles while a well-organized maniac spreads his doctrine of hate and 'Aryan superiority' across Europe and the world.

As we pass through the main entrance, I'm immediately overwhelmed by the semi-chaotic, overcrowded grounds populated with emaciated prisoners. There are no flowers here struggling to exist among the buildings' crevices. The foliage would have been eaten by prisoners long ago.

A stiff breeze suddenly swirls smoke around the chimneys, pressing its malignant ash and embers to the grounds as if seeking burial for the human fragments it carries. Coughing, horrified by what I must be breathing into my lungs, I raise my hand to cover my nose and mouth as I see corpses being dragged out of what appears to be a gas chamber.

At other, like-sized structures, naked women of all ages, some with children at their sides and babies in their arms, stand in lines waiting innocently before buildings that must also be gas chambers. Emaciated prisoners in striped pajamas appear to be half dead as they are pushed cruelly by soldiers being directed, no doubt, to their end. I feel like an icy hand is gripping my heart and squeezing. This is a world of the dead and dying. A world governed by madmen and ruled by Satan.

A coldness settles over me like nothing I've ever experienced. It penetrates my flesh, my bones, and this premonition, for that's what this is, rocks my very soul. *'This is the place I'm going to die,'* I know this.

"All halt!" shouts an SS officer at the head of our migration.

We come to a stop next to a large open area, a mud-crusted field of sorts dominated by rows of two-story brick buildings. A tall flagpole stands in front of what appears to be German Headquarters. Its ensign, a red Maltese cross on a white background, flutters in the light breeze.

Approximately a dozen men in civilian clothes, bearing the yellow Star of David on their chests, approach. They also wear armbands on their left arms embossed with smaller Blue Stars of David that identify them as Kapos. I've seen their kind before. Like the Sonderkommandos, they help the Nazis police us, and in exchange, they are given better housing and extra food rations. It's not a bad situation for them if one can stomach aiding the enemy, which most of us would never consider under any circumstances.

A big, rough-looking Nazi exits the two-story headquarters building and addresses us. "Welcome to Birkenau," the officer says. "I am camp commandant, SS Hauptsturmfurer Josef Kramer."

Dov whispers, "This guy looks like he chews nails for breakfast."

Josef Kramer adds, "I see most of you are rather fit, and for your sake, I hope you are willing to work hard. As you have seen, our camp is overcrowded. We are bursting at the seams with you Jews and other undesirables. The sheer volume is killing us." He laughs. "Actually, it's killing you."

Kramer approaches us, motioning for a nearby Kapo to join him. As the man steps forward, Kramer adds, "This is Kapo Hadash, one of your own. He is your camp leader. You will follow his orders explicitly as if they are coming from me. If you disobey him, you will immediately be executed." He gives us a stern look, then says, "Hadash, take over."

Kramer strides off.

Kapo Hadash slaps his truncheon against the palm of his hand and gruffly orders, "Prisoners, follow me."

"I like this game," Dov remarks flippantly. "'Follow the leader.'"

Crossing the grounds, passing innumerable sights of sick and starving prisoners, Kapo Hadash stops us before a nondescript hut. "Prisoners, go inside. Remove all your clothes and shoes. You will then take showers, and after that, you will be disinfected and have your hair shaved. Next, you will be given prison clothes and replacement shoes. Finally, I will take you to your barracks."

***

It is late at night, and we've been jammed into huts that are inadequate. Dov and I have been warned not to use certain bunks, as the last prisoners to sleep on them died from typhus, a very infectious and almost always fatal disease. Having been showered and then deloused with a white powder that still burns our skin, we now wear newly supplied striped pajamas and ill-fitting replacement shoes.

Dov and I find spots on the dirt floor to curl up. But I can't sleep as my thoughts turn to Kaz. Poor fellow. Where is he? What is he doing? Or has he been executed already? Even though I've only known Kaz for a few days, we enjoyed each other's company. Now I imagine that he's gone—forever.

My sigh reaches through every part of me. I recall my family…I imagine their faces…they too, are gone…all of them. "This *farkakte* war," I mumble to myself. "And these *farkakte* Nazis. A curse on Hitler and his Third Reich!"

Why hasn't a country, any country, come to our aid? Are all the Jews in Europe going to be annihilated? These memories, thoughts, and questions keep coming, all without answers.

***

The following day, Kapo Hadash strides up and orders, "Follow me."

He's not much of a conversationalist.

Hadash leads a hundred of us to a canvas-covered area in a corner of the camp with two tables set up beneath an awning where tattooing is being administered by a couple of antiseptic-looking individuals who look like professional wrestlers.

Hadash says, "Each of you will be inked, like the one on my arm." He displays a series of numbers tattooed in black ink on his left forearm. "From now on, these numbers will be your new identity, how you'll be known from this day on. Your birth name will cease to exist."

I murmur to Dov, "Another attempt to make us disappear."

"As an accountant," Dov whispers, "I normally like numbers, but this isn't a plus for math; it's a minus for humanity."

Dov and I have moved up in line, and as the two prisoners ahead of us are tattooed, I watch with interest. From the grunts and groans of the two being tattooed, I assume it's not a pain-free procedure. Within minutes, the newly-numbered prisoners get up and leave the tables. Dov and I take their places.

I am watching ink pens being re-filled when I hear Dov request, "Instead of tattooing numbers, I'd prefer it if you'd ink a nude of Adolf Hitler displaying his tiny penis."

His tattoo artist, a Jew, actually grins. "I could do that, but then we'd both be shot."

Inspired, I ask my tattooist, "I'd like my tattoo to be the Star of David."

"You two aren't going to last long," the second man remarks gruffly. "Put out your left arm."

I do as I'm told. The man takes a long needle attached to an ink pen and pushes its tip beneath my skin. It's uncomfortable but more annoying than painful. I watch tiny black dots appear, staining my skin to form the letter **B,** followed by the numerals **1, 2, 5, and 9**.

"Feh!" the tattooist remarks as he checks his paperwork. "I messed up the numbers. They don't match my record sheet."

"Forget it," his partner says. "He'll be toast before anyone checks his numbers."

"Right," my tattooist agrees. "Move on."

I look at my tattoo. B-1259. Perfect or not, it's what it is. What I didn't like was the putz's remark about me soon becoming toast. I wipe droplets of blood off my arm and rise from the table, joining Dov and our companions. Dov's tattoo reads B-1258.

Hours later, after our entire group has been tattooed, a dozen SS soldiers surround us, and Kapo Hadash announces, "Attention! You will now be taken to your place of work."

Work? Digging our own graves, perhaps?

It turns out that we are continually rotated from digging barrack foundations to digging pits for the ever-growing number of corpses accumulating as thousands upon thousands of Jews are gassed, ending up decaying in piles as the ovens cannot keep up with the ever-growing number of corpses. Even Birkenau's four crematoriums, incinerating thousands a day, can't keep up with the numbers of murdered. The Nazis are resorting to their old system of burning bodies in pits to help with the continuing overflow of the dead.

The smell of burning flesh permeates our hair, our clothes, and the very air we breathe.

At night, we fall onto our hard plank beds. We have found some that we hope are not contaminated. Exhausted but unable to sleep through the night, I am assaulted by nightmares and horrific visions of the dead.

Awake, I hear the man on the cot across from me moaning and muttering about his lost family and friends. I would like to ask him to be quiet, but I know he can't be silent. His demons are my demons. We exist in limbo, hovering between life and death, with death encroaching on us like a shadow. It's not just starvation and the Nazis who are killing us; it's typhus, pneumonia, tuberculosis, dysentery, even colds and the flu.

"I want to go home," Andrej, the older Czechoslovakian Jewish man on the bunk above me, mumbles in Yiddish, repeating this refrain every few seconds, his voice is a cross between a moan and a cry.

Still wide awake at this unknowable hour of the night, I stare at the underside of his planks, only inches above my nose. These three-tiered bunk beds, if you can call them that, were built for two, not our present five occupants. With only two feet of space between tiers, it is impossible for those on the middle and bottom cots to sit up and extremely difficult to turn over. With Dov and my three other bunkmates squished together, it is a major event to crawl in and out of bed.

Dov, who is behind me, is snoring in my ear. How he manages to sleep in these conditions amazes me.

"I'm going to leave now and go home," the Czech moans. "But first, I'm going to kill some Nazis."

I whisper, "Andrej, try to get some sleep. You need your strength."

"No. First, I have to kill some Nazis. They murdered my family. They shot my wife and locked my children into our house, and then they burned it down. My neighbors told me of my children's screams. I hear them in my nightmares. I see my innocent little angels burning."

He lets out a gasp so deep it reaches into me, squeezing my heart.

He adds, "I am not a violent man. But I'm not a man unless I avenge them. God wants me to do this."

"Andrej, I don't believe God wants you to murder anyone. And I'm guessing He doesn't want you to throw your life away by attempting to kill a Nazi. I believe God spared you for a reason, Andrej. He doesn't want you to—"

"You don't know what God wants or that he spared me. It could be nothing but luck."

"I agree. But you're still breathing. That means something. And if you are at all religious, then—"

"I used to be religious, Elias," he interrupts with a sigh. "But it's so hard to believe in God or anything anymore."

His thoughts are heavy. I wish I had the words to help him. But sometimes, the hole of depression is just too deep. Since I've been there, I know how he feels. I will try to help him as my faith has helped me. "Andrej, I experienced having my father starve to death and my mother, brother, and sisters gassed and burned. Believe me, just like you, I, too, thought of revenge. But then I remembered words in the Talmud where God says revenge is His. Those words pulled me back from the edge of despair. I believe those words are sacred."

There is a long moment of silence.

Andrej finally says, "Elias, do you believe God will really avenge my family?"

"I do. Maybe not in a way we understand, but when He says, 'revenge is His,' I believe Him."

There is a long silence, and then Andrej says quietly, "Thank you, Elias. You have given me some peace."

I smile inside. "Good night, Andrej."

***

Dov, I, and our fellow Jews have been working—no, slaving is the correct word—under the most barbaric conditions. We suffer from the rain, cold, mold that grows in our shoes, aching muscles, and blisters that fester and bleed, all on a starvation diet that barely sustains us. I am wasting away, getting weaker by the day. How long do these Nazis expect us to work under these conditions? It's a foolish question. It seems stupid to me. If they fed us an adequate diet, we could work longer and produce more efficiently. But this does not fit into their game plan of ridding the world of Jews. I witness horrors hourly as men and women are pushed beyond the limits of their endurance.

Yesterday, as we marched outside the camp's fence, I noticed a group of female prisoners. They were being forced to manually push four wagons loaded with rocks back and forth, up and down the same short section of rails—non-stop. There is no sense to this other than enforced torture. When one of these poor souls fell with exhaustion, a rifle was pressed to the back of her head, and she was executed.

Why are these Nazis so heartless and cruel?

I have no answers.

Chapter 16

October 1944

I later learned in June of this year, Allied troops landed in Normandy in an operation called D-Day. By August, Hitler's forces were defeated, turning the tide of the war against Germany.

***

After assembling for evening rollcall, we've been standing at attention for over an hour in glacial rain that drips from the top of our caps to puddle in the bottom of our shoes. When the Nazis finally deign to show up and count us, we are counted and given supper: a piece of soggy bread. We return to our barracks, past the point of exhaustion.

It is long after midnight, and I am drifting in and out of an erratic sleep, only half-aware of moaning and fitful tossing around me. Rolling over, I realize I have extra space. I open my eyes to see that Dov is gone. I imagine he's using the latrine.

It is a bit later when Dov climbs back into our bunk. His clothes are stiff from the cold. "You awake?" he asks in a whisper.

"More or less," I whisper back. "You okay?"

"No. I'm a dead man."

"Dead men don't talk."

"I'm about to be a dead man."

"It waits for all of us," I say.

"I'm serious. I lost my cap."

"For this, you're going to die?"

"For this, I will be executed."

I prop myself up on an elbow. "What's this?"

"It's a long story."

"I have time."

Dov lets out a heavy breath. "A few days ago, I agreed to help a Sonderkommando who asked me for a favor."

"I'm listening." But I am also reading lips in the scant light as he whispers so softly.

"I should explain. He's part of a group planning an uprising."

"Feh!" I exclaim in a whisper. "Weak, unarmed, half-starved prisoners are going to attempt an uprising against a hundred or more SS soldiers and guards with machine guns? This is *meshuggah*."

"They're really quite sane. And there are hundreds of them."

I shake my head. "Hundreds with fists, rocks…"

"Winning is not the point. They plan on making a statement to the world."

"Suicide is a statement?"

"Call it what you will. But the aftershocks of this rebellion will let the world know about the horrifying mass murders these Nazis are committing."

"They may already know this and have other priorities, such as winning the war before they can get to us. In any case, I would not associate with any Sonderkommandos. I've heard they're recruited from convicts and the scum of humanity. Any one of them could give you up for helping them and—"

"My first thought. But those I've spoken to are good men, especially the Jews who can relate to us. While they cannot stop the murders and cremations, they treat our dead with the greatest possible respect—unlike some of the non-Jewish Sonderkommandos who treat bodies like garbage. Our Jewish workers pray Kaddish for our dead while doing their hellish work."

"Dov, my advice: stay away from these people."

"Too late. I've already retrieved gunpowder from a drop site and delivered it to them."

"What?"

"Shhh! I'll explain. Four Jewish women working in a munitions factory have been stealing small amounts of gunpowder, wrapping it in little pieces of paper, and sneaking them out beneath their clothes. They drop these packets off at a drop site on the way back to the barracks. It's been going on every day for over a year until this week when they finally have enough to make a few bombs out of sardine tins."

"How big are these bombs?"

"Small, but there's enough of them to take down a crematorium, maybe two. The explosions will be the signal that starts the uprising."

"You said you delivered this gunpowder?"

"An hour ago. My problem is, while heading back to the barracks, a couple of SS guards saw me from a distance and ordered me to halt. Of course, I took off running. They chased me, but I was able to outrun them."

"Did they see your face?"

"No. It was too dark."

"So, what's the problem?"

"While I was running, I tripped, fell, and lost my cap. I searched all over for it, but with the SS breathing down my neck, I had to leave it."

I shrug. "One cap looks much like another."

"I wrote my tattoo number on the inside of the headband."

Hmm, this is a serious problem. "Where you fell, is there anything to mark the spot?"

"The 'bone-crusher.' I fell down next to it. The cap has to be somewhere close by, but it was so dark I couldn't find it."

This bone-crusher machine, I recall, is the talk of the barracks. It's a bulky mechanized contraption about ten feet tall, eight-feet wide, and twelve feet long, set by the entrance to Crematoria 4. It's used to pulverize leftover bones from the ovens. I ask, "When do the Sonderkommandos plan to detonate these bombs?"

"I don't know the exact time, but it's sometime tomorrow. And as daylight is only minutes away, there's no time for me to go back and search for my cap. I have no doubt it will be found. This is why I'm a dead man."

I believe Dov's conclusion is correct. But what can I do? I look out the window. The horizon shows a slight indication that dawn is approaching.

Lightning suddenly flashes, followed by a thunderclap that booms overhead. Rain begins to patter against the window, running down the glass, and I think the drops are like tears, crying for an uprising that is certain to fail.

I am sick at heart. The thought of losing my friend devastates me. I am not a fighter, at least not with my fists or weapons, but I am a friend. And because of this, I know I have to act to do this thing I am thinking, even though it frightens me to death.

I begin to squeeze my way out of the bunk.

"Where are you going?"

"Latrine," I lie. "We'll talk when I return."

I step out into the rain. Lightning illuminates me and the camp; I am crazy to do this!

Except for the steady rain, everything is quiet. I appear to be alone. Very soon, with the dawn, the guards in the watchtowers will have an unrestricted view of the grounds. Fighting back the urge to return to the barracks, I hurry into the shadows, running as fast as I dare toward the 'bone-crusher.'

As I approach the black mechanical monstrosity resembling a great hulking bear, I wipe the rain from my face and peer at the tall wooden fence surrounding crematorium 4. Smoke and sparks spew from its chimney. I have never been this close to a crematorium.

With the next flash of lightning, my attention is drawn to rain-shrouded figures pushing heavily loaded carts toward the fence.

Voices shout.

The fence's main gate opens wide, and light fans out from the bowels of the crematorium.

Overhead, fiery snakes of lightning illuminate the sky and the cargo on the carts. My eyes stare, narrowing, unwilling to acknowledge what they are witnessing. I clench my eyes and reopen them.

Oh, dear God! I am looking at twisted piles of naked bodies: women, children, and small babies.

My throat constricts, a moan escapes me. Tears flow, mingling with raindrops on their way to this sad earth.

Anguish paralyzes me. The sights before me are beyond the limits of my capacity to absorb. I am transfixed, staring at the orange glow emanating from rows of ovens glistening off sweaty, emaciated, half-naked men as they unload the new arrivals. Others are inserting corpses into incinerators. This is a ghoulish assembly line. How many Jews? How many entire families have gone into these ovens? I grind my teeth until my jaw aches and pain reaches my temples. I cover my mouth, stifling a cry. I must control myself.

I stagger back, leaning against the 'bone-crusher,' then jump away as I realize what I've been touching. Feeling a lump beneath my feet, I look down. A cap. I snatch it up, and, with lightning flashes, I am able to read—B-1258—Dov's tattoo numbers.

Headlights flash over me. I turn to see a truck coming down the road. I duck behind the corner of the machine, my heart pumping. Did the driver see me?

The vehicle, windshield wipers swishing, drives slowly by, finally passing me. Releasing a long breath, I turn and run away as fast as I can.

Dawn is lighting the rainy morning as I slip inside the door of our barracks. I stand against the wall until most of the water has stopped pooling from my clothes. I make my way over to our bunk and crawl between Dov and my other three bunkmates.

Dov's is sleeping.

The prisoner on the other side of me moans, "You're wet, damn it."

"Sorry," I reply, moving a scant inch away.

How can Dov fall asleep under these circumstances? It no longer surprises me. I wish I had the same gift.

I don't wake him. I simply place the cap on his head. His life, I know, is still in jeopardy as his name could be revealed if they catch the collaborators. There is nothing I can do about this, so I close my eyes and try to sleep, but I don't.

Thirty minutes later, still pleased with myself that I was able to locate Dov's cap, I am staring at the bottom planks close above me. The room is relatively quiet, aside from the usual snoring, whimpering, and occasional nightmarish shriek. I blow out a long breath, attempting to clear my mind. The bomb, or bombs, as Dov said, are set to explode today.

A whistle blows.

My heart jumps.

Dov stirs. He opens his eyes and discovers his cap. He quickly checks the inside headliner, grins, and looks at me. "How in the devil?"

"I went out for a little walk earlier and stepped right on it. Nothing to it."

I can tell, by his expression, he knows there is more to it than I am letting on. He says, "Thanks, my friend. You've saved my life."

"Hardly worth a 'thanks,'" I quip. "Maybe we should step outside."

"You two ever shut up?" the man beside us remarks.

We laugh and crawl out of the bunk.

After the roll call, we are ordered back to our barracks. This worries me as we should be sent to our workstations. I suspect the Nazis may have been alerted to the planned uprising.

As the day wears on, my anxiety rises. Dov and I wait for something to happen. But when there are no detonations, Dov shrugs philosophically. "They must have been discovered."

"Feh!" I say. "All that work for noth—"

BOOM!

A huge fireball shoots into the sky. Reaching its apex, flaming debris and oven parts rain down as we stare with open mouths.

They did it!

Dov and I look at one another, containing our reactions. Neither of us can be certain our companions can be trusted with the knowledge they have two rebel sympathizers in their midst.

Alarms *scream!*

In the distance, we hear other explosions, possibly from other bombs and other crematoriums.

The grounds fill with prisoners charging headquarters and the soldiers' barracks, a mélange of striped pajamas rushing forth, yelling, wielding shovels, small axes, bricks, and knives. Sonderkommandos lead the way, dashing forward. Some are throwing grenades fashioned from sardine tins, and a few others have small arms that must have been smuggled into the camp.

RAT, TAT, TAT, TAT… machine gun fire erupts from watch towers. Half-dressed SS soldiers and Nazi officers with pistols, rifles, or submachine guns in hand dash out of the barracks to confront the hundreds of prisoners rushing at them, screaming wildly.

It's total chaos.

With a sinking heart, I watch as prisoners, young and old, are hit time and time again, yet they still keep on coming.

A few of the Sonderkommandos reach soldiers, and even as they are shot, they continue attacking with their few pistols and improvised weapons.

This is a winless battle, but we Jews and others have nothing to lose except our lives, which we know are forfeit in any case. Gunfire from the SS is non-stop. The attack is faltering as more and more prisoners fall. The dead and dying pile up, littering the ground. A few who are able to retreat run off. SS soldiers and their officers hurry among the wounded and administer killing shots.

Soon, all is quiet.

The killing is over.

The rebellion has failed, yet the Jews' efforts have not been in vain. Crematorium 4 is destroyed. This alone will save the lives of thousands.

Word of this insurrection will leak out; it must. The world will soon become aware of the genocide that is taking place.

I notice a few wounded prisoners who have not been given the coup de gras are being dragged away. They will no doubt be tortured in an effort to discover the names of the rebellion's ring leaders. Even though Dov had no part in the initial planning, I worry he may be implicated.

I pray Kaddish for Dov's brave compatriots who have sacrificed their lives this day rather than wait to be executed. They have made a remarkable statement. I only hope the world hears of their sacrifice and responds.

A day later, we learn Polish prisoners in Crematorium 1, Hungarian prisoners in Crematorium 3, and rebels in Crematorium 2 joined the uprising. In all, 250 prisoners were killed in the fighting, and a further 200 were wounded and later executed in the revolt's aftermath.

The wounded prisoners who were dragged off and tortured apparently revealed the identity of the four women who supplied the gunpowder, and those brave souls were executed this morning. Of the Nazis, three SS men were killed, while ten were wounded.

We hear rebels in Crematorium One threw a live, particularly sadistic SS officer into an oven. Is any of this true? We can't know for sure.

Fortunately, Dov has not been associated with the rebellion.

During the next few weeks, we learn from incoming prisoners the Nazis were able to suppress news of the rebellion and the ongoing murder of Jews. Also, I have heard that several prisoners escaped from Auschwitz and other camps with the intent of exposing Nazi atrocities to the media and anyone who would listen to them. Let's hope they succeed!

But at least we are now hearing the British, USA, French, and Soviets are directing the full might of their armed forces against Germany and Japan to win the war.

Will they win? Or, if they do, will it be too late for us?

***

Approximately six hundred prisoners stand at attention for morning roll call in front of headquarters. SS Kramer and Kapo Hadash are assessing us for some unknown reason.

Kramer barks, "I have a request for sixty strong men to work in the coal mines. Those of you who think you are up to the job, take one step forward."

No one steps forward. The image of working possibly hundreds of feet underground, trapped by cave-ins, or suffocated by toxic fumes is not appealing.

"Let me put this another way," Kramer says. "Those of you who come forward and appear strong enough to mine coal will live. Those of you who remain or fail your physical will be gassed. Now, let me say this again. Those of you who think you are up to the job, take one step forward."

Dov turns to me, looking pale. "You up to this?"

"Like he's giving us a choice?"

We both step forward, along with almost all of the prisoners.

I watch as Kramer, much like Dr. Josef Mengele, possibly copying a man he admires, begins his selection. Life is to the right, and certain death at the camp is to the left.

After eight of the first dozen men are chosen for life and four for staying in the camp, it is Dov's turn. Kramer stares at my friend and passes him with a wave of his hand to the right. Relieved, I step before Kramer. Without the slightest hesitation, he waves to the left. I swallow, I've failed.

So, this is where it ends for me. This is where I'll waste away until I'm put to death.

No! I spin around and hurry back into the crowd, losing myself among the prisoners before I can be pulled into the 'death' group.

Hunkered down, hiding behind a hundred milling prisoners, I realize I'm a sad candidate for a work detail. I'm almost as skinny and certainly as white as a skeleton.

Desperate to survive, a thought comes out of the air. *Tate?* I don't know. But the message I hear spurs me to push deeper into the throng of prisoners, and then, when I cannot be seen by either Kramer or Hadash, I punch myself in the face several times. It hurts, but that is good as I am hoping the blows bring color to my complexion to make myself appear healthier than I am.

I again get back in line and wait anxiously, pinching my cheeks to keep the color up. I watch as additional prisoners are assigned to the 'stay' group and others to the 'work' group. I can now see Dov, who also sees me and is watching anxiously as I move up the line.

Now I am standing before Kramer. His black eyes stare at me. He frowns, but I've affected a scowl to go along with my reddened face.

Please don't remember me...

After an excruciating moment, he waves me to the 'work' group.

I join Dov, who is so happy he gives me a hug. "Well done, pink face. You really should be an actor."

"*Danke*," I reply with a sarcastic grin.

Chapter 17

Jaworzno Concentration Camp
Camp # 4 - December 10, 1944

By reading the road signs posted with destinations and mileage, I see we are approaching Jaworzno. The first thing I notice about the place is that the concentration camp is located in an isolated forest on the town's outskirts. It's much smaller than Birkenau but looks just as well fortified with guard towers, electrified barbed-wire fences, a variety of military structures, and dozens of prisoner barracks.

To the south of the camp, the hills have been clear-cut, with the trees removed. The denuded landscape is scarred, as if a giant bear has pawed the earth, leaving deep claw marks. In these depressions, men in striped clothing are digging in black soil. It's obviously coal they are excavating. This must be part of the Sobieski coal deposits and mines where we are scheduled to work.

Our trucks turn off the main highway and follow a paved road to the main gate of Jaworzno's concentration camp, identified by a sign on the guard shack beside the entrance. It reads:

NEU-DACH.

Whatever that means.

The trucks pass through the gate, and within minutes, we are ordered out of our vehicles in front of a two-story nondescript wooden building with the customary flagpole in front bearing the Nazi flag. I assume this is the prison's main office.

Two middle-aged SS officers wearing Germany's 'Iron Cross' commendations around their necks exit the building. They are accompanied by a beefy man in civilian clothes holding a truncheon. The civilian I immediately identify as a Kapo with his blue Star of

David armband. Stepping down a short flight of stairs, the trio strides up to stand before us. The taller of the two officers, a man with a thin mustache and hard eyes, observes us quietly for a moment. When he speaks, it's with a thin rasping voice. "Welcome to Neu-Dachs concentration camp, also known as Jaworzno. I am commander SS-Obersturmführer Pfütze. Beside me is my deputy, SS Unterscharführer Weismann, and our camp's Jewish supervisor, Kapo Uri Sokol."

I stare at Sokol, attempting to gauge the man's character, as Pfütze continues, "You have been sent here to work our coal deposits. This requires strength and stamina. You are expected to work eight strenuous hours a day. If you fail to meet our work requirements, you will be returned to Birkenau and be executed. On the other hand, if you work hard and meet your daily quota, you will be rewarded with better food and living conditions than your previous accommodations. So, I leave it up to you: work hard and live, fail to work and die. I will now leave you with Kapo Sokol, who has a few words."

The SS officers pivot and return to their offices as Sokol steps forward.

From what I can gauge by looking at his fighter's broken nose and cauliflower ears, Kapo Uri Sokol is a *kelev,* a vicious dog, probably one of Auschwitz's original convict prisoners.

"My fellow Jews," Sokol says. "I am here to help you learn what is required of you. I can be your friend, or I can be your enemy. It is up to you. Obey the rules, and we will get along nicely. Disobey the rules and, well, you heard what Obersturmführer Pfütze said: execution awaits you. Your group has been chosen to work in the mines. Your hours are divided into three 8-hour shifts. First shift begins at 7 a.m. and ends at 3 p.m. Second shift begins at 3 p.m. and ends at 11 p.m., and the 3rd shift is from 11 p.m. to 7 a.m. Also, each night, one of you will stay awake to make certain the shifts are not sleeping through their work hours and will arrive on time..."

I ignore the remainder of Sokol's words as thoughts of being enclosed in tight, dark tunnels make me shudder. "I'm not cut out for this kind of work," I whisper to Dov.

"Nor am I. I'll request a transfer for us to be sent to the South of France. After all, it's a German possession now. They have beautiful beaches. You like the beach, Elias?"

"I've never been to one. But if you can make it happen, I'm available."

And so, our work in the mines begins. Dov and I are separated, and the remainder are broken into five-man crews. We are transported to the mines in trucks. Our hands are bound, so we will not attempt to escape. As we arrive at the mineshaft, we are untied and directed into a small cage-like elevator. Within minutes, we are dropping into a black hole with shiny walls only inches away. Descending like this makes my heart jitter.

Finally, our cage comes to a jarring stop. I look up and can't see daylight. We must be a hundred feet or more beneath the surface.

A man standing outside our elevator pulls the gate back. "Out. All out. You are to take the tunnel to the left."

All I can see of this tunnel is a murky hole with a strip of dim lights attached to its ceiling, which barely gives off enough illumination to see the first thirty feet; after that, blackness. I have heard about cave-ins and miners trapped and suffocating in what becomes their own tombs.

No, thank you. Not for me, my survival instincts tell me.

I press myself back against the elevator as my four companions step out of the cage. I'll go back to the top and explain that I can't possibly work in enclosed places, but I will work in the open coal pits.

"You!" the gateman shouts. "Out!"

I don't move, explaining, "Sorry, I can't be in enclosed spaces. I have to go back to the—"

"Out!" he repeats, this time brandishing his truncheon. "If I have to pull you out, I promise you, you'll regret it."

Reluctantly, I step out.

"Follow them," he orders, pointing to my companions who are already walking into the blackness.

"Do you have a flashlight I can borrow?" I ask facetiously.

Obviously not a conversationalist, the gateman jabs me with his truncheon. "Funny man. Go!"

With no other choice, I hurry after my fellow workers, afraid I might lose them in the dark and get lost in a maze, never to be seen again. Trying not to trip over a small set of rail tracks underfoot, I stumble along and finally catch up to them.

We reach an area where men in dust-blackened pajamas are swinging picks and axes and using shovels to scoop up chunks of coal that are then deposited into a series of carts sitting on rails next to us. Behind these mostly filled carts is a line of empty ones.

"Shift one, you're finished," says a man. "Shift two, take their tools, and begin filling the empty carts behind you."

The prisoners who have finished their shift look bone-weary and exhausted. They are too tired to speak to us as they get behind the carts they've filled with coal and push them away. None of us is given lamps or helmets. Dark, enclosed places have always given me anxiety. This one is no different.

It is hours later as we return to the surface, barely recognizing one another in daylight as we are covered from head to toe with black dust. Thankfully, we are able to shower nearby.

As I am under the spraying water, soaping myself, one of the guards, always watching us, asks, "You like that soap?"

I ignore him, thinking he's some kind of pervert hanging around watching men shower.

"You should know the soap you run over yourself; it is made from human fat. Jewish fat."

The bar of soap slips from my hand as this horror grips me.

The guard laughs.

I don't know if he's telling me the truth or simply saying what he said to see my shocked reaction. Some of these guards are sadistic.

***

In our barracks, during the off-shift, three of us are assigned to wake each other in a sequence—the 1st wakes the 2nd, the 2nd wakes the 3rd so that the 3rd can wake the entire barracks in time for the next shift.

Tonight, I am in the 2nd position. After waking the 3rd, I promptly go to my cot and attempt to sleep.

The next thing I know, it's morning, and the loudspeaker is announcing the roll call. I turn over in my bunk and see the third individual, who was assigned to wake our 7 a.m. group of miners, is just stirring. Panic suddenly clouds his features as he realizes his slip-up.

The barracks door bursts open, and Kapo Sokol strides in, truncheon in hand. "You're late, damn it! Outside, now! Move, move. Get in line for roll call."

As my shift partners and I pass him, he gives us a few hard whacks with his truncheon to make his point.

We rush outside to be counted and then taken in trucks to the mine. There is no coffee this morning.

I work through my shift with my shoulder aching from Sokol's truncheon. I'm angry at being unjustly hit and blamed for another man's mistake.

As we're returning from the mines, we're confronted by two SS soldiers with whips in hand. They ask us who was on duty last night. The three of us who were assigned to wake up their respective shifts step forward. We explain what happened; two of us performed our jobs, and one slept in.

The ranking SS soldier says, "You are all to blame, and you will all be punished."

Knowing any protest will be in vain, I remain silent, shaking my head at the injustice of this decision.

In spite of my situation, I almost laugh as a funny thought comes to mind, *Justice from a Nazi*?

The SS Officer in command says, "While you are being punished, you are not allowed to cry out or make any sounds. If you do, you will get more lashes. First man, step forward."

I watch as the prisoner who had the first shift moves up.

"Five lashes. Shirt off. Bend over and touch your ankles."

The prisoner removes his pajama top and bends over, doing as he is told.

The first blow lands with a resounding *smack* across his back. The man quivers but does not cry out.

I cringe as the four remaining lashes land along the man's spine. These are wielded with a heavy hand. On the third hit, blood soaks the man's pants. *Can I suffer the same punishment without making a sound*?

Moments later, after the first prisoner has collapsed to the ground and rolls into a ball, weeping silently, the SS officer turns to me. He says, "Ten lashes."

I remove my shirt and bend to touch my ankles, and I pray, *Don't make a sound, Elias. Keep silent.*

The first lash whips across my back. A stinging sharpness shocks me. I almost cry out, but I clench my jaw, determined to remain silent. The following nine lashes are vicious, cutting, bringing tears to my eyes. I had no idea a whip could cause such pain. It's the repetition, hitting the same place over and over until blood drips from lacerated flesh. Still, I keep my silence.

When it is finally over, I take in a big breath and attempt to straighten up—pain cramps my muscles, and I fall to the ground. It's an excruciating, nerve-snaking pain that pulsates through my lacerated skin. My eyes shed tears of agony, and now I watch the 3rd accused and the only guilty one of us receive his fifteen lashes. He, too, maintains silence. As the last whip smacks into his bloody back, he falls to the ground.

The agony raking through me is so debilitating I cannot stand, nor can the others.

Satisfied with their punishment, the SS officers pull out cigarettes, light them, and talk conversationally as they stroll off.

Dov and others hurry over, help us to our feet, and half-walk, half-carry us back to the barracks.

***

It's three months later, and I've yet to see the South of France or any beach for that matter. And, if I'm correct, it's very near the end of December. The only good thing I can say is my backside has healed, and Dov and I are still alive. The bad thing is we are still working in the tunnels, and we are getting skinnier.

I swing my pickax at the black wall in front of me, and vibrations shoot painfully up my arms. Except for the other picks and shovels striking nearby, I might think I'm working alone as the four prisoners beside me are almost invisible. Our clothes and every centimeter of our exposed skin are covered in coal dust, obscuring everything but the whites of our eyes, teeth, and the pink of our mouths. The black faces would be comical if they didn't remind me of burned flesh. It's an image that haunts me day and night.

After I've chipped out a pile of coal, I gather up the pieces and place them into a box-like cart set on wheels, which I then push, with the help of another prisoner, along the almost pitch-black tunnel to the bottom of an elevator shaft, where it is then hoisted up to the surface. From there, this 'black gold,' as the Germans call it, is loaded onto trucks and delivered to a train. It is then shoveled into open freight cars and shipped to an industrial complex to be burned and turned into energy. This energy will be used in the production of armaments and munitions.

My muscles continue to protest as I swing my ax. I have mused about using the tool as a weapon to dispatch my guards and escape—except I am not like the Nazis. I am not a cold-blooded killer. I'm not even a warm-blooded killer. I'm no killer at all. Besides, the chance of a successful getaway is too slim to contemplate.

Lately, Dov and I have begun coughing up black-speckled phlegm, a warning our lungs are suffering.

With our health slipping away day by day, I have a growing feeling I must attempt to do something to help our predicament. Every day, prisoners fall to the ground, too weak to work, and we must carry them to the surface, where they are shipped to Birkenau.

As Dov and I are sandwiched uncomfortably in our bunk this evening, I whisper, "Remember Birkenau when you retrieved those packets of gunpowder for the Sonderkommandos?"

"Yeah, I also remember if you hadn't come back with my cap, I wouldn't be here."

I wave his acknowledgment aside. "What I've been thinking about is another nighttime outing."

"An outing?"

"Come on," I say, wiggling out of the bunk. "This I'll have to show you."

Outside, we keep to the shadows, looking for SS guards, but the grounds are empty. The sentries in their raised lookout boxes are talking quietly.

I nod to Dov, and we make our way stealthily to a low wooden building. I inhale a familiar yeasty aroma. "Smell that?"

Dov breathes in. "Ahh, bread. I think I'm going to like this outing."

Creeping up to a bank of windows, Dov and I silently observe a dozen bakers kneading dough, shaping loaves, removing trays of just-baked bread, and reinserting new loaves into ovens.

"You think we can do this?" I whisper.

"I think we have to do this," he responds quietly.

Our eyes track the freshly cooked loaves as they are placed on metal racks and rolled to the rear of the building. We move down the exterior line of windows until we are only a few steps away from racks of bread left to cool in a dark room with only moonlight from the windows to light them. There is only a thin windowpane separating us from the loaves.

I turn to Dov. "How many do you think we can carry?"

"We can stuff four loaves inside our shirts. But first, we have to get inside."

Dov tries to lift the window frame. It's stuck. He tries again. Nothing. "Give me a hand," he says.

I move up beside him, and we both push on the frame. It doesn't move.

"Harder," I urge.

We push again. Finally, it begins to move, a centimeter at a time, until we have an open space large enough to crawl through,

"I'll go in," I offer, peering into the semi-dark room.

Dov gives me a boost, and I crawl inside the bakery. I quickly glance around and see I am alone, although I hear voices from other rooms. Without wasting time, I take loaves of still-warm bread off their racks and begin passing them out the window to Dov.

"That's enough," he whispers after I have handed him eight loaves.

I crawl out of the window, lower it, and we hurriedly divide up the bread. Once we have stuffed four loaves each beneath our shirts, we tuck our shirttails into our pants to keep them from falling out.

"Let's go," I urge.

"Halt!"

We whirl around.

Kapo Uri Sokol is standing six feet away, his truncheon in hand. His hulking size and grim-faced demeanor say everything. But still, he declares, "Stealing food is punishable by death."

My first reaction is for Dov and I to attack Sokol, attempt to overpower him, and run, but that has no future to it. He knows who we are and where to find us.

Kapo Sokol steps closer. "You have death wishes, no?"

"Bad luck, you showing up," Dov says.

"It could be worse. I could be SS. Then, you would already have bullets in your skulls. What made you think you could get away with stealing bread?"

I wonder what Sokol meant by saying, "It could be worse."

I reply, "We didn't have a choice. Our friends are starving. These loaves we've taken will give them a few more days to live."

Sokol shrugs. "You're just delaying the inevitable. Every Jew in this camp, including me, will be worked until we're no longer useful and then shipped off to Birkenau." His eyes fixate on Dov. "I know what you're thinking. You're attempting to figure out the odds of success if you and your friend attack me or kill me and then leave a couple of loaves of bread beside me so it will look like I'm a thief in an act of pilfering gone bad. A fallout among thieves."

Dov is non-committal, but I see his hands clenching and unclenching.

"This will never happen," Sokol adds. "You two could never best me in a fight."

"We could get lucky," Dov says, his words challenging.

For an intelligent man, Dov can sometimes speak without thinking. At the moment, there's no telling what he may do.

"*Chutzpah*," Sokol remarks. "If there's one thing I admire, it's *chutzpah*, especially against almost impossible odds. You two have this gift. And it *is* a gift. It is saving your lives."

I cock my head. *What did he just say*?

Dov, too, seems at a loss.

Although, if Dov decides to attack Sokol, I will do my best to help subdue this monster.

Sokol slaps his truncheon against the palm of his hand, "This Jew says enjoy your bread. You've earned it."

A wave of relief washes over me. "You're not going to turn us in?"

"Not tonight. Go. Leave before I change my mind."

Without waiting to count our blessings, I mutter, "Shalom." I grab Dov's sleeve, and we hurry off into the shadows.

Chapter 18

The following afternoon, Dov and I feel a bit magnanimous after watching the bounty of last night's thievery divided among the prisoners in our barracks. They are overcome with gratitude as we passed out chunks of the pilfered bread.

The story we told them was that the loaves were on the barracks doorstep where we found them this morning. It was a pleasure to see grins on the faces of half-starved men as they sank their teeth into the succulent pieces.

The memory lingers on, making it one of our better mornings in camp.

Now, after five hours of digging coal below ground, we are topside having a meager lunch on tables set up outside the main mine shaft. It's difficult to express how good a blue sky with its puffy white clouds looks after one has been laboring in narrow black tunnels all morning, but I am enjoying this short respite as I finish a meatless stew, washing it down with lukewarm coffee.

Dov sits across from me. His face and hands are as black as mine from coal dust. In fact, except for the SS guards, all of the close to two hundred 'mine rats,' as we call ourselves, look just like us, including those seated at our table.

As I study the faces around me, I can plainly see we are all suffering in various degrees of ill health. We are slowly dying, being worked to death. When we spit up phlegm, it is speckled black.

Dov lifts his bowl, tipping it over his mouth to get the last bits. Lowering the container, he says, "I could sure eat some more of that fresh-baked bread about now. You want to make a second run at the bakery tonight?"

"If I were suicidal, I might consider it. But I have another idea."

He raises an eyebrow.

"Toothbrushes."

"Toothbrushes? And they have something to do with…what?"

"The fur on my teeth."

"So…"

"With our newly acquired skills at thievery, we should begin looking for possibilities to help our fellow prisoners."

"And you expect to do this by stealing toothbrushes?"

"Run your tongue over your teeth."

"I don't have to. There's enough fuzz on them to make a fur coat."

I grin.

He looks at me and grins back. "Toothbrushes." He lets the word roll over his tongue. "Why not? I suppose there are odder things to die for. God knows we need them. What's your idea?"

"We reconnoiter the camp's pharmacy, and then on the next rainy night, we will break in and help ourselves. I'll also ask Bernie Goldman, that doctor in our barracks, what medicines we should grab. 'In for an ounce, in for a pound,' I believe someone once said."

"I doubt he or she was a prisoner in a concentration camp."

I realize I'm entering a new and dangerous phase in my life. *It is what it is*, I say to myself.

Mindful of my promise to my father, I say a little prayer, *Tate, I'll be careful, but I must help our people.*

The drone of approaching airplanes interrupts my thoughts.

I direct my attention to the sky.

Two V formations of low-flying bombers are coming at us low and fast.

"British!" I exclaim as I see the familiar markings.

Air raid sirens *scream*!

"Their bomb bay doors are open!" Dov exclaims.

My heart jumps. "To the trenches! Hurry!"

Dov and I, along with dozens of prisoners and SS guards, scramble for cover. We have just made it into the closest trench when I glance up.

Long lines of silver bombs glint in the sun as they trail down from open bomb bay doors.

The first explosions hit the concentration camp. Those that follow in sequential bursts—BOOM! BOOM! BOOM!—reach the mines. The earth beneath trembles as dozens upon dozens of bombs detonate, demolishing buildings, vehicles, and equipment.

The mine's main elevator and shaft explode—a direct hit. Additional tunnel openings collapse. Surrounding buildings are blown apart. Infrastructure disintegrates. Debris rains upon us.

The acrid smell of burning cordite wafts by. Flames leap, engulfing what's left of bombed-out structures.

Then there is silence … except for the sound of engines fading away.

I tentatively raise my head. A wall of smoke burns my eyes. "Dov, look."

Dov raises his head. "*Mein Gott…*"

The coal mine structures, even the surrounding buildings, have been leveled. It's as if a monster tornado swept across the earth and destroyed everything in its path, leaving behind flaming, smoking ruins. Bodies of guards and prisoners are strewn about. Others who have survived are burnt and bloodied. Some that can walk stagger about in a daze.

I lend Dov a hand and pull him out of the trench that saved our lives. "Dov, you okay?"

"I think so."

"Everything is gone. Even the trucks that hauled coal are in pieces, just twisted metal. This place will take months to rebuild."

The sound of quickly approaching vehicles diverts my attention.

A black Mercedes sedan followed by an armored military truck is racing toward us, obviously carrying SS officers and soldiers to examine the damage. The vehicles come to an abrupt halt in front of the mine's demolished elevator and tunnel shaft.

Camp commander Pfütze and his deputy, SS Weismann, step from the sedan while Kapo Uri Sokol and several soldiers alight from the truck. They stride briskly around the obliterated buildings and equipment, inspecting the damage.

"I'd love to hear what they're saying," I comment.

"They don't seem to be saying much. They're in a state of shock."

"I'm in a state of shock. Those Brits couldn't have been more on target. And did you notice there were no German fighter planes to engage them? The Luftwaffe must have their hands full."

"I hope the Allies are beating the crap out of them."

Kapo Sokol walks among the wounded and dead. Those still alive are crying, begging for help. Sokol sees us and waves us over to him. "You two, quickly, help the wounded soldiers into the truck."

"What about the prisoners?" I ask.

"Leave them." When he sees the rebellion in my eyes, he adds, "I'll send another truck for them. Hurry. Take the wounded to what's left of headquarters."

Dov and I move to the bloodied soldiers and begin lifting them. They cry out in pain as we carry them to the truck.

"Shouldn't these men go to the medical building?" I ask.

"There is no medical building," Kapo Sokol replies. "The bombers scored a direct hit on it and the pharmaceutical annex. Half of the barracks in the camp have been destroyed. Our food storage facilities and most of military headquarters are gone. It's a total disaster."

Actually, I think. *Adolf Hitler started this war, and the Germans deserve what they have wrought.*

It's sad so many prisoners were killed, but I have no sympathy for the Nazis.

***

It's hours later. Dov and I, along with a large group of prisoners and surviving miners, have been ordered to search for wounded and dead beneath the bombed-out hospital and pharmaceutical annex that is in ruins. *It's ironic*, I think, *that the British, who are fighting to win the war and save us from a certain death, have almost killed us in the process.*

Picking through bombed portions of the buildings, we pull dead and wounded out from beneath fallen ceilings and collapsed walls, all under the watchful eyes of the SS. I recover one male nurse who is covered with debris, but aside from minor cuts and bruises, he seems to be in relatively good shape. Soldiers hurry him off to a medical van.

Dov pulls an elderly man in a patient's smock out from under a portion of the fallen wall. He has a broken leg. Dov carries him to an army ambulance that pulls up beside us. Two men in doctor's smocks treat several wounded patients to the side of us while muffled cries from buried victims spur us to move faster to save those still trapped beneath the rubble.

I am at the far end of the pharmacy ruins when I come across a broken display case, displaying, among other things—toothbrushes. I count more than two dozen. I grab them all. Then, remembering I have no pockets, I take my cap off and stuff them inside as best I can. It makes the hat misshapen and uncomfortable as I settle it back on my head. I hope it won't fall off as I bend over, continuing my search for survivors.

I lift and move broken shelving and wooden beams. I hear soft keening. Moans are coming from beneath a pile of boards along the half-standing back wall.

"Over here!" I cry out.

As others join me, we hurriedly but carefully lift debris away from the sounds of what I now recognize as a female crying. Within minutes, a grateful, teary-eyed young woman in a white smock reaches her hand out.

I take hold of her. "You're safe," I say. "Don't worry. We'll get you out."

I don't know if she understands my words, but she certainly understands my intentions, as she is now weeping with relief.

We carefully remove the last boards holding her down and help the young woman to her feet. Miraculously, she seems to be unhurt. She throws her arms around me, jostling my cap half off.

Two toothbrushes fall out onto her shoulder. She sees them and picks them up. We exchange a quick look, and then, without a word, she hands them to me. I grab my head covering and manage to replace them.

She then kisses my cheek and says, "*Danka. Danka.*"

I smile, holding onto my cap as others hurry over, take her hand, and lead her away.

Grateful I'm able to help with the recovery search while keeping my contraband, I look around to see what more I can do when I step on several small bottles. Fortunately, they don't break. I pick one up. Its label reads "Bayer Aspirin." I am aware of this cure-all. It's for headaches and pain. Knowing it might be helpful to my prison mates, I surreptitiously pick up the five bottles. *Now what*?

I can't fit anything more under my cap or just hold them in my hands. I see the edge of a small paper bag sticking out from under a pile of rubble. I pull it out, and with it comes a small, smashed carton containing, of all things, nail clippers. I pick all six of them up and, combining them with the aspirin bottles, place them inside the bag.

A thought comes to me. *Am I being greedy, taking too much, risking too much*?

I glance around. No one is paying attention to me. This is an opportunity I can't pass up. That settled; now, what do I do with the bag?

Realizing I have no other option, I place it down the front of my pants and roll the top of it over my waistband as best as I can. Then, I cinch it tightly in place with my belt. I hope the paper won't tear and the contents, now heavy, won't drop down the legs of my pants. I move about carefully, like an old man with a hernia. I pray the bag will not slip away before the search efforts end so I can return to my barracks with the bag intact.

Moving cautiously, I continue to look for survivors. Taking in a breath, I am feeling better than I have in the last several hours. It's funny how little things like toothbrushes and nail clippers can become so meaningful. Still, I caution myself, I must transport these 'little things' back to the barrack without being caught—or I will face a certain death sentence.

We work through the night, recovering more wounded and dead bodies. When the causalities are finally counted, there are at least thirty deceased, as well as over ninety wounded. This includes military personnel, doctors, nurses, patients, and prisoners. Considering the loss of the coal mines, the medical and outlying supply buildings, and the destruction of several barracks, with thankfully only a few causalities among us Jews, the bombing was a complete disaster for the Germans.

***

The next morning, after just a few hours of sleep, I sit at a table where we usually would be having breakfast, with my bare feet in front of me as I clip my toenails. All around me, prisoners are busy brushing their teeth and clipping their nails.

There is no breakfast served this morning. The Germans' excuse, and for once I believe them, is that the food designated for us was destroyed during the bombing. Surprisingly, there were very few complaints, and this, I surmise, is because the first thing I did this morning was pass out toothbrushes and nail clippers for the prisoners to take turns with. It's not the most germ-free endeavor, but now they are almost preening as they show off their clipped nails. Others are grinning, having used the purloined toothbrushes with a touch of soap to brush and display somewhat clean teeth. It's a rare and heartening sight. Yes, small indulgences do count, especially among men who have nothing.

"My, what pretty toes you have."

I look up as Dov sidles in next to me.

"It's a Feinzilberg family trait," I respond flippantly. "We're known far and wide for our beautiful toes."

"Lucky you. And I hope you're going to brush your teeth now, morning and night."

"Maybe even after lunch if we ever have lunch again."

"Good luck on that. By the way, Goldberg said to thank you for the aspirin. He's already dispersed two bottles."

Kapo Uri Sokol and two of his assistants approach. "Attention. An announcement."

"What now?" Dov mutters as the prisoners are quick to hide the nail clippers and toothbrushes from sight.

But not quick enough. Sokol has caught sight of one of the prisoners gripping an object in his hand. "You." He points to the young prisoner, who has his hand clenched. "What's that you have in your hand?"

The young man shakes his head nervously. "It's nothing."

"Open your hand."

The boy hesitates.

"Now!"

The young man, shaking now, slowly opens his hand.

Sokol's eyes widen. He steps up and takes the nail clipper from the young man's palm. "Where did you get this?"

The boy's eyes drop to the ground. He remains silent.

"You will answer me, now!" Sokol slaps his truncheon on the palm of his hand.

The boy looks up, his eyes welling. He shakes his head, refusing to speak.

Sokol's face flushes…about to explode. His hand tightens on the truncheon's grip.

"It's mine," I say.

Sokol's eyes rivet to me. Lowering the truncheon, he spits out, "You… You again."

I nod, my heart thumping.

Sokol strides over to me and stands a foot away, glaring. He opens his hand and raises it, showing me the nail clipper. "Where did you get this?"

I clear my throat. "I found it as I was rescuing people in the pharmacy."

Sokol's eyes flutter. "You were part of the rescue party?"

"Yes. And I kept it to give to my friends. I'm the one who stole it. No one else."

Sokol's mouth twists into a smirk, or is it a grin? Is this a precursor to being bludgeoned to death? I can't read his black eyes…they keep staring…

He finally snorts and says, "I like you, B-1259."

I almost fall to the ground.

"You remind me of someone I used to know. Here," he holds out the clippers. "Take it."

I hesitantly lift the nail clipper from his hand.

Sokol turns and walks a few paces away and turns back to face the prisoners. "I have news that affects you all. With the coal mine out of order, possibly for weeks, and your quarters no longer livable, the camp can no longer feed you. You have become a liability. This situation has left the command with two choices: shoot you or transfer you to another camp in need of labor. Fortunately for you,

Commander Pfütze has decided to have you transported to another camp. You will be walking, leaving here in thirty minutes."

Sokol and his assistants stride off.

I watch them go, thinking, *another camp. How many camps have I been in*?

Liebhof was the first. Wittenberge the second. Then came Auschwitz-Birkenau. And now we're leaving Joworzno, going to another concentration camp, which will make it five. Five concentration camps. It doesn't seem possible. I've survived all of them.

I can't help but wonder, will this next one be my last? The odds are not in my favor. Considering the possibility of one's own demise is rather disturbing.

My thoughts are interrupted as Dov asks, "Can I borrow those clippers? I like to make a good first impression when meeting new faces."

"Little chance of that." I pass him the nail clipper.

Starting to clip his fingernails, he says, "Let's hope they're not sending us back to Birkenau."

Birkenau, I know, would mean certain death. But even if it's another camp we're going to, how long can this go on, being transferred from camp to camp? One day, it's bound to end.

Chapter 19

Concentration Camp # 5 - December 15, 1944

Germany launched a surprise attack on Allied forces in the forested Ardennes region in Belgium, Luxembourg, and France. Called 'Battle of the Bulge.' it started on December 16, 1944, and ended with the defeat of Hitler's Army on January 16, 1945

Approximately 200 SS guards are marching 5,000 of us through picturesque countryside on our way to a town called Opole. What's there? I have no idea. All I'm sure of is that we've been on the road for three miserable days. My tongue is dry, my stomach aches, and my feet are blistered and sore. We've had no food or water except for handfuls of snow that have melted on our tongues and made us colder.

My constant worry is that I will fall, be unable to get up, and be executed like so many others. The murdered are left on the roadside to rot. Just minutes ago, two prisoners beside me collapsed and were shot. If there is a medal in heaven for praying Kaddish the most times, I believe I will qualify.

Dov, shuffling alongside me, continuously eyes the terrain, looking for an opportunity to escape. We're so closely watched it would be suicide, but that doesn't deter him. I admire his spirit. My optimism is waning.

I notice a road sign that informs us the town of 'Opole' is twenty miles ahead.

Two German motorcyclists coming down the road stop to talk to the SS officer leading our bedraggled procession. Dov relays he overheard them tell the officer that getting to Opole is impossible as the township has been destroyed by bombs and the road is impassable.

Shortly after the motorcyclists leave us, I notice we are taking another road. This time, the next road sign tells us we are heading for the city of Gleiwitz, on the Polish and German border.

I assume this place must have a concentration camp. At least, I hope so, as we are all on the verge of collapse—and execution.

Fortunately, the city of Gleiwitz is less than five miles away.

The fading sun is turning purple on the horizon as our bone-weary group of Jews limp into the outskirts of the city. We come upon a park where we are brought to a halt.

Raised voices draw my attention to the SS officers leading us. It appears they are arguing. A few minutes later, we are instructed to go into the park and lie down for a rest.

Dov and I find a grassy spot at the far edge of the park. It looks comfortable enough, and we settle down as the other prisoners find their own places.

"I'm not against resting," I say to Dov. "But if the camp is nearby, we should be pressing on to get there before it's totally dark."

"Attempting to figure out the Nazi mind is like trying to unwind a pretzel."

Suddenly, machine guns *fire*!

Prisoners all over the park who have just settled down are being shot where they lay, and others scrambling to their feet are cut down as bullets tear into them.

Screams!

Pandemonium!

Prisoners all over the park are being slaughtered.

"Follow me!" I yell to Dov.

Ducking, I run. Several yards ahead, I dive behind a berm of earth almost entirely enclosed by trees. Dov lands beside me.

"*Mein Gott*!" he exclaims. "Those mumzers are murdering all of us!"

Eyes wide, I witness the bloodbath.

Prisoners closest to the machine gunners have been killed immediately. Others, like us on the peripheral edges of the park, flee for the cover of trees. Some make it, but the majority of prisoners are cut down.

The shooting stops. As the smoke clears and night encroaches, we watch shadowy SS soldiers walk among the dead and wounded. They administer killing shots until it is finally too dark to see anything.

"Let's get away from here," Dov whispers.

"We should stay."

"Are you crazy?"

"In minutes, it's going to be too dark to see a foot in front of your face. With the cloud cover, there's no moon. If we run, we'll hit trees, fall into ditches, who knows what. I say we stay. Get a few hours of sleep, and then, at the first hint of dawn, when we can see where we're going, we run. Run as far and as fast as we can."

Apparently, this makes sense to Dov as he grunts and settles down. "I'm exhausted. Wake me at first light."

Within minutes, he is asleep. As always, in anxiety-ridden situations, I spend a fitful night, sleeping ten, maybe fifteen minutes at a time. Moans and cries drift across the park. There are still wounded out there who have managed to crawl and hide nearby. Their weeping tears at my heart. It's an awful sound, the final utterances of human beings.

Dawn seems to take forever.

Finally, as the sky begins to lighten, I see the full extent of the slaughter. Hundreds, no thousands, of corpses lie strewn across the park.

Suddenly, shutters on a house overlooking the park bang open. A woman peers out sees the bloody and torn corpses, and shouts in German, "*Gutt! mein gutt*!" God my God!

Dov awakens, sees the bloodied bodies, and urges, "Let's go. Now."

"Wait, wait," I say as a black Mercedes, followed by two military trucks loaded with SS soldiers and dogs, drives up and parks beside the SS commander who led our march from Jaworzno and who must surely have ordered the massacre. A high-ranking Nazi, resplendent in his black uniform, exits the car and is met by the leader of our march.

"Elias," Dov urges. "Time to leave."

"Wait. Let's see what happens."

"They're planning our funeral. That's what's happening."

Across the park, I spot a half-dozen German Shepherds being unloaded from trucks. They are on leashes, tugging, ready to hunt us down.

Another heated discussion between a newly arrived SS officer and the officer who led us on our march is taking place.

The soldiers with dogs fan out across the park. Seconds later, the argument between the two officers concludes. The newly arrived SS officer strides to one edge of the park. He shouts, "Prisoners, I am SS-Oberscharführer Richard Stolten, commander of the nearby Gleiwitz concentration camp. A mistake has occurred here. There is nothing that can be done about it now, but I can assure you there will be no more shooting, no massacres if you behave yourselves. I need workers in my camp, not corpses. Now, I have been informed there are survivors hiding in the forest." He raises his voice. "Prisoners, if you are able to walk, come forward. You have nothing to fear. You will not be harmed. You have my word as an SS officer."

"Worthless," Dov remarks.

As I speak very little German, I ask Dov to translate for me, and he does so.

Stolten continues, "On the other hand, if you prefer to stay hidden, I will send soldiers and dogs after you. So now, prisoners in hiding, you will step forward."

"What do you think?" I ask.

"If they didn't have those damn dogs, I'd say run, but…"

"I agree. My buttocks, what's left of them, don't need fangs chomping on them."

We stand. I'm anxious, uncertain if this is a ploy to get us to reveal ourselves so we can then be shot or if this Nazi officer is a man of his word.

I see other prisoners, some bloody, hesitantly come out from the cover of trees; they are not shot. Dov and I step forward, too. We survivors, less than 1,000 of the original 5,000 who entered the park yesterday, gather before this new Nazi officer.

"Prisoners," SS Stolten says. "It is lamentable that so many deaths occurred here."

"Deaths," Dov whispers. "As if they died from natural causes."

"Well, this is a first," I whisper. "A Nazi apologizing, sort of. He needs workers, I think."

Stolten continues, "I have arranged for you to be trucked to our camp in Gleiwitz, where you will be put to work."

Gleiwitz, I observe later as we drive through its main gate, is a relatively new concentration camp. On the west side, facing the road and train tracks is a concrete slab wall topped with tall barbed wire, and on the east side, the barbed wire is strung between concrete posts. I also notice two distinct enclosures. The largest one holds four barracks and hundreds of male prisoners. The smaller one contains three barracks and almost as many female prisoners. Male and female clothing is a mix of striped pajamas and civilian clothing. Everyone appears somber, malnourished, and lethargic.

The grounds are relatively small compared to the other camps I've been in. The electrified fence encircling the perimeter has six low watchtowers where the SS soldiers manning them have an overview of the camp. The two-story main building, obviously headquarters, has the usual flagpole flying the Nazi insignia. Beside it is a small one-story hospital identified by its Universal Red Cross.

Several yards further on is a large open-sided workshop where prisoners are repairing damaged railroad cars. There is also a machine shop, storage facilities, and what appears to be a kitchen, as I can see men wearing white aprons through the building's windows.

Our truck stops beside a fence surrounding the women's compound, allowing a horse-drawn cart loaded with rocks to pass.

As we wait, I notice a lone woman standing so close I could almost reach out and touch her. She is wearing a distinctive green scarf and is seemingly lost in reverie. I can't help staring as she is quite attractive.

Her eyes are suddenly on me, and my heart jumps. She has the greenest eyes I have ever seen. I can't take my gaze off her. If eyes are pathways into one's soul, I am on that path. I am still staring… Who is this woman? Before I can ask myself another question, my truck lurches forward, moving on. I turn, gazing after her until she disappears from sight. I feel an inexplicable loss.

Dov, who rarely misses a thing, remarks, "*Sheinkeit.* Pretty girl."

My thoughts, too, but for some reason, I don't wish to share them. I ignore him.

Being a *mensch*, he persists, "The young woman you were ogling."

"I wasn't ogling."

He grins.

Our small convoy rounds a curve in the drive, heading toward a large building—and the hair on the back of my neck rises. Three prisoners are hanging by their necks from a tall wooden scaffold. I've seen this before, but it doesn't get old. Maybe I haven't become a hardened cynic yet.

"Despicable Nazis," Dov comments. "They could at least have covered their heads."

"Fear control," I suggest.

"It works. Scares the crap out of me."

The trucks roll to a stop before headquarters. A tall SS soldier hurries up to our truck while other soldiers do the same to the vehicles behind us. The rear panel is unlatched and dropped.

The soldier orders, "*Raus*! *Raus*! Out! Out!"

We slide from the truck. Then, following more shouted orders, we begin to line up, awaiting the arrival of SS officers.

Two hours later, we are shivering in a frigid wind blowing across the roll-call square as we await further instructions.

Another half-hour passes. My legs are wobbling. Finally, a Nazi officer accompanied by a Kapo, carrying the ever-present truncheon, steps from the command building and strides down a short flight of stairs to confront us.

"Good day," SS Officer Richard Stolten says. "Welcome to Gleiwitz concentration camp. This man beside me is Kapo Antek Pakierman, your fellow Jew, who will be your supervisor."

I study the Kapo. He's tall, skinny, mid-thirties, with iron-rimmed glasses. He seems fairly normal. *Although*, I caution myself, remembering Dr. Josef Mengele, *first impressions are not always reliable.*

"You will obey his every command as if it comes directly from me. Failure to do so is execution."

I can't help but think these SS camp commanders are all given the same speech to recite to prisoners.

"You are here to work, and work you will. Most of you will be assigned to repair damaged railroad cars. It's our contribution to the war effort to keep our military vehicles rolling. The Fuhrer himself has mentioned the importance of our work here in Gleiwitz."

I turn to give Dov a look. He spits on the ground.

"The remainder of you will be grading earth constructing new barracks, storage areas, and workshops. There is much to be done, and I expect you to perform without complaints…"

I'm half-listening to this speech and the follow-up lecture from Kapo Pakierman. The substance of their lectures doesn't differ much from those of the other camp commanders and Kapos I've listened to.

When their speeches finally end, we are marched to our barracks. Dov and I are assigned to block 20, which I see is in sight of the women's camp. I search for the woman in the green scarf. She is no longer in sight.

Her image lingers with me. I am distracted as Kapo Pakierman refers to a list he holds identifying us, not by our names, but by our tattoo numbers. It reminds me I am no longer Elias Feinzilberg. I will now be strictly known as B-1259.

While we were told we would be put to work, it's been three days of waiting to hear what our assignments will be. During this time, we are given no food or water. *Are these so-called 'organized Nazis' so disorganized they have forgotten us, or do they have troubles that are taking all their attention*?

I believe it is the latter as Dov and I overhear news of the war from new prisoners who recently arrived. If their news is accurate, which it sometimes can be, Germany occupied Hungary during March and April 1944, and the Nazis began deporting Hungarian Jews to Auschwitz by the tens of thousands. This is sad but not surprising. Are all Jews to be eliminated?

I feel a renewed will to live, just to spite this plan of the Nazis. There is also some heartening news: the invasion of Normandy. On June 6, the combined Allied forces of land, sea, and air, soundly defeated the Nazis. It appears the tide of the war is changing as the Allies are sweeping across Europe, routing German forces. And on July 20th, a group of German officers attempted to assassinate Hitler! Unfortunately, he lived.

I give Dov a look. "It's happening. The Allies are winning. Even Hitler's officers are turning on him."

"Maybe I should ask Stolten to surrender."

"While you're at it, see if he'll exchange living quarters with us."

Kapo Pakierman, who entered our barracks a few minutes earlier with one of the camp's high-ranking SS officers, bangs his truncheon against a post. When the room quiets down, he says. "Officer Stoltz has come here to issue a severe warning to all prisoners."

SS Stoltz, another corpulent man, announces with his face florid, "I have been informed there are vicious rumors being spread by prisoners in this barracks. This will stop as of this moment! There will be no more talk of Allied victories! The enemy is being crushed on all fronts. The German Army is invincible. *Deutschland uber alles*!

"I want to make one thing very clear: the Fuhrer will never be defeated. Now, if it comes to my attention that men from this barracks are spreading false rumors, you will pay dearly. I will have every man here, each and every one of you, executed. Let that sink in. Every one of you will be executed. No exceptions. Do you understand?"

Silence.

Stoltz chooses to accept this silence as compliance. He nods. "*Gut*! I hope I have made myself clear."

"Putz," a prisoner mumbles.

Stoltz's face flushes beet red. "Who spoke?"

Silence.

Then, a thin, grey-haired man steps forward. "I did. You're a putz, Stoltz. A Nazi whore."

It's as if a bolt of lightning has transfixed Stoltz. Eyes bulging, his mouth twists.

Suicide, I'm thinking. The old man is committing suicide.

"Tuck your tail between your legs and get out of here," the old man adds.

The barracks is as quiet as a tomb.

Stoltz is shaking, fist tightening around his truncheon. He charges forward, whipping his club across the side of the old man's head, knocking him to the floor. He strikes him again and again. "*Schwein*! Bastard!" he yells, spittle flying.

He continues to bludgeon the old man until his skull is crushed. Panting, gulping breaths, Stoltz backs up, wipes splattered blood from his face, and looks around wild-eyed. "See! See this! This is what happens to any man who insults me. If you remember anything, remember this. I have the power to send you all to the gas chambers and to the ovens. I can beat you to death! You will respect me, or you will suffer the same fate as this swine. Do you understand?"

Silence.

"DO YOU UNDERSTAND?"

A few unintelligible mumbles are uttered.

They are just audible enough for Stolz to accept them as compliance. He adds, "There will be no meal tonight. At 6 a.m., you will assemble outside for roll call. You will have breakfast, and then you will be assigned work details." He gestures to the Kapo Pakierman. "Have this mess cleaned up."

He turns on his heel and strides out of the barracks.

Kapo Pakierman looks down at the dead old man and says almost to himself, "He committed suicide…why?"

I almost speak, but there are too many possible responses to find one answer. With the prisoners murmuring, reacting to the SS officer's savagery, I step over to the dead man, and as I'm about to lift his corpse and take him outside, a silver-haired prisoner touches my arm. "Please, allow me. He was my friend. A braver man you'll never know."

I step back and watch as this old man struggles to lift his dead friend. I step forward to help, but the silver-headed gentleman shakes his head. I understand…this is between friends. Then, when the dead man is finally lifted, and his old friend has him in his arms, he nods to me and then carries him outside. A subdued Kapo Pakierman follows them out.

Dov whispers, "We have to get back at that *farkakte* SS officer."

"Did you see his face? He's not right. He's on the edge. A man can only lie to himself for so long before it starts to eat at him. He has to know his world is coming apart. Leave him alone. He'll destroy himself."

Dov lets out a breath. "You may be right, Elias. But there are times I want to lash out at these Nazis."

"I wouldn't want to be in their shoes when this is all over." I wrap my arms around myself as it's glacially cold in the barracks.

I select a bunk nearby and crawl onto the rough-sawn planks. I see others doubling and tripling up on their wooden slatted beds, lying next to each other for what little warmth this will offer.

"Elias," Dov whispers as he crawls in beside me. "I can't stand this! We have to come up with some way to get back against these Nazis, to kick their tushes."

"I wouldn't mind kicking a Nazi tush or two…if we can live to talk about it."

"The 'living to talk about it' is the tricky part. I haven't figured that out yet. But trust me, I'll come up with something."

I've no doubt Dov will come up with 'something,' but that something can sometimes be too dangerous to contemplate. But I enjoy listening to my friend's schemes. I begin to take notice of the *alter kacker*, the old fellow, who's squeezed in between us on our plank.

He is muttering moanfully, "A *kappore*, a catastrophe. I'm a dead man. A dead man. I am such a fool. A broch on me for being so careless. So very, very stupid. Yet, I am not sorry. If I could only—"

"Excuse me," I say. "Can I help you with anything?"

"Yes, you can strangle me to death. Save me from a torturous murder at the hands of the SS. I am certain they are going skin me alive."

I find this rather surprising as the old man seems harmless. "Why would the Nazis do this to you?"

He turns over. Only inches away, I see the gentleman has tears in his eyes. "It's a long story."

"I'm not going anywhere."

"I've…been doing…things. Things to make the Nazis pay." He pauses.

I wait, my interest piquing.

"These cretins," he adds. "They must pay for their crimes. I want to make them pay. I've made up a list."

A list? This sounds interesting. "What kind of list?"

"I have written down the names and ranks of every SS officer in this camp who has committed atrocities against humanity, against us Jews. Also, of officers from the camp in Drancy where I was until they sent me here. I have many, many names."

A charge of electricity jolts me. If this old man truly has what he says he has, such a list would be a treasure trove of evidence for prosecutors someday to bring charges against the Nazis.

Dov, who has been propped up on his elbow listening to our conversation, leans over me and asks quietly, "Where is this list?"

"In the desk drawer of my podium in the music hall. But first thing tomorrow morning, I've been warned, one of my less accomplished musicians plans to expose me and my list to the Nazis, and that will be the end of me."

I glance around to ensure no one is eavesdropping, and then I ask quietly, "Why would this man turn on you?"

"To have me killed. I am Paul Hermann. I'm a composer and cellist. You have heard of me?"

"No," I say honestly. "I'm not much of a music follower. But I had a sister, Guena, who played the violin. She probably heard of you if you're famous."

"So, so," he responds humbly. "In any case, the Nazis appointed me conductor of the Jewish camp orchestra. Rudy wants my job. This cannot be. Rudy Auer is not Jewish. He is an Austrian Christian, a criminal with a long record, and a man with no morals. I cannot have him become conductor of our Jewish musicians. He plays a violin like a drunken farmer. He is completely unqualified but isn't aware of his limitations. Why is it so difficult for untalented people to realize they have little or no talent? Never mind, don't answer that. Let me explain his motive. As conductor, I get extra rations; that's his whole purpose, extra food. He doesn't care about Jews any more than I care about bed bugs. For a few extra morsels, he will expose me and my lists tomorrow morning. This must not happen. Yet, I don't know how to stop him."

"How difficult is it to get into the music hall?" I ask, already planning to help the conductor if I can.

"It wouldn't be easy. The building is right next to headquarters. Soldiers come and go at all hours. If I weren't so old, I would try to crawl in one of the back windows that I have purposefully left unlatched. But I no longer have the strength to do these things. And the front and rear doors are always locked. So, I am at a loss. I fear tomorrow I will be exposed."

"Where do you keep this list of names?" Dov asks, and I can tell he is now thinking what I am thinking. We have to retrieve that list.

"Inside my conductor's podium. There is only one drawer. It's where I keep my sheet music. My lists, there are six small ones, are in a folder marked 'Richard Wagner.' As you already know, he is Adolf Hitler's favorite composer."

"No," I admit. "I didn't know."

He ignores my response and continues, "My lists are on scraps of paper. I had to tear tops and bottoms off music sheets to find space to write on. So, you see, that is why I have so many small pieces. They are hidden among my musical scores. By sheer accident, Rudy saw me adding the name of a particularly murderous SS officer to one of my lists, and there was his excuse to turn me in." He exhales heavily. "Rudy, I am sure, believes the Nazis will reward him. If I know Nazis, they will probably execute him, too, as he has seen the names. The man is a fool but a dangerous one."

I turn to Dov. "I think we should try to help Paul. If we can save those lists…"

Dov gives me a long look, then nods. “I agree.” He turns to the conductor. “Paul, as we won’t be able to turn on the lights, I need you to explain the layout of the music hall.”

Chapter 20

It's nearly midnight, with a full moon overhead. Dov and I cautiously make our way out of our barracks and to the rear of the music building by staying in the shadows. It's a rock's throw from headquarters, which is terrifying. Paul has warned us that soldiers will be changing shifts and going in and out of the building at all hours. Stopping by the back two windows, we discover the unlatched one. With a little effort, it slides open, and we quickly crawl inside and lower the window.

Squinting, I can see there is just enough moonlight filtering into the hall from the windows that enables Dov and me to make out the insides of the room and its furniture. The layout is as the conductor described.

"That's it," I whisper, pointing to the music podium several yards away, partially encircled by a grouping of folding chairs.

Dov nods, and we pad across the room to the stand that is a little taller than waist high. I open the single drawer and see a stack of musical folios. There is not enough light to read the names on the front covers, so Dov and I each grab half of the contents in the drawer, about five folders each, and carry them over to the window we just crawled through where there is moonlight to read by.

"Richard Wagner," I announce in a whisper as I find the composer's name on one of the folios.

"I've got one also," Dov says as he holds up another binder with the composer's name.

We rifle through the music sheets inside. There are no little pieces of paper with names on them. Laying aside the first folders, we search through two others with Richard Wagner's name on them.

Dov announces in a whisper, "I've found two scraps of paper with names," he says, squinting to read the wisps of paper. "This is good. Officers' names. Identities of Jewish victims. This is gold, Elias. Pure gold."

"Yes," I whisper. "I've found the same. How many do you have?"

"Three. And you?"

"Two. The other one must be here somewhere."

I am paging through the remaining folios when we both freeze—voices outside the front door.

"Time to leave," Dov urges. "Let's put these back. Hurry."

"Not yet. We have to find the sixth list," I say, hurrying now as I rifle through the last binder with adrenalin racing through my veins.

"Sorry," Dov grabs the folios from my hands and runs over to the podium, stuffing them inside the open drawer and closing it.

Just then, keys jingle at the front door's lock.

"Crap," Dov says.

He dashes back toward me, and as we are about to lift the window to escape, the front door bursts open. We duck as two soldiers holding flashlights stagger in. They are singing, obviously tipsy.

We gaze around. There is no place to hide. Except for darkness, we are completely exposed. If they should turn their flashlights on us, we are, to use a coined expression, 'dead meat.'

"Don't move," I whisper, pressing my back into the wall. "If they spot us, I'll lift the window, and you leap out, I'll follow."

"No," he responds quietly, "You go first. I'll follow."

"Shh," I caution him, having no intention of being the first one out.

The soldiers move unsteadily to the small arrangement of chairs with musical instruments beside them that have been set out in an orderly fashion. The tallest of the two men swoops up a violin case, opens it, and lays down his flashlight. He raises the instrument and says something in slurred German.

His companion responds, "Ja. Ja."

The tall soldier lifts the accompanying bow and, laying it on the instrument's strings, begins to play.

Dov and I exchange surprised looks. The soldier plays the violin surprisingly well, even while half inebriated. He is playing a musical number I am familiar with, 'Ode to Joy.' It's a piece my sister, Guena, used to play for the family at our home in Lodz.

For a moment, I am lost, back with my family once again. Then, the violinist misses a note and sits down hard on a chair. His partner starts laughing. I am brought back to reality and the danger we are in.

"Don't move a centimeter," I whisper, feeling extremely vulnerable.

I watch as the violin player laughs along with his partner, gets to his feet, and replaces the violin in its case. The two men begin singing and stagger out the front door, closing it behind them.

"This is something I never wish to do again," Dov remarks. "Let's get out of here."

"We're missing the sixth note."

"I've looked thoroughly in my folders. Did you?"

"Yes," I have to admit.

"Then, that's all we can do." Dov grabs onto the window sash and lifts. "After you."

Realizing we have done our best and perhaps the old man was mistaken in the number of notes, I crawl out the window. Dov follows, closing it behind us.

Whew, I exhale as we disappear into the shadows.

The thought of a missing sixth note lingers with me well past the time I am back in my barracks.

***

Morning roll call. We, prisoners, are assembling before the headquarters building, which is unusual...and troubling, even more so when Paul Hermann tells me that the man in the striped pajamas standing a few feet from SS Oberscharfuhrer Richard Stolen, is Rudy Auer, the man who promised to expose him to the Nazis.

Kapo Pakierman is issuing his typical orders to line up and be counted. As the count begins, I notice two SS soldiers approaching with what appears to be the very folios Dov and I were searching through last night in the music hall.

Dov and I exchange looks—my thoughts on the missing sixth note.

Fifteen minutes later, after rollcall has been completed, SS Stolen, with Rudy Auer waiting nearby, announces, "Prisoners, there is a man among you who is a traitor to the Third Reich. This man, this lowest of swine, has compiled a list of names from the ranks of the exalted German army that accuses them of phony, made-up atrocities against mankind. This is, of course, typical for traitors and an outright lie and will be dealt with severely. I am now asking one of your own, who is a friend of the Reich, to come forward and present his evidence." He gestures to Rudy Auer, who steps tentatively forward, stopping beside the two SS soldiers who carry the musical folios and is several feet from Stolen. "You may proceed," Stolen says.

Rudy, with a smug expression, takes the binders from the soldiers and opens them. He begins paging through them. After a few moments, as he is searching through the notes, his expression changes to a frown and then to a look of stricken angst. He turns to SS Stolen. "They're gone. Someone has taken them."

SS Stolen strides over to Auer, stares at him for a long moment, and then, using his truncheon, knocks the folios from his hands. They scatter all over the ground.

My breathing stops. A single small piece of paper, just like the five Dov and I recovered last night, has fluttered to the ground. It is lying inches from Stolen's feet. Unaware of the scrap, he listens to Auer protest.

"They were here yesterday, I swear! You have to believe me. Someone stole them. It must have been him." He points at Paul Hermann. "Yes, it had to have been Hermann. Somehow, he must have known I was on to him. He's your accuser. He was planning to report you and your soldiers to a criminal court. He has your names, your crimes, and your victim's names. Ask him. See if I'm not right." He points a shaking finger at Paul Hermann. "Tell him the truth, you bastard."

"He's a crazy man," Paul Hermann states.

A few prisoners join in, "Yes, he is crazy."

Rudy kneels on the ground and pages manically through the folios. Finding nothing, he stares at Paul Hermann and shouts, "Tell them the truth! Confess that you took down the names of these soldiers. Tell them, damn you! Tell them!"

My heart skips a beat. The small piece of paper is fluttering in the breeze, mere inches from Stolen's feet. I glance at Dov. He, too, has seen the paper moving incrementally closer to Stolen. I take in a breath, holding it.

Before I can exhale, SS Stolen pulls out his Luger, aims it at Rudy Auer's head, and pulls the trigger. Auer is killed instantly.

The commander orders, "Paul Hermann. Step forward five paces."

I have to stop myself from crying out. *Is he going to be shot*?

Paul Hermann moves forward purposefully as if he were a gladiator going to his death in the middle of the Coliseum. He stares at the commander with steady eyes.

SS Stolen orders, "Take him away."

Two soldiers grab the old man by the arms and lead him off.

Where are they taking him? Is he to be another Jew who just disappears and is never heard from again? These are questions without answers.

I turn back to see SS Stolen and his assistants leave us and proceed to headquarters.

Kapo Piekerman barks, "I need four volunteers to carry the body to the crematoria. Now."

I am one of the first to step forward, followed by Dov and two prisoners. I move to Auer's body, where I can see the sixth note lying inches from his head. I exchange a quick look with Dov, who moves quickly to block the other prisoners from seeing the note by directing their attention to picking up Auer's feet.

As I reach for one of the dead man's arms, I surreptitiously pick up the note and pocket it. Dov nods his approval.

I sigh with a sense of relief, knowing that one day if Germany does indeed lose the war, there will be justice for the many, many Jews tortured and killed. Dov and I buried Paul Hermann's six notes beneath the front steps of our barracks to be retrieved if and when the Allies win the war. I can only hope that by binding the papers in greased cloth, they will still be readable when we next retrieve them if we are able to retrieve them. This is the best we can do at the moment.

***

In the morning, we awake to the sound of artillery gunfire in the near distance.

"What the hell?" Dov remarks.

"It has to be the Allies. What else?" I reply.

We hurriedly assemble outside for the morning roll call. I notice unusual activity surrounding headquarters. SS officers and soldiers are carrying boxes out and placing them in trucks as if preparing to leave.

SS Stolen hurries down the steps to his Mercedes and is driven out of camp.

"I think you're right," Dov remarks.

"Now, what happens to us?"

"It appears that they're more interested in leaving than arranging firing squads."

"Let's hope so."

Kapo Pakierman and two assistants hurriedly stride up. "Attention! I have been ordered to assemble five hundred prisoners, men and women. You will be marched to another camp. You will be among the first to depart. You will leave within the hour."

"Who's going to carry our luggage?" a wisecracking prisoner asks.

A thin smile appears on Kapo's face. "I wish I were accompanying you. I would personally see to it that all of your bags follow you, even if I had to carry them myself." He glances over the crowd. "You are to assemble immediately at the front gate."

"What's the rush?" I ask.

"Can't you hear? Russians," is his terse answer.

Pakierman turns and strides off, followed by his assistants.

Dov grins. "I never thought I'd be happy to hear that the Russians are coming."

As we are leaving, my last thoughts are on seven little pieces of paper, the last of which I was able to add to the first six pieces late last night. Will they survive? Or will they rot in the ground? Only God knows.

Minutes later, gathering at the front gate, a group of two hundred or more women prisoners join the three hundred of us. I search for a green scarf. My expectations fade when the color is nowhere in sight.

Then my heart jumps. I see my lady. She is coming toward us, holding onto the arm of an elderly woman, helping her walk as they join the group.

"Happy now?" Dov asks.

"Mind your own business," I respond lightly.

He grins.

A young, officious-looking SS officer, formidable in his long black overcoat, gloves, and hat, opens the gate guarded by an unusually large number of soldiers. These Germans, I notice with a degree of envy, are dressed in warm winter clothing.

"All out!" a soldier barks, pointing to the road outside the camp. "*Raus*! *Raus*! Out! Out!"

We file through the gate and are directed to a nearby open area.

"Line up in rows of four," the SS officer orders as he comes to stand before us.

We do as we are told. I glance around, looking for transportation.

Dov asks the question I'm thinking. "So, where are the trucks? Or do they expect us to walk to the train station?"

"Attention!" the SS officer announces. "I am Hauptscharführer Friedrich Schmitt. I am in charge of this march. We will be traveling to one of our sub-camps in Germany. I warn you the journey will not be easy. There will be no shelter and little food or water available. I warn you in advance. Many of you will not survive. I will take no questions. You are to follow my orders explicitly. My first order: "Follow me."

He starts walking toward the train station in the distance.

I exchange looks with Dov.

He shrugs.

We, along with the long line of prisoners, follow Schmitt.

At least thirty soldiers, armed with rifles and sub-machine guns, wearing full military backpacks, join us. They walk on the perimeters of our group. A single truck, carrying provisions and what appears to be rolled-up tents, follows.

I glance behind us to where the women are marching but cannot see a green scarf. Yet, I know she is there, which gives me a feeling of relief and anticipation. I would like to talk with her. I know the chance of this happening is remote. But if there is a way…

We approach the railway station, but in a few minutes, we are walking right past the loading platform. Dov and I exchange looks. The prisoners, too, murmur in confusion.

Our combined dismay garners the attention of SS Schmitt, who is only a few yards in front of us. He moves to the side of our column and says in a voice loud enough to carry to the back of the marchers, "One thing I forgot to mention. There are no trains available to transport you. You will be walking."

The prisoners around me grumble. Few of us are in any condition to walk, no matter how long or short it may be.

Schmitt adds, “The camp you are going to is located in eastern Germany, a bit less than two hundred miles from where we stand.”

A wave of moans sweeps over us.

“Save your breaths,” Schmitt says. “You’ll need every bit of energy you have just to survive.”

He raises a hand to stop the truck following us and gets into the passenger’s seat. The truck drives on, leading our column.

“Nothing like taking a bunch of skeletons on an invigorating two-hundred-mile walk in the middle of winter,” I say sarcastically.

Dov, ever the accountant, responds, “If we march twenty miles a day, it will take ten days to reach the camp. That’s ten days over snow-covered roads without shelter, coats, boots, or whatever food they choose to give us.”

“This group will have trouble walking five miles a day.”

“You have that right. This is a *kappore*, a disaster. It’s January. There’s going to be more rain, sleet, and snow. This is meant to be a death march.”

“Leave it to the Nazis, ever thoughtful.”

We exchange a look that says, ‘This is the end of us.’ We are not strong enough to walk ten miles, let alone 200.

A few steps behind us, a frail old man trips and falls. He struggles to rise but is having trouble. A prisoner lends him a hand when a nearby SS soldier steps close and orders, “*Wegkommen*!”

When the prisoner moves aside as ordered, the soldier raises his rifle, aims at the old man’s frightened face, and pulls the trigger. He then drags the body over the snow, leaving a trail of blood, and dumps the body on the side of the road. The soldier then moves on, paying no more attention to the man he murdered than if he had just stepped on a bug.

“Cold-hearted *mumzer*,” Dov mutters. “How do these people live with themselves?”

"It's a sickness," I reply. "Hitler's manipulated the minds of his followers with hate for the sake of his power."

"How can so many people be so blind?"

Chapter 21

At the end of our first night's march, a north wind lashes us with bitter cold, and as usual, we are wearing only a thin layer. Our exposed skin aches and turns blue, and our feet are numb and bleeding. It feels as if our fingers will break if we so much as bend them.

Icicles form on eyelashes and beards, and our breaths are white puffs. This morning, we are like walking corpses, a ragged group of lost souls, stumbling blindly toward more misery and our own deaths. It is becoming more obvious with every step we are to be done away with. There is no food. No water. We eat snow.

Dov is an exception. He is a bundle of suppressed energy. "Here's my plan," he whispers, brushing ice from his eyebrows. "We wait until the next heavy rain or snowfall, and then after we find a weakness in the guard's perimeter, you and I simply walk away under the cover of Mother Nature."

"Brilliant, I wish I had thought of it," I respond with a touch of sarcasm as I am searching the women's group of prisoners, looking for my lady. But then I see Dov's frown and know he's waiting for a response, I add, "It's our old problem. Where can we go? We have no money. We're in enemy-occupied territory with a high chance of being shot. On the other hand, if we stay together, with the Allies getting closer and closer, we have a fair chance of surviving."

He looks at me for a long while, then shakes his head as if in agreement with himself. "This is about your girlfriend, isn't it?"

While I silently acknowledge he's partially correct, I say, "I admit, there's a certain someone. But she's only a small part of the reason I want to stay on this march. I think the chance of an escape is twenty-eighty at best. Common sense says we stay."

"I've never let common sense stand in my way when my instincts tell me it's time to move on, to fight from a distance. Come with me."

"Dov," I respond, shaking my head. "If you're really determined to go, I'll pray for you."

He looks at me…then flashes a grin. "I'll take you up on that. In the meantime, have you found us reservations for the night?"

"As a matter of fact, I have," I respond as light-heartedly as I can manage. "I've reserved you a bed with a feather mattress and a down comforter under that tall oak tree over there."

He glances at the tree. "Excellent. And supper?"

"Hot pierogi. Our health is obviously one of our benefactors' highest concerns."

Dov looks over at the provisional army truck that has been following us and is now parked by the side of the road as we shuffle past.

SS Schmitt is sitting at a portable table with two aides, eating what appears to be a prepared four-course meal with wine. Behind him, several sleeping tents and tables have been set up for his subordinates, half of whom are eating while the remaining soldiers march along with us.

"In my next life," Dov remarks, "I'm coming back as Hitler's mother."

"Why would you want to be Hitler's mother?"

"So I could abort the bastard."

***

We've been on this 'road of tears' now for five days. The Arctic weather is relentless. Those who fall or stop to rest are shot and left by the wayside. Sickness and hunger also take their toll, adding to the trail of bodies in our wake.

At nightfall, we sleep like animals in open pastures. Roadsides are our latrines. We huddle together in a failing attempt to preserve body heat. Yet every morning, prisoners are found frozen to death.

They are stripped of clothing and shoes and left where they die. Of the five hundred prisoners we started out with, close to a hundred of us have perished.

The roads we drag ourselves over, run parallel to railroad tracks where trains laden with German troops, fuel tanks, and flatcars carrying armored vehicles clatter by, all heading for the front where I imagine battles are raging. I pray for the Allies.

There have been no vehicles on the road, though, two hours ago, we had to move to the shoulder to allow artillery pieces pulled by horses to pass us. It seems like a throwback in time to the Great War. I wonder, *Does this mean the German army is running out of trucks or fuel? Interesting.*

This evening, I leave Dov to wander the field where SS Schmitt has decided we should spend the night. Half of the soldiers go through their routine of setting up tents while, as usual, the remaining soldiers keep an eye on us.

I am walking toward the area where female prisoners are settling on the ground. They are separated from the men's encampment by a fifty-foot open space and four guards who, I suspect, are supposed to stop fraternization. I look at the nearest females, searching for my lady. I spot the green scarf and see her sitting beneath a tree with a few companions only sixty feet away.

I step a few feet closer to the unmarked boundary, where an SS guard eyes me suspiciously. I offer him a friendly nod. I receive a scowl in return. I ignore the brute and stand my ground, gazing across the space, willing my lady to look my way. Eventually, she does. To my surprise, she rises and walks toward me.

I cast a cautionary glance at the SS guard, who seems irritated by my stance only a dozen feet from him. He flicks a hand, a gesture for me to move off. Playing naive, I raise my hand and give him a friendly little wave.

His face darkens, and he steps closer. "*Gehen*! *Raus*!"

"*Danke*," I respond, looking past him.

The soldier advances until he is almost in my face. I smile as politely as I can manage and point over his shoulder.

He frowns, turns, and sees the woman in the green scarf approaching. He glances back at me.

I raise my hands in a gesture I hope conveys my interest in meeting the woman.

He unslings his rifle and gestures again for me to leave. "*Gehen*! *Raus*!"

Rather than standing my ground and possibly endangering the woman I've yet to meet, I walk away. I pray there will be another time, another place, and my lady and I will meet for whatever outcome lies ahead, if anything.

***

Since my failed encounter with my yet-to-be gentlewoman, the original five hundred prisoners we left Gleiwitz with continue to diminish.

We trek through snow and ice on roads passing through open country and several small hamlets. The people in these villages peer out of their homes and businesses to stare at us. A few venture outside to hold out offerings of bread for us, only to have the morsels slapped out of their hands by our guards. I wonder what these villagers think when they see emaciated Jews suffering, persecuted, and executed at the direction of the very leaders these citizens have so slavishly supported?

By nightfall, we collapse upon the hard, cold ground. We need to sleep to keep going, but we don't dare, as sleep is the first stage of death by hypothermia. Dov and I take turns watching over each other while one of us sleeps.

The next morning, having survived another night, Dov and I are walking along the road.

He is mumbling incoherently.

After a few minutes, I ask, "What are you saying to yourself?"

"For your information, I'm praying."

When I raise my eyebrows, he explains, "It's been a long time since I've tried. In Lodz, you went to Yeshiva Bible studies, right?"

"Yes," I respond, wondering where this is going.

"Remember the story about the Prodigal son? A father has two sons. One was good, the other a sinner?"

"I do."

"Well, I'm kind of like the sinner."

I nod, curious now.

"So, I thought if I prayed and told God I'm not really all that big a sinner and that I love Him, which I do—I've just never told him so—well, I thought… I thought He might respond to me." Dov shrugs. "At least I'm giving it a try."

"What are you praying for?"

"Rain. A heavy rain or a blinding snowfall, something to cover my escape before we reach Gross Rosen. What do you think?"

"I think what you're planning to do is crazy. But if you're set on going, then praying is worth a try."

Two days later, snow begins to fall, lightly at first and then with gusts of blinding flakes that swirl around us as if we were inside a shaken snow globe.

Dov, accompanied by two prisoners he has rounded up to join in his escape plan, moves close to me. "Elias, my friend, this is where we part. I look forward to seeing you when this insane war is over. If I make it, I'll leave word for you in Lodz at Chaim Rumkowski's office."

"I'll do the same. Good luck, Dov," I say with a heavy heart.

I am tempted to go with him, but I think my odds of living are better if I remain with our group. And I now have another reason to stay in the camps; I haven't seen her in days, and I worry that she won't make it through these appalling conditions.

Dov and I embrace quickly. He gives a cautionary glance around. The snow is falling so heavily that it is now difficult to see ten feet in front of us.

The outline of a German soldier appears as he accompanies our slowly moving line of prisoners. Then, as the guard moves off, Dov whispers, "*L'Chaim*."

"*Mozell tov*," I respond, wishing him luck.

Dov and his two companions leave the road and begin jogging across a field that climbs up to a bank of trees. They disappear in a veil of white.

Moments later, the wind changes direction, and the snow temporarily lets up. Dov and his companions are exposed, laboring uphill through knee-high snow, heading for the cover of trees.

Gunfire shatters the stillness!

Horrified, I watch as Dov and his friends are hit, their bodies jerking as they spin and plummet to the snow, only a few feet from the tree line where they might have found cover. All three prisoners lay motionless where they fell.

Snow flurries gust once more, whirling around their bodies, covering them from sight. The scene is too silent.

I am frozen with shock. My insides feel as if a giant hand is physically squeezing them. The few tears my body can produce well and brim over, turning to ice on my cheeks.

"*Raus*! *Raus*! Move!" the German guards shout, prodding us along.

I continue to gaze after the bodies of my fallen friend and his companions even though the snow has obliterated their images. Then, without realizing it, I am moving on, following the line of prisoners.

My breathing is ragged, my steps unsteady. My lips are moving; I am praying, reciting Kaddish for the lives of so many of my departed friends: Dov, Adam, David, Avram, Kaz, my Mame, my Tate, my brother and sisters, and my Jewish acquaintances and neighbors from my old Lodz neighborhood. I exhale so hard my lungs ache.

I trod on, snowflakes wiping out everything around me. I am in a cocoon of whiteness, isolated and alone. There's a heaviness in my legs with each step I take as if the weight of the cruelty in this world is heavier than my body can bear. God and His ways are beyond me.

I believe He exists, but my belief is being tested. I think of stories in the Old Testament of Jews who were persecuted and murdered and then of Jews who, despite persecutions, never gave up—and survived.

These latter thoughts give me a scintilla of hope that God has not abandoned us and that He will see to it that we endure and make it through these worst of times.

I pull myself out of the depths and, remembering God is always with me, I once again begin thinking about what I, a single Jew, can do to fight the evils of our oppressors. Probably not much. But not much *is* something.

I inhale, and a sense of my old resolve reasserts itself. I am not giving up. And while I struggle to survive, I will continue to do all I can to help destroy everything Hitler represents. I am not doing this for myself but the plight of Jews everywhere.

***

Time passes slowly, painfully, as we trudge through snow and slush with temperatures dropping below 0 degrees Celsius at night. More of us freeze to death or die from starvation, exhaustion, and endless executions.

Thankfully, it has stopped snowing as our haggard group comes across a sign.

Willkommen in Deutschland

The marker must be left over from the pre-war days when there was a border between Poland and Germany. The landscape is the same, except the towns have industrial complexes. Many of them have been damaged or destroyed by, I assume, Allied bombings.

At one village, we are enlisted to clear rubble from a cratered manufacturing plant so German military equipment can pass through. Several times, we cross paths with haggard-looking Wehrmacht troops on their way to the front lines; they don't know what haggard is.

It is overcast and dark, but ahead of us, there are lights burning in the village we are approaching. Colored lights.

I hear singing. And then I see a group of thirty or more people on the steps of a church, singing Christmas songs. Across from the church is a line of six German Panzer tanks. Their crews sit on top of their vehicles, listening to the carolers. By their uniforms, I see they are Wehrmacht military, a far cry from the callous SS soldiers guarding us.

As we draw closer and come to a stop, I look at the faces of these Germans as they sing their Christmas carols. How can these well-fed, well-clothed Germans, supposedly religious Christians, not see their sins as we, a ragged group of emaciated, half-dead Jews, appear before them? Yet their faces, seemingly caught up in their religious fervor, do not acknowledge our plight.

They sing with a passion that ignores the truth that Jesus was Jewish and that the persecution, torture, and murder he suffered is much the same as we Jews are now suffering under Nazi rule.

I look around at my companions and see tired faces that recognize a spiritual connection to singing, yet they, too, are conflicted by the hypocrisy of the Germans.

While the harmonies of song can lift the heaviest of hearts, mine is weighted down by the reality of antisemitism: how this doctrine of hate can turn many church-going Christians into sinners who follow the rule of Adolf Hitler and break God's Tenth Commandant 'Thou Shalt Not Kill.'

The choral group begins another song, and even though the words are in German, I understand the melody.

Stille Nacht! Heilige Nacht!
Alles schläft, einsam wacht,
Nur das traute hochheilige Paar
Holder Knabe im lockigen Haar

Schlaf in himmlischer Ruh
Schlaf in himmlischer Ruh

The German tank core joins in. Their faces are reverent. No doubt, the soldiers are filled with memories of home and family.

The song ends, and at the request of bystanders, it is repeated.

All around me, as SS guards watch nervously, the choral group begins to sing. The tank core again adds their voices. A few prisoners, obviously non-Jews, begin to sing hesitantly. A woman in the column behind ours sings in English, "Silent night, holy night,

All is calm, all is bright,
Round yon virgin, mother and child,
Holy infant, tender and mild,
Sleep in heavenly peace,
Sleep in heavenly peace.

When the final words drift into the night, I look around. People have come out of homes and apartments, flooding the street with offerings of cookies and little pastries, and some of the Wehrmacht soldiers pass out cigarettes.

I am given a cigarette. I thank the soldier, and as I don't care for cigarettes, I give it to another prisoner.

An SS soldier, a few feet from me, pushes a German lady's arm away while handing cookies to the prisoners. "*Nein*! *Nein*." the SS soldier orders. "These are Jews! Do you not know this?"

"I don't care," the lady responds, ignoring him as she continues to pass out treats.

The SS soldier appears anxious. He looks around at villagers moving among the prisoners, giving them pastries and little candies. Resigned, he takes a few steps back and simply watches.

A smiling woman hands me a little biscuit, saying, "Lebkuchen."

I take the delicious-looking cookie, which is warm and smells like spice.

"*Danke*," I say gratefully.

I hold the little treasure in the palm of my hand. My thoughts immediately take me back to Lodz, 1939, when Mr. Dornitz, who owned the bakery shop, gifted me a cinnamon rugelach. I can still almost taste its succulent flavors. And now I am holding another treasure as I make my way through the mass of prisoners with one thought on my mind.

I push my way past SS guards who seem at a loss from the Christmas happenings around them, and then I am at the edge of the women's group.

Moments later, I am standing before her. She is alive!

As our eyes meet, I am spellbound. She offers a tentative smile and then says in the most lyrical voice I have ever heard, "I am Esther."

Gazing into her green eyes, I manage to respond, "I am Elias. But please call me Eli."

"I am happy to meet you, Elias…Eli"

"I am happy to meet you, too." I hold out the cookie. "For you."

"Oh no. No, Eli, I can't, I—"

"Please," I insist as I place the cookie in the palm of her hand.

Once more, I am losing myself in her eyes, which have little gold specks highlighting the emerald green.

Whistles!

Stern guttural voices.

I am roughly pushed away from Esther by an SS putz. He and his comrades are attempting to separate prisoners from the villagers to stop the flow of gifts.

Angry voices rise.

Truncheons lash out. Prisoners are struck viciously.

I catch a glimpse of Esther looking after me as I am pushed and shoved as soldiers attempt to separate prisoners from the townspeople.

Gunshot!

The crowd freezes.

A tall Wehrmacht officer beribboned with citations, including the Iron Cross, stands on a Panzer tank, the pistol he fired in hand. His face tells me he is not happy with this display of violence on Christmas.

Silence.

SS Hauptscharführer Schmitt, his face flushed beet-red, pushes through the crowd and strides up to the officer's tank. He yells angrily at the Wehrmacht commander.

The beribboned soldier jumps down and calmly walks up to Schmitt until they are nose to nose. He speaks quietly to Schmitt, who responds angrily.

The Wehrmacht officer raises his pistol and aims it at the Nazi's forehead.

Schmitt blanches.

The commander speaks too softly for his words to carry beyond the two of them.

Schmitt's face contorts. He simmers for a moment and then glances around. The Wehrmacht soldiers have drawn their pistols. It is obvious they are prepared to back up their commander if this war of wills becomes physical.

Schmitt growls inaudibly, turns on his heel, and walks back to his subordinates. He glares at the townspeople, a tick in his left cheek pulsating.

I've thoroughly enjoyed this moment of decency displayed by the tank commander and his troops, although we may suffer for it later. The village inhabitants, moving hurriedly now, pass out their remaining gifts.

SS Schmitt barks an order, and within minutes, we are leaving the village behind.

Christmas carols start again and drift away as we march along the road. My thoughts turn to Esther, the few words we spoke. I know her name. I repeat it to myself, 'Esther.' And now she knows who I am. This is a momentous achievement, as I still feel the soft touch of her hand and the gentle intelligence of her eyes.

Our column trudges over snow-covered roads, through more picturesque villages and hamlets where people's lives go on with no acknowledgment of the horrors inflicted upon us. Perhaps they are aware of our suffering, but the Nazis would shoot them if they were to attempt to help us.

We are continually ushered aside as military vehicles rush by, splattering us with cold, slushy mud. Despite the discomfort, the presence of Esther in our column is reassuring. I am relatively content knowing she is close by, but worried for us all.

Day by day, we pass a surprising number of concentration camps. I learn from fellow prisoners that the Gross Rosen area where we are headed has close to sixty sub-camps in eastern Germany and occupied Poland. I have no idea which camp will be our destination, but I am sure now none can be good.

It's the dead of night as our haggard group finally arrives.

Chapter 22

Gross-Rozen Concentration Camp
Camp # 6 - January 1945

I watch the sun linger on the horizon and then slip away, leaving an array of orange, gray, and purple. The colors fade as darkness creeps over us, and we trudge through ankle-deep snow, marching toward the camp's entrance.

It is a long single-story structure with a two-story block in its center. Its upper level is beige plaster with stone facing on the ground floor, incorporating an open arch for vehicles to pass through. On the wall over the archway, again, is the Nazi axiom,

ARBEIT MACHT FREI

I know its meaning by now—'Work Sets You Free.' A sick joke. Only death sets one free in these camps.

Since leaving Gleiwitz ten days ago, I would guess of the 500 male and female prisoners we started out with, our numbers have been reduced to approximately 300. The poor souls who died or were executed were left by the wayside, over half of them with bullet holes in their skulls. Others didn't wake in the morning; they had become blocks of ice.

A very few, driven by starvation, thirst, and disease, went mad and attacked the soldiers. They were kicked and clubbed to death. These Jews should be alive! They should be living surrounded by family and loved ones. I wouldn't want to be in Nazi's shoes when they die and have to face God for the people they have so cruelly murdered.

Inside this sprawling camp, with patches of snow everywhere, are thousands of men and women segregated into separate barbwire enclosures, all under the watchful eyes of prison guards and low watch towers.

As we move deeper into the camp, I catch a glimpse of Esther as she is led toward the women's enclosures. I am relieved she has survived. There has been no possible way for me to help her.

Moving on, we pass what appears to be a twenty-foot-tall mound of lumpy goods. Dusted with snow, it's difficult to make out what I'm looking at. As we move closer, my step falters. I see now that these 'lumpy goods' are discarded shoes! Thousands upon thousands of them—far too many to count. There are varying sizes, men's, women's, children's—all that's left of once living, breathing people. Absorbing this gruesome sight for what it is, I want to lash out at the Third Reich and the evils of Nazism—and the man most responsible for this obscenity—Adolf Hitler.

Emotionally drained, aware of the horrified reactions of those around me, I feel I am sinking into the depths of depression. I close my eyes and rub my temples, attempting to massage away the pain, but it's impossible.

Opening my eyes, I see we are moving around a block of buildings, led to a large enclosure where skeletal men in striped pajamas are loitering. *When will their shoes be added to the pile*?

I glance around at the grounds. Overall, this camp is unkempt and filthy. This is surprising, as Germans usually insist upon extreme order. Perhaps this is a sign of the Third Reich's deterioration. One can only hope. Or maybe they are just overwhelmed by the huge number of prisoners whom we see here.

We are assigned to barracks and crowded into barren quarters where two dim lights dangle from wires attached to the ceiling, allowing us to see the usual lack of flooring, blankets, and pillows. The bunks are three tiers high with bare boards. Again, five to six of us are forced to sleep in spaces meant to hold two people. Torture is Hitler's prerequisite for the care of Jews.

Night does not come gently but slams upon the earth like a curtain falling on a stage. Will this be the camp where we are eliminated? I have been sure other camps would be my end, but I have made it through. This time, I see no way out. It seems the Germans are becoming more and more desperate.

We climb into our cots and squeeze in between prisoners, attempting to find un-cramped positions. It's impossible.

Sleep eludes me as I lay wedged between bunkmates. The image of the shoe mound floats into my consciousness, haunting me. *Dear God, why are these Nazis so heartless? So evil?*

With a willful effort, I push the image away, allowing my mind to drift to memories of my family, lost friends, and Esther.

Ah, Esther.

The one bright spot in this dark world.

Now Dov comes to mind, his companionship and his passion for fighting Nazis. I miss him, his bantering, and his eagerness to fight. There is something to be said about friendship; it will not be replaced overnight. It takes time for a relationship and trust to build.

I close my eyes, trying to sleep. I pray for my fallen friends, my family, Esther, and the Allies to win the war quickly.

Whistles startle me awake.

It's morning already.

Stepping outside, I hug myself as a gust of bone-chilling air blows over us. Doesn't the temperature ever warm up in Germany?

Shivering, I gaze around at the unkempt surroundings. Weeds, peeking through the snow, are growing against and between buildings. There are broken vehicles left to disintegrate where they have stopped, and a general run-down look to the grounds.

I line up with hundreds of prisoners in front of tables where lukewarm coffee is being distributed. All of us are malnourished, and the air of desperation on the prisoners' faces frightens me. *Do I look as wretched? Perhaps.*

I sip my coffee with the realization that there is no way out.

"Good morning," I say to the men sitting by me.

Two respond in Yiddish, and the others in languages I don't understand.

I quickly learn that Gross-Rosen is a camp where Jews have been brought from all over Europe. There are also Gypsies, homosexuals, and Christians who are not pure Aryans or have spoken out against Hitler's Third Reich.

I nod to one of the men who speaks Yiddish. "How long have you been here?"

"Five weeks. I am Dasan. This is my son, Amiel." He nods to the pale-faced, skinny sixteen or seventeen-year-old youth sitting beside him. "We were sent here with twenty fellow Yugoslavs. All are dead now except me and Amiel."

I sip my cold coffee, digesting this response. Finally, I say, "I'm Elias, from Lodz, Poland. How did your friends die?"

"Die isn't the correct word. We work the quarries. My friends were beaten and starved to death, and some were thrown into acid pits. There were suicides also. Life expectancy in the diggings is two weeks."

When I respond with alarm, he adds, "You heard that right, two weeks. If you're sent to the quarries, every day, you'll pass an open graveyard. Take a look; it's where thousands of bodies lay rotting, mostly Jews like us. We're being murdered faster than they can bury us."

Sorrow and anger, no strangers, compete for my attention. I close my eyes and pray Kaddish for these poor souls.

After a few moments, with a clearer head, I resolve to survive. If it's remotely possible, I will at least try.

"Attention!" orders an SS officer who has arrived to stand before us. The silver skull and bones on his cap glint in the weak morning sunlight. I later learn he is SS-Sturmbannführer Johannes Hassebroek, the camp commander. He is accompanied by a Kapo, whose father could have been a Neanderthal. Apparently, Schmitt, who led us to Gross-Rosen, will no longer be with us.

Johannes Hassebroek adds, "Welcome to our camp. You will be treated as you deserve. Obey our rules, or you will be … bla, bla, bla…"

Having heard this harangue before, I tune his voice out, and my thoughts turn inward. Without Dov, I feel isolated. I have no friends, and I'm in another camp where my keepers are, at best, marginal psychopaths. I've long given up attempting to reason why so many people in the world treat Jews like we shouldn't exist. Are Jews so different from others?

I've heard there are German groups who, for years now, under the direction of Adolf Hitler, have been brainwashing children to hate us. The Third Reich's philosophy is to get them young, indoctrinate them into a sick philosophy, and you will soon have an entire generation of Jew-haters. These same children are now adults who hold the power of life and death over us.

Hitler and his ilk have succeeded in twisting the minds of almost the entire population of Germany. Those who reject Hitler's plan of indoctrination must either keep quiet to live or, if they speak out against the Fuhrer, they are eliminated. How can an entire country allow themselves to be so brainwashed? How did it happen? That is the question that will be debated for many years. But at the moment, there is nothing I can do about this. I wonder, *Is my life in the hands of Nazis or in the hands of God*?

I don't know the answer to this.

"… and as of this moment, prisoners are no longer allowed to talk to one another," Hassebroek says. "You will not speak to a guard or Kapo unless you are spoken to first. You will now receive your assignments from Kapo Lewinski."

Hassebroek turns on his heel and leaves.

Kapo Lewinski stares at us for a long moment, then says, "All of you will start working this morning in the granite quarry. It's a twenty-minute walk. You will work twelve hours a day. Roll call is at 6 a.m. Breakfast follows at…"

Bla, bla, bla, I think as I again tune out our itinerary and threats of punishment and death, and my thoughts drift to Esther. *What is she doing*?

***

We are walking toward the quarry when we come upon the open graveyard my Yugoslav acquaintance mentioned. I have seen many terrible things in the past few years, but this sight is like a visit to hell. Thousands, literally thousands, of naked bodies of men, women, and children have been thrown into haphazard piles. This hideousness makes my heart descend to a bottomless cavern within my body.

I look away, clamping my mouth shut, struggling to hold down my coffee. I pray Kaddish, and I pray the whole world will one day soon bear witness to Hitler's atrocities and his mentally ill followers.

We reach the grotto. Before us is a large outcropping of solid granite; it extends over a hundred yards with several pools of water fronting it where excavations have taken place.

In the nearest pond, two dead prisoners float just below the surface, their bodies ghost-like. Behind me, our two hundred or more prisoners murmur anxiously as they watch emaciated Jews already at work, pickaxing and chipping away at huge slabs of stone. Other prisoners are struggling to push carts packed with granite chunks to flatbed wagons, which are then loaded and wheeled away. The men bear bloody marks of abuse.

Dozens of SS guards oversee the prisoners, all thin-skinned skeletons. I see a worker fall. Unable to get back up, he lies there. An SS guard casually walks up, shoots him in the head, and orders two prisoners to haul his body off.

For the first time, I notice another stack of at least a hundred dead workers on the west side of the quarry. I can now believe the life expectancy here is two weeks. *How long will I be able to last*? *I think I will perish here*.

Kapo Dvorak, a skinny, thirty-ish Czechoslovakian who wears a wooden cross on a leather cord around his neck is followed by a half dozen SS soldiers as he walks to the front of our group and addresses us. "Jews, this is where you will be working. You will be divided into groups of six each, and then you will go to the east end of the grotto to get the tools to cut and chisel. The least hint that any of you plans to use these tools as weapons will be met with instant execution. You will work without talking. Each of you will be given a work quota that you must fulfill every day. Failure to do so is twenty-five lashes for the first shortfall. If a second shortfall occurs, you will be shot. If you work beyond your quota, you will be rewarded with an extra ration of bread. For those of you who…"

I again tune out the threats and lose myself with memories of the early years of my life, light-hearted years in which I would never have imagined death would hang over my head like a guillotine blade. I am certain now that the Nazis will not be satisfied until every Jew in Europe is dead. May the Allies continue to root out the Germans and defeat them, hopefully in time to save us.

Cutting and hauling stone drains my strength far quicker than I ever imagined. I swing my hammer and use my chisel against the rock like a robot. My mind is blank as I chip away at a slab of granite. My hands are blistered and sore, and my throat is so parched it is difficult to swallow.

I've witnessed two killings this morning, as well as several beatings. There is no medical help. If a prisoner is debilitated by work or punishment, he is shot.

I feel myself edging closer and closer to the grave as I hammer away at a slab of stone that is defying me. I wipe sweat from my eyes; this work is indeed a killer. It's as if I'm trying to carve out steel with a fingernail file.

To make our lives even more miserable, none of us is allowed to take breaks. We work steadily despite bloody blisters, muscle spasms, and sheer exhaustion.

I hear loud voices and turn to see Kapo Lewinski is back with us, yelling at Amiel, who has fallen onto a thin ledge six feet below the edge of the grotto's eighty-foot hill of granite. The gravel beneath Amiel's feet is falling away. He reaches his hand up, begging for help. Kapo Lewinski appears above Amiel, but instead of offering the boy a hand, he simply watches as Amiel loses his grip and falls. His scream is short-lived as he hits the rocks below.

A second later, a man's anguished voice screams, "*Nein*!"

I look up to see Dasan, Amiel's father, charging Lewinski. He tackles him—and they have disappeared. Both have gone over the edge of the precipice, falling eighty feet to the rocks below.

From where I'm standing, I see no movement from the three figures splayed out on the rocks.

A Kapo from a work party below runs up to the bodies and checks them for signs of life. After a quick prognosis, he announces, "Dead. Both dead."

All I can think of is *a waste of life.*

Kapo Dvorak, who is at the edge of the precipice looking down, turns back to us. "Excitement is over. Return to work!"

I've just witnessed the death of three men, two of whom were fellow Jews. This doesn't seem to register with the other prisoners as we return to work. I am in a world where human beings have ceased to respond as human beings.

Whistle!

I ignore the shrill notes, knowing it is too early to quit work, but when I hear the whistle a second time, I turn to see it's Kapo Dvorak blowing the signal. I wipe grit from my face and pay attention, as do my fellow workers.

He stands on an outcrop of rock across a wide expanse of grotto where the main body of prisoners has been cutting and chipping granite. We wearily wait for him to speak.

"Prisoners, today is a very fortunate day for you. It is New Year's Eve. Work stops now, an hour early. Put down your tools and follow me back to the camp."

I let out a sigh and toss my hammer and chisel aside. 1945! Tomorrow will be the first day of the new year.

As I make my way toward other prisoners lining up to march back to the camp, I begin to calculate how long I've been a prisoner. How much time has passed since I made the promise to my father to survive? So long ago!

I remember my father and I standing on Limanowski Street and watching the Germans roll into Lodz on that prophetic morning in 1939. Over five years ago! Miraculously, by the grace of God, I'm still alive.

As we trudge back to camp, I overhear a forbidden conversation whispered between two Polish men who have been conversing with newly arrived Polish/Soviet POWs. They are talking about the American General George S. Patton. His army defeated the Germans in Ardennes on the Western Front. It appears that German forces are retreating all across Europe. The Soviet Army crossed into Poland, and the tide of war continues to change in favor of the Allies. After hearing this welcome news, my step has a bit of a bounce as we enter the camp.

"Meat," I say with surprise, keeping my voice low as talk among the prisoners is forbidden. I hold up my fork. Speared on its tines is a small piece of sausage.

"And we were given an extra slice of bread," a young prisoner sitting across the table says quietly.

"New Year's should come every day," I whisper.

"Have you noticed the soldiers?" the young man asks, whispering as he glances around. "I think they've been drinking."

As I look closer, some of them do appear to be tipsy. The SS are drinking, but few are smiling and only occasionally laugh; even then, it seems forced. Even the music coming from headquarters is Wagnerian-heavy.

I am at a loss until a fellow prisoner, again breaking the rule of silence, tells me he has overheard two soldiers talking. The Soviet Army has broken through the German lines on the Polish border and is even now advancing in our direction. Now I understand the subdued celebration of the New Year. The German Army is retreating. How long will it be before the Soviets reach our camp?

Kapo Dvorak, leading a line of prisoners, hails me. "B-1259. Over here. All of you. Fall in line. We're leaving immediately."

My companions and I join a growing line of prisoners, not sure what's going on. There is excited talk of the Russian advance, and for the first time ever, there is a sense of optimism among us.

Dvorak and several SS soldiers lead us out of the main gate. I have no idea where we are going. This leads back to worrisome thoughts again.

We reach the train station as a coal-fed locomotive prepares to pull its attached line of cattle wagons from the platform. Our transportation is open to the elements, with a series of thick metal bars enclosing us like a jail cell.

We stumble on board, and I find myself in a corner and notice, surprisingly, that there's room to sit. I plop down and brace my back against metal bars.

Earlier, on our march from camp, I was very aware there were no women being transferred. *Esther...*

What will become of you?

The odds of us meeting in the future are remote at best. Even though we have never had the opportunity to have a real conversation, I believe I know her as one knows an old friend. In my thoughts, she has become more than a friend. She is my hope. And hope gives me the strength to continue, to survive. Optimism, my mother always told me, is part of who I am or who I was… There is still a glimmer of hope inside me—the German army appears to be failing.

The train begins to move, shaking me out of my deliberations.

As snow-covered trees, meadows, and farms begin to roll by, a disturbing thought surfaces again. *Will the war end in time to save us*?

Chapter 23

Buchenwald Concentration Camp
Camp #7 - February 1945

Hours later, passing through the city of Weimar in central Germany, I sit up with interest. This sprawling city is in a state of near ruins from what was surely Allied bombing. Once beautiful, historic buildings have been partially or completely reduced to rubble, as have many factories, businesses, and homes. This sight, more than anything, impresses upon me the growing plight of the Third Reich. If this large city has almost been destroyed, others all across Germany could be suffering the same fate if they haven't already. The Germans are losing the war. Where does this leave us Jews? Will we be set free? I don't know what to think.

As twilight turns into night, I am still ruminating on our fate.

Our train rolls to a stop. The gate to our cattle wagon slides open, and the first thing I see is a small rail station. I notice a single light over a sign.

BUCHENWALD

All my hopes to survive crash into my lungs, taking all my breaths with it. This is one of the Nazis' notorious killing camps. I can't help but think that this is where it ends.

Barking dogs divert my attention.

Nazi officers, SS soldiers, two Kapos, and the ever-present dogs are waiting for us on the loading platform.

A tall Kapo orders, "*Rous*! *Rous*! All out!"

Five hundred of us, leaving our dead behind, begin disembarking. Is it me, or am I sensing the same tension in these soldiers as I witnessed among the Nazi staff at Gross Rosen? Certainly, these soldiers must be aware that Russian troops are flooding into Poland and beginning to cross into Germany. It's certainly part of the reason we're here, being moved further away from the front lines with each passing week. Of course, the other part of the reason we're here is simply that here at Buchenwald, the Nazis can exterminate us faster than ever.

Minutes later, we are marching away from the railway station and up a long lane called Caracho Road, bordering a flat plain populated with scattered farms. The Russian word 'Caracho' means "good," I learn this from a Russian prisoner, but it is far from good for us.

When the SS men call out, "*Caracho!*" We inmates must run on the double, on blistered feet blackened by gangrene and frost. We are spurred on by rifle butts and dogs who bite at our legs.

Fear propels me, my muscles straining and aching as we climb a steep forested hill. The weakest among us fall to the ground.

The inevitable gunshots resonate behind me, but I do not turn to look. I recite Kaddish for the souls of the fallen.

Reaching the top of this tree-encircled mountain called Ettersberg, I see by the lights of the camp ahead black smoke and sparks billowing out of a tall brick chimney. This sight, which has become common in these camps, is still able to stir a rage within me.

We are marched through the camp's main gate, which bears a metal sign that reads:

JEDEM DAS SEINE

A fellow prisoner informs me the words translate loosely to, 'To each his due.' I have no idea why the Nazis put this here unless it is cynical, which is probable.

The camp, I'm beginning to see as we march inside, is huge. It's spread over a flat mesa that stretches out for what must be close to two miles. A high barbed wire fence encloses its entire perimeter, surely charged with electric current and fortified with a substantial number of guard towers.

There are rows and rows of prisoner barracks, open latrines, outbuildings, and a large brick building that I assume is SS headquarters. To the west, just outside the fence, is a large two-story home, a villa, where a woman in a maid's uniform is shaking out a small carpet. I imagine this home belongs to the camp commander.

In the center of the compound are upgraded brick barracks. These must be for SS officers and soldiers. There is also a structure bearing a Red Cross symbol—a hospital. I can readily assume it is for Germans only, as most camps offer no medical care to prisoners.

Additional wooden structures appear as we march further onto the grounds. There are workshops, a sawmill, a carpenter's shop where men in stripes are stacking cut lumber, a vehicle repair garage with mechanics working on military trucks and motorcycles, and several other buildings of undetermined industry.

We are directed to an area with a brick factory and gravel pits.

I am surprised to see a small zoo on the west side of the camp when I march toward the distinctive brick headquarters building. I see two zebra and several deer. There's also an aviary. It holds a lone eagle, and in adjoining cages is a brown bear, a couple of foxes, and a few mystery containers that certainly hold some other animals. Or, perhaps, Jews? I find this thought not so impossible, and then we come upon a barbwire enclosure filled with hundreds, make that thousands of men. They are emaciated souls, barely able to walk. For the most part, they ignore us.

As we pass another enclosure, my heart squeezes as I recognize haggard and malnourished women and children. They, too, pay no attention to us as we pass by.

Ahead is the camp's crematorium. It is surrounded by a wooden fence, at least eight feet tall, blocking my view of all but its sixty-foot chimney, from which black smoke curls. As I'm observing this, a breeze swirls the grey-black ash around and brings a black veil down upon us. My skin crawls as this dark curtain settles over me. I don't know what to do. Shall I brush the ashes off? Will it be disrespectful? What do I do?

I look around. Other prisoners are realizing the composition of this deathly rain. Some attempt to brush ashes off, others simply walk on, tears in their eyes.

If only the outside world could be made aware of these murders that go on every day, every week, every month, without stopping. One must see this atrocity to realize the evils of the perverted Nazi mind.

I glance around at the hundreds of half-dead Jews behind their barbwire enclosures.

How soon will they be turned to ash?

A vile smell gags us as we round a corner; confronting us are hundreds upon hundreds of wasted, decomposing bodies laid out like firewood. One can never forget this stench and depravity.

"Attention!"

Jarred, back to reality, I realize we have arrived at an area fronting the camp's headquarters where my fellow prisoners and I will have to listen to yet another SS officer who has appeared before us. He introduces himself as SS-Oberfuhrer Hermann Pister. He is slim, of medium height, middle-aged, with the demeanor of a mortician.

The Adam's apple in his scrawny neck bobs up and down as he fills us in on camp procedures and rules, including what he expects of us as workers, all of course enforced with threats of death—nothing new here.

He informs us that we are no longer human beings; we are lower than swine. If he knew what *I* was thinking of his status in the world, I would be shot.

Pister goes on to tell us we will be known only by our tattoo numbers. This is meant to further humiliate us as if this were possible. And we are again told that we'll be putting our lives at risk if we look a guard straight in the eye. We must stare at the ground when addressed. Also, Christians, gypsies, homosexuals, and Jehovah's Witnesses will be favored over Jews, who will be given the hardest work and the least amount of food. Jews will cut trees, dig latrines, build barracks, and cut stone in the grotto. As the camp currently has a shortage of living quarters, new arrivals will be sent to temporary huts. And even though Buchenwald has no gas chambers, only crematoriums, he makes it a point to tell us they run continuously.

"There is no way to survive in Buchenwald," Pister emphasizes. "But you can extend your life through hard work. Your Kapo Fritz Fuchs will come shortly and take you to your barracks."

It is almost completely dark now, and the rain has become a torrent as we stand in the downpour, waiting for our Kapo to arrive. Pister has left us long ago and gone to the shelter of his office.

I lose track of time as we stand in the freezing rain, waiting for Kapo Fuchs to appear. The storm does not let up. The night drags on and on. We shift from foot to foot, our legs and backs aching, our feet numb as they sink into thickening mud. Struggling to stay upright, I hear rather than see prisoners falling around me, where they will surely die.

Finally, dawn breaks and the weather clears. Kapo Fritz Fuchs appears. There is no apology for his tardiness, but as he looks at the dozen men who lie dead where they fell during the storm, he says, "The dead are better off, believe me."

He orders us to follow him.

Kapo leads us, who can barely walk, across the parade ground to a low building. We are ordered to disrobe entirely and then have short showers as if we need them after our thorough soaking during the night. Shortly after our showers, we are sprayed with white disinfectant, and those of us who are again in need of hair removal have our body hair shaved off.

We are now led to our barracks, or rather our 'hut' in the 'small camp' as they call it. When I see the inside of this small rectangular wooden box with its dirt floor and one window, I realize this is the worst quarters I have yet seen. Our sleeping arrangements consist of ten rows of triple-decked shelves; each shelf consists of a twelve by twelve-foot pallet with, once again, only two feet of height between each layer.

Kapo Fuchs tells us each pallet will sleep twelve men or more, but I can't imagine how.

Our old clothes have been discarded and new ones supplied. They are piled in a lump in the dirt. We are told to pick out new garments and to meet outside within ten minutes for supper.

Outside, dressed in ill-fitting striped pajamas, we are given a single tin bowl with a spoon to be shared with multiple prisoners. There isn't enough watered soup for everyone, so they ladle out smaller scoops, giving each person a minuscule portion.

Kapo Fuchs, I come to learn, is not as bad as others in his position have been. While waiting in line for our supper, he happens to stop beside me. I ask, "How long have you been here, Fritz?"

"Since 1941."

"Four years," I respond with surprise. "What's your secret for living?"

"I obey orders. When you're in the grotto chipping limestone, you'll be tempted to speak back to the guards, don't. Remember, you're expendable. Do as you're told. Obey orders. That's how I've lived this long. How I intend to live longer."

I nod and glance around and see what looks like an old stable a couple of hundred feet away. "They keep horses here?"

"Hardly. You don't want to be sent there. That's a private murder factory."

While I am absorbing this gruesome information, he adds, "It's where Soviet prisoners-of-war are executed."

"Just Soviet prisoners?"

He's silent momentarily, then adds, "One of our former camp commanders fought on the Russian Front. He was wounded, captured, and horribly tortured by the Soviets. He escaped and ended up here. That building is where he has personally supervised the torture and execution of close to 9000 Soviet prisoners of war during the last two years. When the camp runs short of Soviet POWs, Jews are substituted. At last count, over six thousand Jews. The Jews will soon outnumber the Soviets. Normally, with our labor shortage, they only execute those who are sick or are too weak to work. And, of course, those who don't keep up with their work quotas. But lately, there are more being killed…"

"Does this apply to you, too?"

His eyes swivel to me. "I more than keep up with my duties, specifically camp discipline." After a moment, he adds, "The barn also serves as a medical experiment facility where SS doctors use Jews as guinea pigs."

Very little shocks me anymore, but I am curious. "What kind of experiments?"

Unblinking eyes stare at me. "They choose specific test subjects according to the nature of the trial. Some are injected with Typhoid bacteria, strychnine, and sometimes just air. This way, they test all sorts of serums. Few survive the after-effects of the injections. Also, I hear they are using phosphorus to burn the skin on test subjects to see what will work to heal Germans injured by mortar bombs, grenades, and the like. I've heard it actually burns to the bone."

"Killing Jews for science..." I remark, barely containing my revulsion.

"It is what it is," he responds with a shrug. "Nothing I can do about it. Probably the most heinous acts take place in the pathology block. It's where Nazis with abhorrent sexual proclivities have been known to torture and murder their victims, usually the cream of Jewish youth."

"I've heard rumors."

"They're real. The saddest of all are the experiments on children."

Shaken, when I thought nothing could shake me anymore, I can only stare at Fritz as my mind attempts to grapple with this. I finally say, "I pray for the Allies to win the war."

"Your prayers may come true. The Germans are being crushed on every front."

Ah, so that is why the soldiers seemed tense today.

"If you want to live to see the end of the war, my advice to you: obey the rules. Otherwise, you'll be fuel for the ovens."

"I can do that." I look over the camp, at the living and the dead. I ask quietly, speaking more to myself than to Fritz, "How did we Jews ever come to be so persecuted?"

"I'm not an educated man," Fritz replies with a sigh. "If I were, I still don't think I'd have answers for you. Remember my advice, 'obey the rules,' and you may live long enough to find these answers yourself, but probably not."

Fritz Fuchs walks off.

I do believe there is a just world outside of this place and that I will survive to find it.

I'm momentarily lost in this thought when a voice interrupts, "Elias, is that you?"

Surprised to hear my name spoken, I turn to see a skinny old man in striped pajamas staring at me. He looks vaguely familiar.

"It is you, is it not?" he asks.

I answer hesitantly, "I'm Elias Feinzilberg."

He grins, showing a missing front tooth. "I thought I recognized you when you entered camp with the others. I'm your father's old friend from Lodz, Aaron Orlanski."

I recognize him now. He is much thinner, and his hair, what little he has left, is white. "Aaron, I do remember you."

"Come here with me." He motions to the side of the barracks.

I follow him to an area that offers the scantest bit of privacy.

"Elias, I am happy to know you are alive. I was sad and troubled to hear about your father's passing and your family being sent to Chelmno." He shakes his head. "Life is difficult. Losing family and friends makes it more so."

I nod in commiseration, happy to see someone from Lodz. "How have you managed to stay alive all these years?" Before he can answer, I add, "And how is it you can walk around so freely?"

"I have certain privileges."

"You're a Kapo?"

"Never." He spits. "I am the camp's mechanic."

"A mechanic?"

He nods. "I service and repair cars, trucks, anything with tires. The Germans need me to keep their armored vehicles, motorcycles, and automobiles running." He points to a wooden building a short distance away. It houses an assortment of vehicles in three open bays. "That's my garage. I manage the camp's motor pool. Were it not for my mechanical skills, I would have been toast long ago. This brings me to your situation." He gives me a long, pensive look, then asks, "What do you know about car engines?"

"Nothing."

"Are you a fast learner?"

"I believe so."

"Good. You're coming to work for me."

"How can I do that? I was just told I would be working in the grotto."

"Forget it. The camp needs mechanics much more than rock cutters."

"Aaron, I'm not a—"

"Not to worry. I'll teach you all you need to know. You'll learn to replace spark plugs, fan belts, and change oil. Nothing to it."

"You can hire me?"

"Sort of. I can make a request. I was on my way to headquarters to tell them I need more help when I spotted you. When I explain I just found one of the best mechanics in Poland, they'll be happy to let me hire you. Germans love their vehicles, especially Commandant Pister. I keep them running." He lowers his voice to a whisper. "Except for the ones I don't."

My pulse quickens. *Is he saying…?*

He winks at me.

I grin at this implication. “Aaron, I would love for you to teach me to be a mechanic.”

“That’s settled then. Now, let me see your number.”

I offer him a look at the tattoo on my arm.

“All right, B-1259. Wish me luck.”

As Aaron walks off, I wonder if he can actually persuade those in charge to let him hire me. If so, it will very likely save my life. I silently pray, *Thank you, Tate, for having a good old friend. And thank you, God, that we met.*

***

The following morning, I haven’t heard a word from Aaron Orlanski. I’m nervously drinking a cup of cold coffee while waiting in line to be sent to the grotto with the other prisoners.

“B-1259,” Fritz Fuchs says as he strides over and pulls me out of line. “You’re to report to the car garage.” He gives me an inquiring look. “How did you manage this?”

I shrug. “An old family friend recognized me.”

“So?”

“I’ve been working in car garages all over Poland,” I’m surprised how easily this lie rolls off my tongue.

“Really?”.

“Yes,” I compound my lie. “I’m quite a good mechanic.”

“Hmm,” he replies, scrutinizing me as if I’m an oddity of some sort. “Do you know where the garage is?”

“I saw it when we arrived yesterday.”

“Okay, go. If anyone stops you, have them contact me, and I’ll verify your transfer to the garage. Good luck to you, Mr. Mechanic.”

“Thank you.” I turn away, feeling like a bird in a cage, as its door suddenly springs open.

I walk away from the prisoners as they are marched off to a day of back-breaking labor. With a continuing sense of relief, I realize I’m going to work at a real job. And even though I know nothing about cars, I will learn.

A few minutes later, I am whistling, surprising myself. I can't remember the last time I whistled.

As I approach the garage, I notice its three open bays. The nearest one holds a green military vehicle where a prematurely balding young man in overalls is changing a rear tire. The second bay has a small car of a make I don't recognize with its rear end propped up on pedestals. The farthest bay contains a large black sedan with its hood up. Drawing closer, I see a man's feet sticking out from under the chassis.

I glance around at the garage's interior walls. Plastered on the walls are an assortment of automobile posters along with a large, framed photograph of Adolf Hitler. I scowl at his image, then turn my attention to a row of new tires lining the back wall, along with various vehicle parts stacked neatly on shelves. A variety of tools are spread everywhere. These instruments are as foreign to me as chopsticks.

I approach the young man, noticing his overalls are worn over striped pajamas. Also, he is skinny as a rail, but that is the look of the day.

"Hello, I'm Elias Feinzilberg, I'm looking for—"

"Elias, yes," he interrupts. "Aaron told me you'd be coming in this morning. Welcome, I'm Zev."

He wipes his palm with a cloth and offers it to me. We shake hands, and he points to the third bay. "He's under that big monster."

"Thank you, Zev."

I proceed to the impressive-looking automobile just as Aaron scoots out from under it on a board with small wheels attached to each corner. He, too, wears overalls over striped pajamas.

"Elias," he says as he gets to his feet and moves to the front of the car. "Welcome to our garage. You're just in time to learn how to change oil. After that, we'll get to spark plugs and the distributor. I'll make a mechanic out of you in no time."

I grin at his enthusiasm as I admire the black sedan. "Powerful looking car."

"Yes, it's a Mercedes-Benz 770. One of the fastest grand sedans in the world. It used to belong to Ilse Koch. She was our last camp commander's wife. You've heard of her, no doubt?"

"No."

"She was known as the 'Witch of Buchenwald.' A notoriously sadistic woman who murdered hundreds of prisoners for her own amusement. And, if they happened to have an interesting tattoo, she had her victim's skin flayed, to be made into book covers and lampshades to decorate her villa."

Appalling. I shake my head with disgust. "Is she still here?"

"No, thanks be to God." Aaron reaches under the Mercedes hood and unscrews the oil cap on a tube running up the side of the engine. "Her gruesome habits were too much even for the Nazis. She and her husband, SS Commander Karl Koch, her accomplice in many of her cruelties, were arrested shortly after her skin-flaying episodes, and that's when her 'medical research' trophies were discovered. She collected internal organs from prisoners and kept them in jars in her office. Her idea of 'medical research.'"

I let out my breath. "Dear God! What became of her?"

"She and her husband are going to trial. My guess is they'll have to be hanged. That's all I know, but good riddance."

A short time later, I am watching Aaron unscrew a cap on the tube to the side of the Mercedes's impressively powerful engine.

He explains. "This is where we add oil. I've already drained the engine's old oil. Now, I'll add eight new quarts. For peak performance, these cars need to have their oil changed every 5,000 miles. Watch how I do this, and then I'll show you how to service the car's lube points. Those are small nipples we use to infuse grease into joints to protect anything that moves from wear and tear. After this," he says, picking up a can of motor oil and puncturing its top. "I'll show you how to change spark plugs and adjust timing points inside the distributor cap. Before you know it, you'll be a first-class mechanic."

I watch as Aaron affixes a spout to the can and pours its contents down the tube. He continues this process with seven additional cans.

"Have you heard the latest on the war?" Aaron asks.

"I've heard that the Allies have the Germans on the run if we can believe the rumors."

"Actually, this time, they're true. I get my news by eavesdropping on SS drivers who chauffeur the camp's commander and his cronies around. The Germans are getting clobbered. The USA, British, and Soviets are continuing to defeat Nazi forces all over Europe. To top that off, there's been an assassination attempt on Hitler."

"I did hear that. Too bad it failed."

Zev walks up and hands Aaron a piece of paper. "More crap."

Aaron closes the Mercedes hood and reads. "Ah, another proclamation from Berlin. Himmler has ordered the liquidation of all ghettos and camps in the Baltic states."

"Where does that leave us?" I ask.

"Even more crowded."

An SS soldier arrives. He and Aaron exchange a few words, and then the man gets into the Mercedes 770 sedan and drives off.

Aaron says, "The woman I was just telling you about, Ilse Koch, she and her husband have just been acquitted by Germany's highest military court. So much for Justice."

Somehow, I don't find this news surprising.

"I hope we never see that bitch again," Zev remarks.

"Back to work, Zev," Aaron says. "Elias, come with me. I'm going to show you how to drain a car's differential and replace its fluid."

I follow him to the car in the second bay.

And so, my 'first-class mechanic' education begins. While I'm learning the basics, I'm also observing the camp. The women's section reminds me of Esther, but I have lost hope of seeing her again. I just pray she is not suffering.

Seeing children behind a barbed wire fence brings sadness to my heart. How young they are to be separated from parents they'll likely never see again. They may not even live. Why am I still alive? I don't know the answer.

***

I've been in Buchenwald for less than a week, and working in the garage has somewhat lifted my spirits. Aaron is teaching me to service cars, motorcycles, and trucks. And while I still have to master the art of being an apprentice automobile mechanic, I am fascinated by the vehicles I work on. I also feel guilty in the evenings when I return to the barracks, knowing the meager meal my mates had at noon while Aaron, Zev, and I have shared a marginally better offering supplied by SS motor pool drivers. They do this so we will take special care when we service their vehicles.

In the morning, when I rise to go to work, there are always men who have passed away during the night. We must always carry the dead to roll call, where personnel will then dispose of them. At least their suffering is over. But these poor souls didn't have to die. All this misery and death is rooted in one man. I pray there is another attempt on Hitler's life and that it will be successful.

I am working in bay 1, changing oil on a Nazi officer's car. It is late afternoon. Aaron is releasing an automobile he has serviced to an SS driver in bay 3. Zev is in bay 2, changing brakes on a motorcycle with an attached sidecar.

After Aaron's customer drives off, he comes over to me, motioning Zev to follow.

"I've some grim news," Aaron says.

Zev and I move closer to him as he adds, "We're being replaced."

"Replaced?" Zev responds with shock.

I, too, am surprised. "By whom?"

"Military mechanics from Berlin. They'll be arriving tomorrow to take over the garage. Apparently, every able-bodied prisoner is needed to help produce oil for the Third Reich, and that includes us."

"Are they crazy?" Zev asks, "We don't know anything about producing oil."

"We're able-bodied or a step up from death, anyway," Aaron explains. "That's all they care about—laborers."

Zev throws a tire iron across the garage in disgust. Aaron would normally smack him for that, but he ignores the infraction.

"I just got here!" I say. "Where are they sending us?"

"Bisingen concentration camp."

Zev and Aaron continue to discuss this new turn of events while my thoughts are already reviewing plans I've come up with during the last few days for possibilities here in Buchenwald to, in effect, throw a monkey wrench into the German's military pool. With this latest news of imminent departure, it is imperative I now act fast—tonight.

"Bisingen?" Zev inquires.

"Yes," Aaron replies. "The Germans have a petroleum facility there and they're desperate to produce oil to keep their armor moving."

Zev states, "I'm not an oil rig monkey."

"They don't have rigs," Aaron says. "They produce oil from shale rock and flowers."

"Flowers? How does that work?"

"Apparently, we're going to find out. We leave in the morning."

"First I've got work to do," I say as I glance around the garage with a growing sense of urgency. "I'm going to create a little 'going away present' for our hosts."

Aaron gives me a look, understanding my implication. "Not without me, you're not."

Zev, looking puzzled, says, "What 'going away present?'"

My attention is drawn to two soldiers who stop outside to have a smoke and talk. To avoid the possibility of being overheard, I whisper in Zev's ear.

Zev's face blanches.

"Not to worry," I say, attempting to calm his fear.

Zev turns to Aaron. "Not to worry, he says."

"Shh," Aaron whispers.

"This is suicide!" Zev exclaims in a whisper. "They'll know we did it and track us down." He raises his forearm to emphasize his tattoo.

"It's a problem," I admit, continuing to whisper.

A possible solution comes to me. "Follow me."

I grab Zev's arm and lead them into Aaron's small office.

I lift a pen from the top of Aaron's desk, uncap it, and touch its point to my tattoo, B-1259, on my left forearm. While Aaron and Zev watch, I apply black ink to the black-inked tattoo, and I alter the numeral 1 to a 4. My tattoo has changed from B-1259 to B-4259.

"Very impressive," Aaron says. "But the ink looks a bit different."

I rub my fingers across the floor. I then blow on the ink to make sure it is dry and lightly rub grime over the altered tattoo. The new ink blends with the old.

"Good," Zev remarks. "It looks good."

"With these alterations, the Nazis will never be able to track us. Give me your arm."

Zev stretches his forearm out. His number is B-3691. I use the pen again and change the 3 to an 8. His tattoo transforms from B-3691 to B-8691. I blow the ink dry and smudge dirt over the tattoo.

"I can't tell it from the original," Aaron says. He sticks his arm out. "Do me."

His tattoo reads, B-2823. I alter the 3 to an 8. I blow on it and rub grime over the ink. It now reads B-2828.

"It's good," Aaron says as he appraises his altered tattoo. "No one can tell it's been changed."

"The ink will wash off in a few days, and the original letters and numerals will become visible," I say. "But by then, the Nazis may have given up looking for us. And, if by chance they are still hunting for us,"—I put the cap on the pen and pocket it— "I'll save this and redo my artwork."

Aaron nods. "Good for me. Zev?"

"I'm in. Where do we start?"

Ssssss...

I have punched a hole in the side of a tire with a screwdriver, and even though my hands are shaking like a palsied old man, the sound of escaping air thrills me. Only minutes ago, Aaron, Zev, and I finished demolishing the garage's vehicle batteries, as well as slashing the entire inventory of new automobile tires and engine belts. Now, we are destroying the larger tires on over twenty military vehicles in the camp's motor pool in the rear of the garage.

We neaten the inventory so none of the damage is too obvious. Prior to our assault, we unscrewed lightbulbs on two of the four most glaring floodlights that light the yard. Still, it wouldn't surprise me if we were discovered and shot on the spot.

Disabling the motor pool may not have been my best idea, but it was the only one I could think of on such short notice. And, if we get away with this, it's unlikely our handiwork will be discovered until later tomorrow when the new mechanics arrive. At least, that's what I'm *hoping*.

"We're done," Aaron says as he and Zev hurry to my side.

"Me too. Let's get out of here."

We leave the motor pool and go our separate ways back to the barracks. Tomorrow will be an interesting day.

I say a prayer, asking God to protect us. They say prayer works miracles. I've found that sometimes it does, and sometimes it doesn't. But prayer does give me hope, and I need that right now, so I silently add, *God, thank you for helping me to survive this long. I hope I'm not asking too much to ask you to help us get out of this camp alive.*

***

The first rays of sunlight peek through our window. I rise and follow my hut mates out into the yard, where we undergo another roll call and then have coffee for breakfast. My nerves are on edge. I am expecting us to be apprehended at any moment.

Kapo Fritz Fuchs, his assistant, and several guards are lazing about.

This a good sign.

Aaron and Zev join me in line.

Aaron says, "So far, so good."

"Nothing's good until we're out of here," Zev remarks.

"It's all timing," I say. "If the new mechanics arrive early, or if someone goes to the motor pool to take out a car before we leave, we're dead."

Aaron nods. "There's the old saying, 'eat and run.' Of course, with us, it's 'drink your coffee and run.'"

"I'll settle for getting out of here any way we can," I respond as I am handed a cup of coffee.

Aaron and Zeb grab mugs, and we find a place to sit on one of the benches. Aaron downs his coffee.

"I think I ate too much," Aaron remarks, patting his stomach. "I'm stuffed."

Zev swallows the last of his coffee. "Me, too."

It's an old joke that has worn itself out but communicates so much more.

My eyes flick from headquarters to the garage, where the bay doors remain closed, and back to the prisoners who are drinking their coffee far slower than I would like. I silently urge, *Hurry up. Drink*!

Minutes later, Kapo Fuchs orders us to assemble.

Aaron, Zev and I are the first in line.

Kapo Fuchs raises an eyebrow and shrugs, and then we follow him as he and several guards lead us and others out of Buchenwald's front gate.

In the distance, our locomotive sits in the railroad yard with smoke curling into the sky. Attached to the engine and coal car are a dozen cattle wagons, our normal transportation.

I want to hurry along, but our pace is frustratingly slow. Glancing over my shoulder, I let out my breath. *So far, so good.*

There are no SS soldiers chasing after us. The destruction we left behind has yet to be discovered.

Chapter 24

Bisingen Concentration Camp
Camp # 8 - March 1945

With our cattle wagons rolling through the countryside and small towns, I notice plumes of dark smoke staining the air as we approach a large, sprawling city. A sign on a passing railway station identifies it as:

Stuttgart, Germany

Peering through the wagon's rails, I see devastation all around us, mile after mile of it. The city has suffered recent bombings as the ruins of many structures still have flames and smoke billowing from them, adding to the dark clouds hanging over the city. Many churches, buildings, and apartments in the city center have been reduced to rubble. Other structures are mere shells, with one or two walls still intact, relics of the past. *This is encouraging.*

But how many civilians were killed during the bombing? German citizens are paying a terrible price for Hitler's war. But looking at this destruction, my sympathy is limited. The Germans allowed a war to start by embracing the maniac's doctrine, and now they're paying for it.

Fear is still my close companion. Will the war end quickly enough to save us?

It's a short time later that our train rolls to a stop at a small railroad station. Looking past the passenger platform, I see three rail spurs leading to a large yard where several black oil tankers sit. In my fantasy, I imagine them exploding in flames. I am becoming more than a little obsessed with my desire to see Germany's war efforts come to a quick end.

As we disembark with the usual contingent of SS officers, soldiers, and dogs, I notice a group of buildings ahead of us, many of which show signs of bombardment.

"Bisingen," a prisoner behind me identifies.

The town appears to be small. Its main architectural attraction is a bombed-out church, missing half its roof and all its windows. The iron crucifix once affixed atop its tall spire hangs by a bent metal strap as if God has abandoned one of His homes. I don't blame Him.

SS guards stand by the church, directing a group of prisoners who are attempting to repair the roof. The remainder of the town is an assortment of homes, apartments, shops, and small factories.

A half-mile beyond is a barbed wire-enclosed group of one and two-story buildings, obviously Bisingen concentration camp. From a distance, it appears to be grimmer than most, if that's possible.

The surrounding countryside is stony, devoid of trees and grass, with mining structures set amidst a large series of low rock ledges. These formations look like 'shale rock' from which oil is extracted. Hundreds of men in striped clothes labor on these ledges like worker ants, using picks and long iron bars to dig and break large rocks into smaller pieces. The fragments are loaded onto wagons and pulled by teams of horses to a group of buildings and dumped there. Tractors scoop up the payload and transport the rock to a moving conveyor belt, which is dumped and carried to a large crushing machine.

"No one's checking tattoos," Aaron remarks as he looks around the train platform. "It doesn't appear anyone's searching for us."

"Not yet," Zev says nervously.

"We're going to be okay," I remark, with more optimism than I feel.

"Maybe not," Aaron adds, nodding toward a group of soldiers being led by a tall, stern-looking SS officer who begins shouting.

While I can't understand his words, my stomach tightens as he passes out pieces of paper to the guards. I believe I know what's on those papers. Now, I can only hope my 'artwork' passes inspection.

I glance at my forearm. The tattoo looks good to me, but will it pass Nazi scrutiny?

The SS officer leaves abruptly, and a skinny, bearded man about forty years of age comes to the forefront of the guards. He wears civilian clothes and has a blue armband with the letters KAPO embroidered on it.

He carries a truncheon and slaps it against his thigh as he speaks. "I am your Kapo, and as such, I oversee all Jewish prisoners. My name is Lucian Andrei. I am a Romanian Christian, one who does not blame you Jews for the death of Jesus; you'll be happy to know. My first order of business is to have you submit to an identification check before you proceed to your barracks. We have been alerted that there may be saboteurs among you. Criminals, listen to me! The SS has your tattoo numbers. You will save them and me a lot of time by stepping forward now and receiving a quick and painless death. Or if you refuse to confess and we must go through the time-delaying process of discovering your identity—and the SS will find you—I can assure you they will administer a long and torturous death. Now, please, guilty ones, please step forward."

No one moves.

Kapo Andrei slaps his truncheon on the palm of his hand. "Don't say you weren't warned. You will now proceed down the steps to the table being set up on the field below. There, your identity numbers will be examined." Andrei slaps his truncheon once against his palm. "Prisoners, go now."

Aaron, Zev, and I are first in line by the stairs.

I exchange looks with Aaron and Zev. My concern is Zev, who is sweating heavily and licking his lips. Aaron is a rock. I give Zev a reassuring nod. He glances at his forearm. We both see it at the same time—sweat has made the tattooed O smear. Zev's eyes widen in panic.

I grab his arm. "Easy," I whisper. "We'll get through this." I lick my thumb and run it over the edge of the O, attempting to wipe the smudge away.

"You," an SS soldier yells. "At the head of the line. Move!"

My heart leaps. Zev is ready to bolt. The smudge is still visible. I reach down to my right shoe and swipe my hand across its bottom. I rub soiled fingers over Zev's tattoo, leaving a film of grime over the O letter.

The SS soldier who yelled is striding toward us.

"Elias," Aaron urges. "We must go."

I start down the flight of steps. Aaron, Zev, and the prisoners follow. Aaron pushes up next to me as I move up to the inspection table. We show the SS soldiers our forearms. They inspect our tattoos, check them against pieces of paper they hold, and then, seeing no match, they wave us through to the open field beyond.

I turn to see Zev step forward to be examined. He offers his forearm. The SS soldier stares at his tattoo for a long moment, then nods and passes him through.

My breath leaves me. Hopefully, my pulse will return to normal.

Zev walks over to us with a relieved grin.

"Well done," I say.

"*Danke*," he replies.

"Well done to you, Elias," Aaron says quietly. "You may have a new career ahead of you as a tattoo artist."

"And I was hoping you'd make me a master car mechanic," I retort.

"You're much too destructive to work in any garage."

I enjoy my first smile in days.

After the prisoners have all been vetted and no anti-Nazi criminals found, Kapo Andrei and a few dozen SS soldiers and dogs lead us down a road turned to mud by recent rains. As we slog toward the concentration camp, our feet sink into the ooze, and as we pull them out, our shoes are sucked off. We must stop to dig them out again and again before we can replace them and proceed. It's a slow and tedious process. We plod along in this fashion for more than an hour until we finally reach Bisingen's main gate.

Kapo Andrei leads us past armed guards and barking dogs, and we march into camp. A hundred yards ahead, a Nazi flag hangs listlessly from a tall pole in front of a long wooden building. It has to be the camp's headquarters, but the building looks timeworn as if the structure had once been an old factory. It is fronted by a sea of puddles and more mud for us to plod through. I notice rows of muck-splattered tents; beyond them are newly constructed wood barracks with others in the process of being built.

Hundreds of men in dirty striped pajamas are at work on these buildings, digging trenches for new foundations. Muddied equipment of all sorts is scattered about as prisoners labor under the attentive eyes of guards in surrounding watchtowers.

"Mumzers," Zev suddenly remarks.

I follow his gaze and see an open pit filled with piles upon piles of dead human beings. Their naked bodies are nothing but skin and bone. I clench my jaw and murmur yet another Kaddish for their souls.

As we continue toward the main building, I wonder, after having beat the odds at so many camps, how long can it be before I end up on one of those piles, discarded and unknown, with no one to say a prayer over me?

Passing headquarters, I am surprised there is no SS Officer on the porch to give us a welcoming speech that ends with the usual 'You will work, or you will die.' I suppose they are aware we have heard it all before and consider additional threats a waste of time.

Entering the camp's main yard, I observe many starving, rail-thin men working on various construction jobs. Several dead lie on the ground beside a horse-drawn cart where former workmates are stripping their clothes and shoes off. I remember once seeing an artist's painting of hell; the only thing lacking here is fire and brimstone.

The wretched condition of my surroundings, over-crowded with prisoners like Buchenwald, leads me to think the war might indeed be changing in favor of the Allies, as these Nazis seem no longer able to manage the ever-increasing number of inmates. If the Germans lose the war, the Nazis must be held accountable for their inhumane treatment and murders. Perhaps the most egregious criminals will hang.

The pain and misery the Nazis have wrought upon us is incomprehensible. I wonder, *Can a human being ever forget the evils and depravities he or she committed? Or experienced?*

I often reflect upon my belief in an 'all-loving' God, and I always come back to my faith that He has a plan, a purpose. I know to many, this is incomprehensible, but I no longer question the existence of God, even with all I've been through and witnessed.

For as long as I can remember, I have an ingrained belief that springs from childhood and my religious upbringing. This belief, you can call it optimism if you like, continues to carry me through these dark days, weeks, months, and years.

"The first eighty prisoners are assigned to barracks at the end of this row," Kapo Andrei orders as he leads us to a stop beside a row of low buildings. "Count off as we pass and claim your barracks."

One of Andrei's assistants, a Kapo about sixteen or seventeen years of age, supervises the counting.

Aaron, Zev, and I are in the first group. We enter number 6, our feet padding upon a dirt floor. At least it's solid earth and not mud.

I glance around. There are no glass panes in the windows, and our cots have no mattresses. The beds are four feet wide and three tiers high.

"German hospitality is *farkakte*," I say to Aaron and Zev.

"I'll send a complaint to Adolf," Aaron responds. "He's sure to give us an upgrade."

The young Kapo ignores us and orders, "You will all share beds, four to each."

Aaron remarks cynically, "No blankets or pillows?"

"They arrive on the second Monday of next week."

"Hey, that's funny," Aaron responds. "You must be Jewish."

"Yes," the Kapo retorts. "But I am not a comedian. After you've claimed your space, gather outside. You have ten minutes."

"Well," I remark after he leaves, "at least there's a roof."

"It leaks," Zev says as he points to scattered pools of water.

***

Moonlight filters through the windows, but the glow can't penetrate the darkness I hear in the mumbled voices around me. There are many different accents, but the prevailing language is Yiddish. They talk of home, missing relatives and friends, and the temperature in the barracks that must be below freezing. Some manage to drift off. I, like many others, find sleep elusive.

I close my eyes. If I do fall asleep, I wonder if I'll wake in the morning or be discovered as a frozen chunk of meat.

"Someone, speak to me."

My eyes open.

"Talk to me, please. I need someone to talk to."

I listen to the plaintive voice of a man on the top bunk across from me.

"Talk to me," the voice again pleads. "Please, I'm begging you. Say something, anything. I'm going to die. I don't want to die without talking to someone. I'm so alone. Someone, say something, please."

"Shut up," a prisoner yells directly above me.

"Please say something," the man continues to plead.

The despair in the man's voice touches me, yet I am at a loss as to how to respond. *Say something*? *All right, I will try*. "You're not alone. You have friends here."

"Who are you?"

"I am Elias. Elias Feinzilberg from Lodz, Poland. What's your name?"

"Arie Nosek. I am from Vilna, in northeastern Poland."

"Quiet!" a gruff-voiced prisoner behind us complains. "I'm trying to sleep."

"I've never been there," I respond to the voice across from me. I attempt to take his mind off his loneliness. "What's Vilna like?"

"It's a beautiful city on the Neris River. My family had a home there overlooking the water."

"It sounds very nice. How did you end up here, Arie?"

"The Nazis evicted us from our homes. Those who refused to go were executed; my mother and father among them. I am the only one left of my family. I was sent to a labor camp. After that, I was transferred here. I suppose they plan to kill me, but I'm going to rob them of that pleasure. I'm going to kill myself. In the morning, I'm running into the fence."

"For God's sake, go to sleep," a fourth prisoner complains.

I ignore these complainers. Running into the electric fence is a sure way to die. I understand Arie's depression. I have felt the wretched loss of family and home. And, while I've never considered suicide, I know of men who have taken that path. I am against it. I feel no matter how bad life is, and these Nazi camps can't get worse, I believe God gives us the strength to suffer through these trials. But how can I convince Arie of that? That suicide is wrong? I finally say, "Suicide, that's one way to let the Nazis win."

"I don't care."

"I want you to know I care. I care about you and your life, Arie."

He scoffs. "You don't even know me."

"Yes, I do. You're not much different from me or anyone else in here. We're all suffering. We've all lost everything we value. But there's one thing that keeps us going in spite of all the beatings, tortures, and killings."

"What's that?"

"The knowledge that if we survive, we will have beaten the Nazis."

Silence, except for the wind whistling around the corner of the barracks.

Arie finally says, "I never thought of it that way."

"As long as there's a chance to live, there's a chance to win. To beat the Nazis. You must not give up on life, Arie."

"Give up already!" the man above me responds.

More silence descends on us, and the wind dies to a whisper.

Timbers in the ceiling creak. Then Arie's voice, carrying a bit of optimism I haven't heard before, says, "Thank you, Elias. Thank you for that thought. I'm not going to let the Nazis win. Good night."

"Good night"

Closing my eyes, I think of Tate's council to me all those years ago on the steps of our apartment when he asked me to survive. I smile as I realize I am now passing his advice along to others. If I can send little sunbeams and words of encouragement to others, I believe more of us will survive. I say quietly, "Good night, Tate."

***

The Germans lose no time putting us to work. My first encounter with oil production comes a few hours later inside an old warehouse. I, Aaron, Zev, and a group of around fifty prisoners are given instructions, surprisingly, on how to burn sunflowers until the kernels crack open, then remove the seeds and place them in a press. The seeds are squeezed until oil is extracted. It is a lot of work for very little return. I imagine the Germans must be desperate for fuel if they are resorting to such extreme measures to make oil. I really don't know how they turn this flower oil into fuel, but that's not for me to worry about.

I've learned that the remaining prisoners from Buchenwald have been put to work breaking up shale rock for processing, which produces quite a bit more oil. This is easier for me to comprehend as shale rock oil is a fluid that I recognize as a lubricant. I am grateful I am not doing this work.

The next few days turn into weeks. Aaron, Zev, I, and the rest of us work in the flower processing plant, laboring from dawn to dusk. At least it's warm by the fires used to burn the kernels.

Meals, if you can call them that, have been reduced to twice daily, morning and evening. Because of increasing air raids by British bombers, lights are forbidden in camp. We eat our supper in darkness.

During daylight hours, the fearful drone of British planes increases day by day, with bombs falling nearby, hitting targeted factories. We hold our breath when we hear these explosions, as we all know our oil processing plant is certainly a target. Sometimes when this happens, the Nazis hide, and we prisoners run outside so the pilots can see us in our stripes. With new prisoners arriving every day to replace those who die from starvation and executions, we begin to hear additional rumors of the Germans losing the war.

Our SS guards appear more and more apprehensive every day as they, too, must know Hitler's Aryan hallucination is turning to dust. This growing reality doesn't stop them from beating, torturing, and murdering prisoners, but I've noticed now that their former enthusiasm is gone. They are worried. And they should be. Once this war is over, there should be trials set up to prosecute them. We can only hope all those who participated in atrocities will be held responsible.

***

It's raining, and I am inside listening to drops pattering the factory's tin roof as I stand at my station running the oil-extracting machine. It didn't take me long to learn how to burn sunflower seeds until the hulls cracked open, releasing their seeds, and pressing them into oil.

Aaron and Zev stop by, each carrying a load of flowers.

"Elias, good news," Aaron says. "The United States army is taking one German city after another. Partisan groups all over Europe are joining the Allies. Concentration camps are being liberated. Soviet troops have taken Auschwitz, arrested the Nazis, and set the prisoners free. Even now, the US is closing in on Buchenwald."

Zev adds, "The days of the Third Reich are ending."

"Too bad we're not at Buchenwald," I say, feeling hopeful.

Aaron says, "The German high command has ordered all gas chambers and crematoriums destroyed."

"The bastards are trying to hide their crimes," Zev remarks.

Aaron nods. "This very camp is being evacuated and torn down starting tomorrow. We're being moved to Dachau in the morning."

I grimace. "Dachau is strictly a killing camp."

"They're going to murder us all," Zev states.

"It appears they're going to try."

***

As if I don't have enough to worry about, my morning starts on the wrong foot, so to speak. I swing out of the bunk and reach for my shoes. My fingers touch the floor and then search the surrounding area. "My shoes… Anyone see my shoes?"

I look around for the possibility that they may have been kicked aside. Nothing. "Some creep has stolen my shoes!"

"What?" Aaron asks as he and Zev roll off the bed to stand beside me.

"My shoes, someone's taken them!"

"That's really low," Aaron remarks. "Let's check around."

"I'll look on this aisle," Zev says, then hesitates. "Elias, how can I tell your shoes from anyone else's? They're all caked with mud."

I see his point. Attempting to locate shoes with no identifying characteristics other than muck makes it impossible.

My thoughts are distracted by Kapo Andrei's morning whistle shrilling outside, summoning us to breakfast.

I shake my head. I'm mad enough to wring the culprit's neck if I can find him. I recall the wretched mound of shoes from our last camp, but I've seen no such outdoor collection here. "Maybe they have a warehouse here with clothes and shoes where I can find another pair. That is if the guards let me go through them. It's morbid, but I don't have any other choice. Let's go."

I pad barefoot out the door with Aaron, Zev, and the other prisoners following. The frozen rocky ground prickles the bare soles of my feet as I look at the other prisoner's shoes, hoping to identify mine.

No such luck.

Disgusted, I hop from foot to foot, trying to avoid sharp gravel and frostbite.

Kapo Andrei, his assistant, and at least fifty SS soldiers, accompanied by those ever-present dogs, are waiting for us beside a long line of trucks.

"Prisoners, give me your attention," Kapo Andrei announces. "Bisingen is closed as of this morning. It's being broken down as I speak. German headquarters has ordered the immediate transfer of prisoners to Dachau concentration camp."

I exchange looks with Aaron and Zev. We are well aware Dachau is our destination and a final one.

Kapo Andrei continues, "You will be transported in these trucks. Each vehicle is to carry forty prisoners. My assistant will count you off as you begin loading. You are now to proceed to the trucks."

"Hey, Andrei," a prisoner calls. "What about our coffee?"

"No coffee."

There is an uproar.

"Silence!" Kapo Andrei orders. "Silence! You do not have a choice in this matter. Any of you who refuse to immediately go will be executed. These are explicit orders from SS headquarters. No further outbursts!"

As the tirade diminishes, I comment, "No coffee. No shoes. Transferred to Dachau. Not a good beginning for the day."

One of the prisoners asks, "How far is Dachau from here?"

"By car, about one hundred and fifty miles," Kapo Andrei replies.

Aaron quips, "Will they have a hot meal ready for us when we arrive?"

"Of course," Kapo Andrei replies. "I've ordered sauerbraten with spätzle along with hot apple strudel and vanilla ice cream for dessert, to be served as soon as you arrive."

"Putz," I murmur.

"Move out!" Kapo Andrei barks.

Within the next thirty minutes, a thousand prisoners have boarded the line of trucks, and we are now driving out of Bisingen on the road to Dachau, the extermination camp.

***

The ride to Dachau takes us through thick green forests and valleys with grazing cows and bubbling streams cascading over rocks. The sky is blue with wisps of white feathery clouds. As beautiful as the scenery is, it does nothing to lift my spirits and those of the others around me.

As the hours pass, we travel through towns and hamlets whose residents seem oblivious to the war that rages on only a few hundred miles away. What I notice most about our journey is the line of German troops trudging alongside the road that parallels the railroad tracks. These soldiers, who only months before marched with discipline and pride, have been reduced to a haggard group of war-weary men, many of them with bloody bandages. They seem dispirited, as if unwilling to reenter a fight that has turned against them. I wonder how long these combatants will continue to take orders from their officers when they realize the Third Reich is a lost cause?

In the meantime, I remind myself that speculating about the soldiers' morale doesn't help us Jews, especially now with the Nazis planning to remove all evidence of their atrocities.

I have lived through so many camps and come so close to death, and somehow I've survived. Why is this? I don't know. All I know is that I will continue to do everything in my power to keep my promise to my father. One day, I know I will die. Will it be in Dachau? Only God knows.

Our truck bumps along, hitting potholes, knocking me out of my morbid and frightening thoughts. I gaze at two soldiers sitting by the rear loading panel. Their submachine guns are on their laps, pointing at us as if they know we have nothing to lose by attempting to escape. They seem fully prepared to shoot us if we try. Yet I believe I would be able to overpower them with Aaron's and Zev's help if it weren't for the vigilant German Shepherd sitting between them. These dogs send chills through me.

The older of the two guards glances at my bare feet. I look at his muddy boots. My size? Close enough that I envy him. Envying another person's dirty boots sounds strange until you're barefoot with ice-covered toes. The truck's cold metal floor doesn't help. The guard grins, possibly knowing I would like nothing better than to be wearing his boots, feeling their warmth.

I turn to other thoughts. Esther instantly comes to mind, and the first time I saw her as a young woman in a green scarf. Where might she be? I often think of her in the quiet moments before falling into an exhausted sleep. Her eyes, I reflect, the loveliest shade of green I've ever seen. They have reached into my soul in ways I can't explain. I say a prayer, *Dear God, if Esther is alive, please help her to survive.*

Chapter 25

Dachau Concentration Camp
Camp # 9 – April 1945

The sun is drifting low on the horizon as our truck convoy comes to a stop outside Dachau's guarded front gate. As at Auschwitz, the comforting slogan, "ARBEIT MACHT FREI," 'Work will set you free' is set into a wrought iron gate under the stone arch entryway. I would have thought Germans would be more original with their signage, but they must be too busy torturing and murdering.

SS guards wave us into a large, rectangular prisoner complex enclosed by the ever-present electrified barbed wire fence and guard towers. I count seventeen barracks in two rows, with a parade ground separating them from Headquarters and the administration offices. Clustered nearby are what I imagine to be cooking, laundry, and shower facilities. At the far end of the camp, there's a vegetable garden. The crematorium is just outside the camp; I can see the smoke.

Surrounding the camp but separated by open spaces are what look like manufacturing plants. Railroad tracks bisect these structures.

As our line of trucks pass through the grounds, I see guards leading masses of emaciated men, women, and children to outlying areas. There are also ragged-looking prisoners of both sexes behind segregated barbed-wire enclosures. A group of a dozen prisoners are in a band playing an assortment of musical instruments. I believe they could be playing a Bruckner piece, but it's beyond me to identify it. No one pays them the slightest bit of attention.

Our truck comes to a stop at the edge of an open area. Our two guards lower the rear panel and jump to the ground, the Shepherd following.

"*Schnell*!" the oldest guard commands, gesturing for us to disembark,

As I follow the others sliding from the truck, gravel bites my bare feet, a painful reminder to tread carefully.

"*Schnell*," the second guard yells.

He barks out additional orders as if we can understand his guttural German and then leads us to the center of the parade ground, where we stand, awaiting further instructions. Glancing around, I cringe at the sight of a wooden gallows where three women and two children are hanging by their necks, dead. Close by, two bloodied men are chained to poles hanging upside down. Somehow, they are still alive, writhing in pain. *These Nazis are on 'borrowed time*,' I tell myself.

Beyond this tableau is the all too familiar dark column of smoke rising from a chimney housed in a low brick building.

My attention is drawn to a group of women and children who are being herded across the yard by SS guards. They are so close I can see their frightened faces. Rifle butts prod those who have trouble walking.

A young girl, maybe ten years of age, trips and falls. The guard nearest to her yells. She attempts to rise but falls back, weeping. The Nazi places the barrel of his gun against her skull, leans down and yells. She looks up at him with teary eyes and shakes her head. She is unable to rise. He pulls the trigger. Her body shudders in death as he kicks her aside. The killer moves on as if she were nothing more than a momentary inconvenience.

Rage and sorrow, no strangers to me, surge. I am moving toward the killer when Aaron grabs my arm. I spin around.

His sad eyes bore into me as he whispers strongly, "No…"

I stare defiantly at him.

"No..." Arron repeats, this time quietly.

The soft tone of voice gets to me, defusing my rage. I now allow him to hold me back while I seethe with helpless fury.

I finally nod, letting Aaron know I am under control. He releases my arm. How is it these Nazis have no morality? No conscience? I've asked myself this over and over. I've not found an answer that even comes close to satisfying me.

Suddenly, I hear happy, funny music. Recognizing the tune, 'Three Blind Mice,' I turn to see the band I noticed earlier. They are accompanying a ragged group of over a hundred women and small children as they are crossing the parade ground, escorted by an SS officer and several soldiers. My mind flashes to images I witnessed in Auschwitz-Birkenau—carts of men, women, children, and babies being delivered to the crematoria and thrown into ovens. I open my mouth to yell a warning but hesitate. There is nothing I can do. My warning would only terrify the children.

The happy tune plays in stark contrast to the emotion on the faces of the mothers, who are aware of the hellish fate that awaits them. The mothers sing bravely along, forcing smiles, attempting to distract their children.

"What's happening?" Zev asks.

"They're on their way to the 'killing wall,'" Aaron responds. "From what I've heard, Dachau has no gas chambers, except for a small one, Barracks X, that they never use. The Nazis constructed a special area just outside the fence where prisoners are lined up against this 'killing wall' and machine-gunned to death. When the camp is jammed like it is now, they ship prisoners off to gas chambers at Hartheim Castle near Linz, Austria. Trust me, nothing's going to stop these Jew-haters from trying to annihilate us."

Only yards away, the unseeing eyes of dead Jews who lie in piles no longer witness this living tragedy.

As the group nears the main gate, the mothers, unable to keep the charade up any longer, are openly weeping yet still forcing themselves to smile in an effort to keep the children unaware of their fate. Seeing their mothers crying now, the children begin to sense something is wrong. They hug their mothers and cling to them.

Guards rush in and brutally push them out of the main gate, even as the cheerful, happy music plays on, although it sounds more ragged now. I imagine the faces of the musicians are wet with tears.

"*Raus*!" orders one of our guards.

He motions us to move along until we are near the end of the camp, close enough to smell the tainted air of decomposing bodies stacked against the crematorium where Sonderkommandos are scavenging through piles of the dead, twisting gold wedding bands off stiff fingers and prying mouths open in search of gold fillings. There are far more bodies than can be loaded onto carts and pushed inside the crematorium.

I thought Buchenwald was hell. This is beyond any concept of it I've ever imagined.

The Nazis are seemingly racing to kill us as never before, to remove evidence that they have murdered so many. It's impossible. They will never succeed. But that's not stopping them from trying.

There must be tens of thousands of Jews from many countries, gypsies, Jehovah's Witnesses, the disabled, and homosexuals in this camp who are marked for execution. The Germans, overwhelmed with their grisly tasks, seem to be on the verge of panicking.

Our only hope lies with the Allies. But will they arrive in time to save us? Obviously not for some, and maybe not for us.

Standing beside Zev and me, Aaron remarks, "I hate every one of these Nazis mumzers. With the war coming to an end, they could let everyone go. But no, they have to continue to murder us, even the women and little children, and play their sadistic farkakte music as they do so. There's a sickness in the Nazi mind only death can cure. I was wrong, Elias, stopping you from attacking that SS soldier who executed the young girl. Seeing that senseless killing and this 'death parade' is more than I can stomach. I'm about ready to attack these mumzers myself. I'm willing to die in the process."

Surprised to hear the defeat in Aaron's voice. I say, "Says the man who just saved me from a bullet."

He shrugs as we gaze after the mothers and children being led away as the band plays on. “I’m just tired, Elias. This life is no life.”

“You’re running into the electric fence?” Zev asks.

“No, I won’t do that. I’ll try to take one or more of these Nazi mumzers.”

“All you’ll get is a bullet in the head,” Zev says.

“Aaron,” I say. “This war is coming to an end. If we survive, we may live to see these criminals face a firing squad or the hangman’s noose. You should want to stay around just to see that.”

Aaron lets out a long breath. “You’re right, Elias. You’re right. Thank you. That alone I will live for.”

Gratified, realizing we’ve saved each other’s lives in the past few minutes by not doing something stupid, I take a step to the side, grimacing as gravel cuts into the bottom of my bare feet. Desperate, I glance around. Not thirty feet from us is another pile of dead, at least three hundred of them. These bodies have yet to be stripped.

My eyes focus on the men’s feet. A man about my size still has his shoes. I begin to walk toward him, expecting the guards to yell at me or shoot me, but I reach the pile of corpses without incident. I quickly remove the dead man’s shoes and, holding them tightly to my chest, hurry back to Aaron and Zev.

I put them on—they fit well enough. With mixed emotions, I remark, “These will do.”

I take a few steps in a small circle, feeling relieved and thankful. “Remind me to say Kaddish for the poor man’s soul.”

Zev asks, “How does it feel, walking in a dead man’s shoes?”

“I feel guilty, but not guilty enough to take the shoes off. I believe the dead man’s spirit will rest better knowing I am going to put his shoes to good use.”

***

Three days without food. We have been ordered to stay beside our barracks since we arrived. We have not been assigned jobs or sent on work details. Every day, we witness hundreds of prisoners being led to their execution.

The sky over the camp is shrouded by a dark mass of clouds that arrived last light and has lingered, hovering over us, depressing our spirits, and we think of death. It's obvious to me we are in some sort of rotation, waiting for our time to come. The inevitability of our executions has made the prisoners in the barracks talk of desperate actions: attacking our jailors, escaping, suicide, anything to cheat our oppressors of the gratification of executing us.

We continually hear firing squads. We've learned that when Russian POWs arrive, and there are thousands of them, the camp Commandant Martin Weiss immediately orders them sent to the 'execution wall' where they are executed. This murder factory, for that's what Dachau is, is too much for my brain to grasp.

In the meantime, we are starving, and it's painful. We're becoming Muselmann, those prisoners who've been reduced to skin and bone, awaiting death.

So far, I have not been able to come up with a plan to help our situation. Our only positive news is that some of our SS officers and enlisted soldiers are leaving Dachau, deserting their posts. It's no secret Germany is losing the war.

I've noticed apprehension on the guards' faces. They know the end of the Third Reich is near. They discuss it openly. Yet, most of them stay, programmed to obey orders. And this is what they are doing: obeying orders to kill us as fast as is humanly possible.

The number of prisoners in Dachau is in the tens of thousands, with thousands more arriving daily. Our time is running out. I can feel it. I must do something, but I cannot think. My brain isn't functioning.

It's now April 27, 1945. I know this because our Kapo, Emil Hadash, announces it's his birthday. He's thirty years old today. In observance of his natal day, he has arranged to have small cubes of bread passed out among us. We are grateful, even though it turns out to be just enough food to make our stomachs cramp and remind us we are starving.

After this forgettable morsel, we are lined up again.

"Prisoners, attention!" Kapo Hadash announces. "We will now march outside the camp. There, you will board a line of trucks that will transport you to the railroad station. You will be taking the train to Tyrol, an area in the Austrian Alps. There, you will be put to work repairing rails damaged by recent bombardments. You will be happy to know while you are in Tyrol, you will be fed three full meals a day."

This last information is met with approval, although I find this sudden promise of food difficult to swallow, so to speak.

"A one-way trip?" Aaron asks, always suspicious of Nazi intentions.

"Wouldn't surprise me."

"I don't want to die," Zev mumbles fearfully.

"Think of it this way, Zev," Aaron says. "The Austrian Alps will be a far better place to die than in this hellhole."

An hour later, we're loaded into cattle cars and on our way to the mountains. What awaits us in Tyrol is uncertain, but the very fact this trip is so bizarre troubles me. Aaron could be right about this being a one-way trip. After surviving eight concentration camps, I have no intention of simply giving up and becoming a target for trigger-happy Nazis.

The clatter of wheels and the sway of the cattle wagon will hopefully jar my dormant brain so I can come up with a plan to survive. While I await an epiphany, I think a prayer might help. *Thank you, God, for this reprieve. I only hope I can come up with an idea to free us from a firing squad or whatever else the Nazis might be planning. If it's not possible, well then, I suppose I'll be able to tell Tate I tried my best.*

***

The train's engine labors noisily. Our drafty cattle car is slowing, losing speed. It's as if we're being pulled up the steep Austrian pass by an exhausted animal. The incline is becoming too much for the tiring beast.

Time passes slowly as the locomotive crawls up the grade. With the increasing altitude comes a drop in temperature. Soon, it's freezing, and our thin 'pajamas' do little to protect us. We huddle together, attempting to block the drafts from the car's loosely slatted sides. Lack of food adds to our discomfort. But we do have a communal barrel of water that tastes like a urinal. We drink from it anyway.

Finally, the wheels grind to a stop. I peer between the slats. We're in the middle of a forest paralleling a dirt road.

German voices shout.

Footsteps hurry to our car.

Metal clinks.

I believe we are being uncoupled. It must be to separate our cattle wagons so the train's underpowered engine can pull a smaller load up the grade.

German voices yell stridently.

I hear the locomotive begin moving, but our car remains idle. The train, lighter now, must be pulling the first half of the cars up the grade.

"What's happening?" Aaron asks.

"I believe they've split the train in half. The engine is pulling the first half of the cars up the mountain. After they unload at the top of the grade, you can bet they'll be back for us."

I peer through the slats. Twenty or more SS troops have been left by the tracks.

My brain begins firing. I am relieved for the delay, yet still anxious as I push my way through the prisoners. I am searching, looking for a weakness in the car, a hole, a broken slat. My eyes scan the roof, the floorboards, the ceiling.

"What're you doing?" a prisoner asks as I push him aside.

"Looking for a loose board, anything we can use to make an opening."

"If we try to escape, they'll shoot us."

"I'm not 'trying' anything," I respond. "I'm planning to get us out of here if it's possible."

Minutes later, with many of the prisoners joining in, we scoured the cattle wagon for any weakness in its construction, but none of us could locate a flaw in the sturdy wood. Disheartened, I plop down beside Aaron and Zev.

"Hopeless, huh?" Zev comments.

Not appreciating his pessimism, I ignore him.

***

Hours later, I am half asleep when Aaron suddenly jumps to his feet.

"Oak versus pine," the old car mechanic mutters.

He moves to the barrel of water set against the wall and begins wrestling with it in an attempt to turn it over.

I watch him, curious to see what he's up to.

When the barrel doesn't move, Aaron bends, places his shoulder against it, and pushes with all his strength. It tips up…and over…splashing water in all directions. *What's this going to accomplish*? I wonder.

The prisoners mumble, irritated that our only source of water is now dripping through cracks in the floorboard.

Aaron kicks at the top ring of metal holding the wooden staves together. When he manages to get it part way off, he leaps on top of the barrel and begins jumping up and down on it. Several wooden spines begin to crack, and then, suddenly, they break apart from each other.

"That make you feel better?" I ask.

"Yes, it does," Aaron replies, gasping for breath.

He hands me a splintered slat with a sharp end.

I heft the hardwood in my hand. *Does he think we can use these staves as spears against the SS? No, he's smarter than that. Then what?*

"It's harder than pinewood," Aaron adds.

It only takes me a second to grasp what he is suggesting. I turn to Zev. "Grab a couple of these. We're going to start digging our way out of this box."

Without waiting for them to join me, I begin using my length of wood as a pike and attack the floor. Moments later, with prisoners crowding around us, Aaron, Zev, and I are thrusting these improvised 'spears' at the floorboards.

Crack.

One of the planks splinters.

"Daylight below," Aaron announces.

Encouraged, I jam my pike into the opening and lever it up to widen the fissure.

Creak...

A three-foot section of flooring breaks away. Below, I see the railway bed and creosote-coated rail ties.

"It's working," Zev gasps.

I urge, "Place your staves under the board next to mine, and we'll push up together."

Aaron, Zev, and I, shoulder to shoulder now, struggle to pry up the protesting length of pine.

The board moves slightly and squeaks… but doesn't lift.

"Give it your all," I say between clenched teeth.

We redouble our efforts. The plank suddenly breaks away, leaving an eight-inch gap. A communal release of breath from the prisoners. Sweating now, we hurriedly pry the neighboring planks apart, widening the hole.

Finally, the opening is big enough for a man to crawl through.

German voices approach.

We freeze.

Then, to our horror, a snarling, barking German Shepherd appears in the escape opening.

The boxcar's door is slid noisily open, revealing SS guards. The Officer in charge yells, "*Raus*! *Alles aus*! Out! Out!"

"Feh…" Aaron curses.

"Escape was too good to be true," Zev comments.

"*Meshuga*," I mutter as I stand and kick the barrel's broken debris over the hole covering the dog.

I move to the door with the others and leap to the ground. Looking around, it appears the German Shepherd that discovered our potential escape hole departed before garnering anyone's attention.

The soldiers now lead us away from the rails to an open area slightly uphill. Walking alongside the tracks, I am distracted by the train's whistle. I look up at the mountainside.

Our train, with the first half of the boxcars, is backing down the incline, pushing the empty cars before it. I assume it is returning to hook up to us and transport us back up the mountain to join the first contingent of prisoners, wherever they may be.

SS soldiers yell additional orders, and we are led to the dirt road paralleling the tracks.

Strange, I think.

Then, my eyes focus on three groupings of soldiers. My stomach curls. They are positioned on the rail side of the road, standing about thirty feet apart in front of three knee-high tarp-covered bundles.

Aaron sidles up next to me. "I don't like the look of this."

"Nor do I."

"Any ideas?"

"Halt!" yells the German officer leading us. "All halt!"

Our line of prisoners stops before the trio of guards standing behind their shrouded bundles.

I glance behind us. The forest has given way to a large outcrop of solid granite. There is no place to run in that direction. I watch as our SS guards and their dogs split into two groups; each faction moves to either end of our line, cutting off those possibilities of flight. As for the three twosomes in front of us, the train is now backing up behind them to recouple with the abandoned boxcars, effectively cutting off the last possible avenue of escape.

The locomotive brakes to a stop.

The officer in charge, yells, "*Die weffen legt an*!"

I don't need an interpreter to tell me he's ordering his men to prepare to fire!

"It appears I'm getting my wish to die in the mountains," Aaron comments.

The trio of soldiers whip tarps off, revealing, as I suspected, three heavy-caliber machine guns mounted on tripods.

"They're going to kill us!" Zev exclaims.

"Not without a fight," I say grimly. "Rocks. There's rocks all around us."

I raise my voice. "Everyone, pick up the sharpest stones you can find. We're going to throw them at the gunners and charge them."

"It's suicide!" Zev protests as the prisoners quickly begin gathering rocks.

"Standing still is suicide! If we can disable one of the gunners, we can grab his machine gun and turn it on the others."

Zev shakes his head. "I don't think—"

"Pick up some *farkakte* rocks!" Aaron yells.

The SS Officer, seeing our intentions, quickly yells, "*Waffen vorbereiten*!"

Gunners quickly sit on ammunition boxes behind their weapons as their partners attend to adding 'ribbons' of bullets to breaches. Machine guns loaded—they are cocked…

Chapter 26

"L'Chaim!" I yell.

"Stone them!" Aaron shouts.

A deafening roar of automatic gunfire erupts!

Rock still in hand, I freeze. My jaw drops at the sight unfolding before me. Blood is spurting from the heads and torsos of machine gunners, SS officers, and German soldiers on either end of our line as they are hit and topple to the ground.

Breathless, I see flashes of gunfire erupting from open doors on the portion of the train that has just backed down the grade. The firing stops as quickly as it has started.

As the smoke clears, my eyes take in a sight I thought I would never live to see: Nazi bodies lie everywhere—many are dead, others are wounded, dying.

Then, there is stunned silence, broken by voices yelling in Polish and Yiddish, "For Poland!"

"For Jews everywhere!"

"For freedom!"

"For Warsaw's Jews!"

Dozens of armed men in civilian clothes begin jumping from the train. They are Polish partisans! Partisan fighters! They quickly finish off the wounded Nazis.

Not quite believing what I'm seeing, I cautiously begin laughing and crying; all of us are amazed and astounded, and wholehearted cheers erupt. We drop our rocks and rush to greet our rescuers. Our two groups meet and embrace with a cacophony of Polish and Yiddish.

Then, I hear a voice I never thought I'd hear again. "Elias!"

I turn and almost fall to the ground. There is Dov with a big grin on his face. He's grown a bit of a beard, but it is him.

As he steps over to me, my eyes blur with tears. I touch him to make sure I am not dreaming. Dov is real, and he's alive! My dearest friend from the camps is alive. It's surely a miracle. I saw him shot and killed all those months ago on the snow-covered hill, attempting to escape the Nazis.

"Dov…" is all I can manage to say as we embrace like long-lost brothers.

Holding onto him, my heart beating joyfully, I pray, *Thank you, God, thank you*.

We break apart, and I take a ragged breath and ask, "How? How is this? That you're alive?"

"By the grace of God, the Nazis missed me that day. As bullets tore all around us, I jerked my body like I had been hit and fell to the ground. Thankfully, the soldiers were too lazy to climb up the hill and check on me. So, I lived. But you, look at you. You're skin and bones."

"I'll fatten up once I eat."

"Elias, my friend. I am so happy to see you. We have much to talk about. This war is coming to an end. The Soviet Army has Berlin encircled. They're about to deliver the final coup de grace."

I stare...*Did I hear correctly*? "Say that again."

"I'm saying the Third Reich has all but surrendered. The concentration camps, Auschwitz, Buchenwald, Bergen-Belsen, Sobibor, Mauthausen, almost all of them have been liberated."

While I know the war won't end until Adolf Hitler is dead, I feel a sudden sense of lightness. I could fly if I only had wings.

I hear excited voices. The partisans must be informing the prisoners of Berlin's pending fall.

"Dov," I say, indicating my two companions, "these are my friends, Aaron and Zev. We've been through some tight moments together."

Dov says, "Hopefully, that's over, we're—"

"Tanks!" Zev interrupts.

"*Farkakte*," Aaron mutters with a frown. "This war isn't over yet. There must be a dozen of them. And troop carriers."

A long line of lethal-looking armored vehicles is winding down the road coming at us.

"They're friendlies," Dov identifies. "The tanks belong to USA's 20th Armored Division. And the troop carriers are transporting soldiers from the 42nd and 45th Infantry Divisions. We're all together, headed for Dachau. We plan on liberating the camp before the day is out."

I really cannot quite believe this is happening.

"Yahoo!" Zev yells with relief. "The Yanks are coming!"

All around us, prisoners let out 'whoops' and 'hollers.' They are crying, laughing, and cavorting, relieved to be alive as they watch the Allied forces drawing near.

I feel rejuvenated as a portion of my old optimism returns.

Dov says, "We were with the Americans this morning when they took Tyrol and killed or captured the German forces. We caught the mumzers as they were drowning prisoners."

"Drowning?" I ask with confusion. "Why drowning?"

"Our guess is they were running out of ammunition."

"How could they possibly drown hundreds, if not thousands, of Jews?"

"They tied their hands behind their backs, placed burlap bags over them, and threw them off a bridge into the local river."

"Swine," Aaron remarks.

"Elias," Dov says. "You and your friends need medical attention. There are Red Cross trucks and medics up the grade. The train conductor will take you and the others back up." He waves to the passing vehicles. "My men and I are hitching rides to Dachau. So really good to see you, my friend. We'll catch up later."

"I'm going with you."

"Elias, you're not in any condition to join us. You need medical attention, rest, food, and water."

"That can wait. As we speak, Nazis are killing Jews. I'm not staying here when I can be of help. I'm coming. We should hurry."

With one eye on the passing vehicles, he responds. "No, Elias, you are not. If I remember rightly, you don't know one end of a gun from the other. Besides, in your condition, you'll never keep up with us. Don't even think of arguing with me. Understand, Elias?"

I glare at him. I do understand. I am a liability.

Dov nods, accepting my silence as acquiescence. "Get yourself and your friends to the medics," he says as he hurries off, calling to his partisan fighters.

Within seconds, they have all hopped onto troop carriers for the trip to Dachau—where a fight is sure to ensue.

I say a prayer for him, for the Allies, and for the Jews and others who, at this very late moment, are still being exterminated.

As the last armored troop carrier passes us, I begin to run after it.

Why? Because I can't stand by when help is needed.

I hear Aaron and Zev call after me, but I ignore them.

I am running now, running as fast as I can.

Gasping, stumbling, feeling I am about to collapse, I somehow catch up to the last truck's tailgate. My legs, weak as a baby's, falter, yet with one last effort, I lunge forward, reaching my hand out. I yell the only English word I can think of, "Help!"

An iron grip encases my hand. The American soldier pulls me up like I'm a feather and lifts me into the truck bed. I fall to the floor, gasping for breath. I find myself amidst a group of grinning young men.

One claps me on the back, and I feel my ribs rattle, but I can only smile with gratitude. Others are saying things I don't understand, but I know they are congratulatory. One gives me a 'thumbs up.' I gather my thread-worn pajamas close as I feel a sort of shame at my appearance in the presence of these uniformed warriors.

The soldier who hauled me on board twists the cap off his canteen and offers me a drink. I stare at him. He is so dark-skinned that it takes me a moment to realize I am looking at the first African I have ever seen. I quickly smile to modify my unintentionally rude stare and gratefully accept the canteen. I guzzle half of its contents.

Sighing at last, I nod my thanks and offer the canteen back to him. He refuses, gesturing that I should keep it. I settle down among these strong, well-armed soldiers, and a thrill courses through me. I am with the Allies. This long nightmare may finally be coming to an end.

I hear sporadic gunfire as our truck, the last in the vehicle convoy, enters Dachau. We brake to a stop beside a tangle of tanks, armored cars, troop carriers, US soldiers, and German prisoners. At least a dozen dead SS soldiers are sprawled on the parade ground, with many more standing in groups, hands above their heads. Using my very limited English, I quickly call out to the Yanks, "Thank you. Thank you."

I slide off the back of the troop carrier as a breeze blows heavy black smoke and ash across the camp.

The U.S. infantrymen might think they are downwind from a chemical factory, while others may compare the acrid odor to the sickening smell of feathers being burned off a plucked chicken. None of their prior combat experience will have prepared them for what they are about to encounter.

What the Soldiers discover next leaves an indelible impression, sure to produce a lifetime of nightmares. The images of the atrocities they see will never leave them. The human mind at first refuses to believe what the eyes see, and then vile reality seeps in. All the stories of Nazi horrors these GIs have heard about were underestimated rather than exaggerated. They can see this now.

In a warehouse, the soldiers uncover over 4,000 bodies of men, women, children, and babies, and over 1,000 more dead bodies are discovered in the barracks. And then there are the grounds surrounding the crematorium where the US soldiers, accustomed to witnessing death, are horrified. They are sick, throwing up, having no stomach for the furnace rooms stacked almost ceiling-high with tangled human bodies, a maniac's woodpile, as they now understand the acrid smell.

Dachau's 32,000 prisoners begin emerging from barracks and barbed-wire enclosures. Walking skeletons is the only way to describe these poor souls. Their clothes are rags, they are covered with dirt, sores, lice, bloody injuries, and weeping wounds, with many suffering from disease. Despite their mental and physical agonies, they hobble forward and grab at their liberators' uniforms in disbelief as they connect what is happening and realize that their abysmal ordeal is finally coming to an end.

Joyous exclamations fill the air. "Americans! Americans!"

"Liberation!"

"It's over!"

"Liberation!"

"The war is over!"

I stare at this heartening bedlam. *Am I dreaming*? If I'm dreaming, it's the most promising dream in the world.

In the midst of this jubilation, I also feel sad as memories of my parents, Tate and Mame, my sisters and little brother, Guena, Reizl, Hanche, Pearl, Rivka, and Avi, flash before me. All gone. I manage to take in a breath, attempting to settle the deep ache in my soul, but my pain comes out as a wail of grief. I cup it in my hands, trying to muffle it.

Tears course down my cheeks. I collapse to my knees. I don't know for how long I am kneeling when I feel a light hand on my shoulder. I look up to see a shadow of a man, one of the prisoners, so emaciated a strong breeze would surely blow him over. He is trying to comfort me. His eyes, too, are full of tears, not from pain but from compassion. And I realize, for this man and for all of us, the fear can finally be let go. Yet the mourning will never pass.

A short while later, after the old man has left me, I see Yanks pulling out canteens of water, C-rations, and dozens of Hershey bars and passing them to half-dead prisoners.

Food! I hurry over and stare with wide-eyed amazement at the feast before me. My stomach gurgles with anticipation. Within seconds, I am opening packages, tearing off wrappings, right alongside the others, seeing food I've only dreamed of—beef, chicken, cookies, chocolate—in short, Heaven!

The wind, blowing from the east, changes direction, bringing with it the stink of burning flesh and thick, acidic smoke that curls around me. Quickly gathering up my gastronomic treasures, I scurry off to find a scent-free area. I settle down beside a barrack. Eating a Hershey bar and licking chocolate from my fingers, my attention is drawn to several Allied soldiers chasing down two SS soldiers. Catching them by the latrines, they shoot and kill them. This triggers an outpouring of pent-up feelings among my fellow prisoners. Seeking revenge, they yell, "Find the Nazis! Kill the murderers! Don't let any of them get away! Find them! Hunt them down!"

These declarations are met with resounding cheers. Eating cookies, I cheer right along with them as the more able-bodied prisoners run about, picking up anything they can use as a weapon: a shovel, a rake, a piece of lumber. They begin searching for their former tormentors who have abused, tortured, and killed so many of us. If these 'beasts of Dachau' wish to live, they had better surrender to the Yanks. I sympathize with my fellow Jews who have suffered so horribly at the hands of the Nazis, but much of my own urge to retaliate against the enemy, if I ever really had one, has dissipated.

From the far reaches of the camp, sporadic gunfire bursts out. More retribution? Possibly. Do I blame them? Not at all. It's just nothing I wish to participate in. It's time for a new beginning.

I turn away from the sounds of violence and watch as Jews and other prisoners walk about, roaming free—free at last. A growing sense of joy fills my senses. Here I am, alive, free! It is hard to trust that I am finished with the horrors of war.

I eat the remainder of my candy bars and C-rations and stand up, overwhelmed with happiness. I begin to yell, sing, jump, cry, and go wild. I am luxuriating in the heady, overwhelming delight of having a full stomach and being liberated. I am free!

"Are you auditioning for the theatre?"

I turn to see Dov and a few of his partisans approaching.

They, too, are smiling.

"Actually, why not?" I respond with a grin. "I may become the next John Barrymore."

"You don't take direction very well."

"I never have," I reply, feeling only a smidgen of guilt. "Besides, I couldn't miss this. It's an historic moment!"

"Yes," he agrees as we turn to witness frail prisoners walking and limping with the help of others.

I am suddenly angry at myself for eating before helping them, many of whom are still in their barracks, too weak to leave. How many are dying? How many more will die because the war didn't end in time to save them?

Red Cross vehicles come into view, threading their way through this mass of army vehicles to park alongside the barracks. Doctors and nurses alight, carrying medical bags, and hurry into the prisoners' quarters. There are not nearly enough of them to administer to the hundreds, thousands, of the ill and dying.

"Dov," I say, "I must go and help. There are prisoners who can't get out of their bunks, who can't walk. I have to go to them to see what I can do—"

"No, my friend. Look at yourself. You're in no condition to help anyone. You're ready to fall over."

"No, I have to—"

"Stop arguing with me, Elias."

For the first time, I realize how true Dov's words are as I suddenly feel as weak as a newborn. My stomach rumbles, then cramps. Grimacing, unable to stand, I bend over, and then the ground rushes up to me.

Chapter 27

A very auspicious day, May 8, 1945

Voices. Foreign. English.

I open my eyes to find myself in a barracks that has been converted into a clinic. There are at least fifty cots in the room filled with ex-prisoners attended to by military doctors and nurses wearing white Red Cross uniforms. *My God, I'm in a proper bed with a mattress, a pillow, and a sheet covering me.*

Moving my arm, I discover an IV needle in one of my veins on the back of my hand, its plastic tubing running to a bag hitched onto a metal pole, and the clear liquid moves through snake-like coils. This is Dov's doing, I surmise. I must have passed out, and he pulled some strings with the Americans to get me here, as I imagine he is some sort of a partisan hero.

I like the bed and pillow but don't like being confined when so much is happening.

I glance around. A US army nurse, a big fellow who speaks German, tyrannizes a harried group of young German soldiers, who are being made to mop the floor, change bedpans, and wash patients. This is quite a surprise. Nazis are waiting on Jews. It makes me wish I spoke German so I could order, "Clean the windows too! Scrub down the walls! Iron my laundry!"

As if I had any laundry to wash.

A pretty woman in a white uniform and wearing a Red Cross armband comes over to me. "Awake, I see. I'm your nurse, Miss Mariam."

Polish! Thankfully, she speaks Polish.

"How are you feeling, Mr. Feinzilberg?"

My name, my proper name. When she mentioned it, I thought she had misspoken. I am no longer going to be recognized as B-1259! Never again.

Lifting my left forearm, I see the numbers are still there. The tattoo will always be part of my identity, a reminder of a time when evil tried to conquer goodness and almost did.

"Mr. Feinzilberg, are you feeling alright?" Miss Mariam repeats with a concerned frown.

Aware she is waiting for my answer, I realize I haven't had time to think about my stomach. It's sensitive but better, much better. I respond, "Good. I feel good. How long have I been asleep?"

"Two days," Mariam says.

"Two days!" I respond with shock.

"Yes. You were starved and badly dehydrated. Your system wasn't prepared for all that food you consumed. The IV is giving you vitamins and nutrients, and we'll be feeding you soup until your stomach is ready for something more substantial."

Soup? This sounds suspiciously like the swill I've been fed for the past several years. "No, thank you. No soup. I don't ever want to ever see soup again. I'd like more C-rations if that's possible."

She shakes her head. "That's what brought you here."

"I think it was the Hershey bars. I ate six of them, maybe more."

"Yes, not good for a starving stomach. Just to let you know, the soup here is like a stew, very nourishing. It's chicken noodle. I believe you'll like it."

"Soup with chicken?" It sounds promising. "I'll try it."

"Good. If you can keep it down, we'll have you up and out of here in a few days."

"A few days? No, no. I'm ready to leave now."

"Mr. Feinzilberg," she says a bit too firmly. "It's best if you stay here until you can hold down solid food and regain some of your strength."

"And how long might that be?"

"It depends entirely upon you. You're very malnourished. Three or four days at least."

"That's almost a week."

"You have someplace you have to be?" Mariam asks.

A good question. I realize there's no place I have to be. I respond, "I have nothing urgent at the moment, but I'd like to be up and about. When can you remove this needle in the back of my hand?"

"Maybe the day after tomorrow."

"I would like to have it out now so I can leave as soon as I feel better."

She sighs. "You're not a very good patient, Mr. Feinzilberg. The IV is to help you recover."

"I feel good now."

"You won't say that if you stand up, trust me."

I let out an unhappy grumble.

Mariam raises her eyebrows. "If I give you some very good news, will you stay until the doctor says you can be released?"

"It would have to be some very, very good news."

"I promise you it is."

"All right. What's this very, very good news?"

"Word just came in that on April 30th, the day after Dachau was liberated, Adolf Hitler committed suicide in his Berlin bunker."

I am speechless. *Hitler is dead*?

I let out a long breath. "This *is* very, very good news. Thank God that evil monster is gone."

"I have even more good news. On May eight, the Germans unconditionally surrendered. The war in Europe is over."

If smiles could break one's face, I'm sure mine would fall to the floor in pieces. And if I felt a bit stronger, I would jump out of bed, grab Miss Mariam, and dance with her around the room. *Thank God, the war is finally and completely over*!

I tune in to Miss Mariam as she is saying, "… and the Doctor told me to inform you that when you are released, you will be transferred to a rehabilitation camp called Feldafing. It's outside of Munich, not far from here. You will be cared for—"

"Germany? No. No. I don't want to stay in Germany. No, thank you. I wish to go to…" I realize I don't know where I wish to go. Or where I can go.

I have no money and no clothes besides my striped pajamas that I intend to burn at my first opportunity. I have nothing. And then I remember my father mentioning his uncle, Benjamin Tenenbaum, the brother of my father's mother, who has a business in Guatemala, in Central America. Perhaps I could write to him and see if he would offer me a job. It's a long shot, a very long shot, but maybe…

"Elias," Mariam interrupts my thoughts, "I understand how you feel, but Feldafing is in the American sector, staffed by the Red Cross, and it's a place where you can recover and stay until you decide what you wish to do with your future. Trust me, it will be a very welcome change from the life you've been living. If I were you, I would take advantage of this extraordinary offer. It's open-ended. You may stay as long as you wish, with all the comforts you need available to you. Good food. New clothes. Not only that, but you'll have complete medical and therapeutic services for as long as you need them. Compliments of the USA and the Allies. I really recommend you at least try it."

I don't know what to say. How can they afford to do this? But, instead of questioning my good fortune, I nod. "Ok. I'll try it."

"You won't be sorry, I promise you."

"Do you happen to have writing paper and a pen I could borrow?"

"No, but I'm sure I can find something. Now I have my rounds to make. I suggest a nap."

"Gladly. And thank you," I say as Mariam leaves.

I realize I am tired. I close my eyes and lay on this comfortable mattress. It's really very comfortable.

My thoughts drift to the day in Lodz, sitting with my father on the front steps of our apartment. *When was that*?

I remember. 1939. So many years ago… So many concentration camps… Nine. Can that be right? Yes, I confirm after I've recounted them.

I'm amazed I'm alive. *Tate, I pray silently*, believing he can hear me. *Somehow, I've managed to keep the promise I made to you—to survive. And now, with the help of God, our heritage will also survive.*

"Elias."

Hearing my name, I open my eyes to find Aaron and Zev beside my bed. I smile. How good it feels to see my friends and to smile again.

"Glad we found you," Aaron says. "How are you feeling?

"Better. I should be out of here tomorrow or maybe the day after. What are you two up to?"

"We're leaving, but we'd like you to join us. We'll wait for you if you'd like to come along."

"Where are you going?"

"Warsaw. I've heard the Germans have been cleared out of the city. My family owned some property there that the Nazis confiscated. It's not much, but I'll claim it and convert one of the buildings to a garage for car repairs. Elias, I want you to join us. I'll make you a partner."

I am flattered. *A partner in a car garage*?

"I'm going to own twenty percent," Zev says proudly.

I raise my eyebrows, giving Aaron a look.

"It's true," Aaron confirms. "I'll make him earn it. And, Elias, I'll give you twenty percent also. What do you say? Partners?"

I am touched by Aaron's offer, but I know it's not for me. "Aaron, thank you for your generous offer. I really appreciate it, but I have other plans. Besides, we all know I don't have the talent to be a good car mechanic."

Aaron's eyes crinkle. "Elias, I could teach you." He sees my skeptical look and adds, "Ah, you're probably right. We did some good things together, didn't we?"

"That we did," I acknowledge, remembering our night of disabling the Nazi's motor pool of army vehicles. "I'll miss the two of you.

"I'll miss you, too," Zev adds, offering his hand.

"Goodbye, my friend," Aaron says.

We shake hands and share quick embraces, knowing we may never see each other again.

A sense of loss settles over me as I watch them walk out of my life.

***

The next morning, I'm still in bed and composing a letter, thanks to Miss Mariam, who located writing materials for me. I am writing to my father's uncle, Benjamin Tenenbaum. I am asking him if it's possible he can give me a job. Any kind of job. I let him know I will be staying in Feldafing, at the rehabilitation camp outside of Munich, and he can write to me there. My problem with this letter is not its content but that I know absolutely nothing about my relative other than his name and that he lives in Guatemala City. What I don't have is his home address. So, with not a lot of hope but having no other option, I address the envelope:

Senor Benjamin Tenenbaum
Care of Guatemala City's Main Post Office.
Guatemala, Central America.

Senor, the only Spanish word I can remember hearing, may help.

It's a long, long way from Germany to Guatemala, and there's no guarantee my letter will arrive or that if it does, it will somehow find its way to Senor Tenenbaum. I have no choice but to leave it in the hands of the US Army Postal Service to deliver—and to the Almighty to guide its arrival.

"How's the patient this morning? Good, I hope."

"I'm good," I respond as Dov walks up to my bedside.

"Elias, I'm leaving today, but before I go, I want to make you an offer, a proposition."

I look at him, wondering what this proposition might be.

"I'd like you to consider coming back to Lodz with me to start our lives over. I'm an accountant, as you know, and a damn good one. But I'm going to need office help." He sees my skepticism and quickly adds, "I know accounting is not your forte, but we can work that out. I like you, Elias. You're an honest man, and I know you're one of the bravest non-combatants I've ever met. And I don't want to lose you as a friend.

"Will you come to Lodz with me? We can make things work. You're a kind, gentle man and very likable. In the past, I noticed even some of the worst Nazis were charmed by you. I, on the other hand, charm no one. I'm outspoken and don't care to change my ways. Despite everything that's happened to us, you still have an optimistic outlook on life; it exudes from you. It's who you are. You lighten my burden simply by being my friend.

"Elias, I need someone like you in the accounting firm I'm going to start, someone to soothe all the feathers I'm sure to ruffle. What do you say? Represent me. Be my personality."

Completely overwhelmed, I am quiet for a moment as I digest Dov's offer. This is the second partnership I've been offered in two days. And yet, neither one is something I will consider. "Dov, I can't go back to Lodz. It would be opening an old wound. So many sad memories, so many losses. No, no, as much as I would like to take you up on your offer, Dov, I can't. I'm sorry."

He gazes at me with sad eyes. "I understand, Elias. I do. I'll miss you, my friend. I wish you well in whatever undertaking you pursue. I'll be leaving this afternoon. And, by the way, remember Paul Hermann?"

I nod. How could I forget the brave composer/conductor who wrote down the names of criminal Nazis who murdered Jews? "Yes, and his six notes."

"I retrieved them. They were a bit smudged but were surprisingly still readable. I turned them over to the Yanks. They're going to track down those Nazi butchers and see they're brought to trial and, hopefully, hung."

"Good," I say, thinking about the brave musician who risked his life to keep a record of SS names.

I wonder if he's still alive. I'll probably never know. So many of us just disappeared.

"Elias," Dov adds. "You can locate me through the Jewish Council in Lodz. And I'll expect a letter from you when you're settled."

"You'll get one. I'll let you know where I end up."

I hear a jumble of voices outside. "What's happening?"

"General Walker's ordered the entire adult population of the city of Dachau to be marched through the camp to witness first-hand the atrocities the Nazis inflicted upon us Jews and Hitler's other 'undesirables.' I've also heard the US Army and news media is photographing the camps as they were discovered with all of the tortured, starving, and dying prisoners, as well as the piles of dead, the gas chambers, and the crematoriums, so that there will be undeniable proof that the Holocaust, that's what our suffering is being called, did in fact happen. These truths can never be denied."

"Smart man," I respond, suspecting that in the future, antisemites will once again appear as they always have and very possibly try to deny the evils the Nazis brought on us, dismissing them as 'exaggerations' and 'propaganda.' It is our history.

"Shalom, my friend," Dov says as he reaches over and squeezes my shoulder.

"Shalom," I reply quietly as I watch another friend walk away, passing out of my life.

Thinking of the atrocious sights the people of Dachau are now witnessing, I remember one of my father's favorite quotes that our rabbi translated into Yiddish several years ago. It's paraphrased from the writings of an Irishman, Edmond Burke, "The only thing necessary for the triumph of evil, is for good men to do nothing.'"

Looking back and contemplating Germany's invasion of Poland and the rest of Europe, all to satisfy a madman's quest for power and the elimination of the Jewish race, it appears a lot of good men initially did nothing.

Chapter 28

Feldafing Rehabilitation Camp - September 1945

I now live in Feldafing, the first all-Jewish displaced persons' facility for concentration camp survivors. It is twenty miles southwest of Munich in the American zone of occupation. The director of the camp, who welcomed me upon my arrival, is Lieutenant Irving J. Smith. Like all the other administrators, he is Jewish despite his English name. I almost feel at home; at least I'm comfortable with my surroundings as I walk through the camp of approximately 4,000 Jews. Perhaps my calm comes from the knowledge I'm finally safe and the threat from Nazis is a thing of the past.

The camp is clean, well-maintained, and comprised of stone and wooden barracks and a few individual homes. The inhabitants of Feldafing, I've learned, are mostly survivors from Dachau. The lodge I am assigned to holds just twenty of us. It's roomy and has comfortable beds. I really appreciate a pillow and a mattress as never before.

I'm wearing new clothes, part of two sets I was given upon arrival.

I soon learn educational and religious life is flourishing in the camp. There's a religious community supported by a rabbinical council, with several schools for adults and children, including a Talmud Torah, a yeshiva, and a library with a religious book collection. Yes, there are children here, women also.

The 450 children and adolescents, all orphans, are housed in a separate kinderblock. The women have their own barracks. I was surprised to discover two small newspapers published in the camp, *Dos Jiddishe Wort* (the Jewish World) and *Dos Fraje Wort* (The Free World).

I sit down to lunch at the end of a long table with benches for men and women on each side. At least thirty of these tables are in the enclosed hall, where meals are served on a rotation basis.

Across from me is an older, bald gentleman and a younger man beside me. The bald man says, “I’m Beny Schwartz. You new here?”

“I arrived a few days ago. From Dachau.”

The younger man says, “I’m David Gutenberg, welcome.”

“I escaped Dachau a while back,” Beny says, “killed a dozen or more Nazis in the process and stole a tank. A Panzer it was; could have been one of General Rommel’s. Ran out of gas, or I wouldn’t be here.”

My eyebrows rise. But then I see David touch fingers to his temples as if to say, ‘Beny isn’t all there.’

I nod surreptitiously and respond to the older man, “Congratulations.”

“No need. I self-congratulate. Have you tried the vanilla ice cream?”

“No. Not yet.”

“I’ll get us some.” Beny rises from the table and enters the kitchen.

David explains, “Beny was a physics professor at the University of Berlin. The Nazi party attempted to recruit him to develop their flying rocket program. When he refused, they arrested him and gave him a series of shock treatments to try to convince him otherwise. The shocks didn’t do what the Nazis hoped for, so they increased the electrical currents and irreparably damaged his mind.”

“So sad.”

“Being a Jew is never easy. I used to own a kosher restaurant in Munich. Nazis closed it down, executed my wife and my employees for no other reason than they were Jewish. I missed death by ten minutes. I had left to pick up some loaves of challah.”

“My family’s gone too. Similar story.”

Beny returns to the table with two plates, each with a large scoop of vanilla ice cream. He hands me one, sits down, and eyes me expectantly.

Ice cream is new to me. We didn't have an ice cream store in the Lodz neighborhood where I grew up, but it looks interesting.

I pick up my spoon and take a bite. The vanilla flavor meets my tongue—delicious! It's one of the best tastes I've ever experienced. I smile. "Beny, this is positively wonderful."

"I knew you'd like it," he replies with a grin. "I gave David the recipe, didn't I, David?"

"Yes," David says, keeping a straight face. "I believe that's so, Beny. Thank you."

"I have a recipe for brisket that I may give you tomorrow."

"I'll look forward to that, Beny." David turns to me as I take another bite. "It's homemade. Wait until you try the chocolate. We'll be making that tomorrow. By the way, I'm the head chef here. You know how to cook?"

"Not really."

"Want to learn?"

And that's how I became a junior chef in Feldafing's kitchen. I am quick to learn that working in the kitchen is not just learning how to follow recipes and cook but, at least in our camp, also entails cleaning the pots and pans, the stoves, taking out the garbage, and learning how to fix small cooking appliances when they break down.

Today, I have been given the task of replacing the electrical cord on a large mixer. I have been advised of the procedure, and with David supervising, I have taken the mixer out into the eating area to work on it, as there is no room in the kitchen. I plug the original cord into a nearby wall socket to make sure it is indeed dead. I flip the on switch at the side of the mixer. It works. The mixer is running. I turn to David.

"It still has to be replaced. The rubber on the wiring is frayed and dangerous."

I nod, unplug the cord from the socket, and take off the mixer's housing. Seeing where the old wires connect to the motor. I unscrew two screws, free the end of the old cord, and discard it, then reach for the new cord.

"Peel back the ends," David instructs.

Sitting at the table only inches from the mixer, I use a sharp knife I brought from the kitchen to cut and peel the rubber back on two connecting ends. When I have an inch of naked wire showing, I wrap each end around the connectors and screw them into place. I sit back and review my handiwork. *Not bad*, I congratulate myself.

"Good job," David says.

He reaches down and plugs the cord into the wall socket.

"Ahh," I scream as electrical currents zap through my buttocks, sending me backward, crashing to the floor as I wonder what hit me.

"Sorry, plugged in the old cord," David says apologetically as he pulls the offending cord from the wall socket. "Too bad you were sitting on its end."

Yes, it is too bad, I'm thinking, wondering if my tush is burned and if my trousers have a hole in them.

I stagger to my feet, and as I am feeling for a hole in the seat of my pants, I hear a cacophony of English voices.

"Well, will you look at this," David says and then quickly adds, "You have a comb? That hair of yours is a rat's nest. Pat it down. Do something, hurry."

My hair? Hurry? What the…?"

I turn to see a large group of American military men and a gaggle of what might be news people coming toward us.

The military officers, tall, strong men in impressive uniforms, stop at tables and, using interpreters, talk with Jews recovering from mistreatment at the hands of the Nazis.

"Pretty interesting, huh?" David asks.

Yes, I'm thinking as I watch the military men. They talk to everyone and shake their hands, and while I can't understand what they are saying, the words bring smiles to faces.

My eyes widen as they reach me, and I see the number of stars on the soldier's uniform leading them: Four stars! My hair, still in need of combing, stands straight up.

The four-star general speaks to me, and his interpreter repeats, "How are you feeling, sir? Better, I hope?"

Tongue-tied, I nod.

"I'm General Dwight D. Eisenhower, and this gentleman beside me is General Walton Walker."

I don't need the interpreter to translate as I immediately recognize Dwight D. Eisenhower's name. He is the leading general of the entire Allied Army!

Through his interpreter, General Eisenhower congratulates me on my survival and wishes me a long and healthy life. Surprisingly, Eisenhower and the general beside him each shake my hand, and then they file out of the clinic.

General Dwight D. Eisenhower and General Walker, these world-famous military leaders who helped win the war, have just visited me!

David, standing a few feet away, remarks, "Impressive."

"Yes, yes…" I say, still in awe.

Then, I hear a vaguely familiar voice, "Eli? Is it really you, Eli?"

An even bigger shock courses through me—I know that voice! I turn—and there's Esther!

She is standing right before me.

Not so many months ago, with so many people killed in the camps, I lost all hope of ever seeing my Esther again, but here she is, and now I am staring into those eyes…those beautiful green eyes…

Esther!

Her lips part, "Eli…"

I can only stare…

She, too, is staring…

Tears well…

I reach out my hands.

She takes them in hers, and we hold onto each other.

The tears make their way unashamedly down our cheeks. We are mute.

"Am I interrupting something?" David asks.

I glance briefly at him. He seems puzzled.

As I gaze back at Esther—we simultaneously burst out laughing. Another dam has broken. Hopes I had dared to entertain return, and after a few seconds, our hilarity ebbs, but our eyes remain on each other. My heart thumps, about to burst with joy.

"I don't know what's happening between the two of you," David says, looking flustered. "But I think you'd better go someplace where you can talk. Don't worry about the mixer, Elias. Go. Just go."

We release each other's hands to wipe our faces. Still, at a momentary loss for words, I take her hand in mine, and without a word, we hurry out.

Several steps outside, we catch our breaths and find a place to sit.

"Eli," Esther says, moving a hand to her breast. "My heart is beating like the wings of a hummingbird."

"Mine, too," I respond, barely able to squeeze the words out.

"I couldn't believe it when I saw you. It's a miracle. Oh, Eli, with all that's happened. All of the…" she hesitates, unable to go on.

Then, a radiant smile appears. "I am so very happy you are alive. For so long, I have prayed for you. That you would survive, that we would meet again. I still can't believe we are here, free, sitting next to each other. Pinch me."

I pinch her arm. "I am here, Esther."

Her words, 'I prayed for you,' have affected me in ways I cannot express. I finally say, "For the longest time, I have also prayed for you and that we would meet again, but then…"

"I know… I know. Say no more."

"Esther, we barely know one another. We've only spoken a word or two, yet somehow, I feel we are friends. No, actually, I feel we might be more than friends."

"I feel the same." She suddenly chokes back a sob. "Eli, we truly are more than friends."

"Then perhaps it's time I know your last name."

Esther laughs. "I am Esther Szpigner."

"I am happy to meet you, Esther Szpigner. I am Elias 'Eli' Feinzilberg."

"It's a pleasure to meet you, too, Elias 'Eli' Feinzilberg."

Somehow, as implausible as our situation is, we are much more than friends. I won't question how this phenomenon happens or why; I just know I want to know more about this woman. "Esther, I am off work in half an hour. If you have some time, I'm hoping we could share a walk together."

"I would like that, Eli."

A short while later, Esther and I are walking along a path that takes us around the camp. We are talking as easily as if we have known each other all our lives.

Esther is saying, "… and I was born in Warsaw. My parents and my older brother were in the flower and produce business. My brother had his own shop, and I worked there ever since I could count Zoltas selling fruit and vegetables. When the war broke out and the Nazis invaded, my parents made arrangements for us to escape to Russia. My brother and sister-in-law, who just had a baby, decided to stay behind and try to live with the invaders. I stayed with them to help care of their new baby."

"That was brave of you."

“And not altogether smart. If only I could have convinced my brother to leave earlier.”

“The ‘if onlys’ in our lives. I have many.”

“A few months after my parents left, the Nazis swept through the city, arresting and killing Jews. My brother tried to get us all out, but by then, it was too late. He was executed, along with my sister-in-law and her baby. I was shipped to Skarzysko-Kamienna, a concentration camp in Poland. I was put to work in a munitions factory. Little did the Nazis know that my fellow prisoners and I were loading shells with half the amount of gunpowder to make them less effective. I stayed working in the factory until I was transferred to Majdanek, another concentration camp, where I was again placed in a forced labor group. Then, two years later, I was transferred to a third concentration camp, that’s where I first saw you.”

“You remember that?”

“Yes, Eli. You have very nice blue eyes. I’ve never forgotten that first glimpse.”

I swallow. My heart is surely swelling. “I’ve never forgotten your eyes either, Esther. They have kept me company when I needed company.”

“Then, when the war was deteriorating, I was again transferred, this time to Dachau. I thought for sure, this will be my end.”

“I’ve had those same thoughts.”

I feel her fingers brush hesitantly against mine. I cautiously encircle her hand. She squeezes me in return. A pleasant jolt of electricity makes me happy as we walk on. However, I hesitate to speak. I am not willing to break this moment. Finally, searching for neutral ground so I don’t babble something stupid, I ask, “Whatever happened to your green scarf?”

“Oh, that?” she replies with a little laugh. “Someone ‘borrowed’ it while I was in Majdenak. I never found out who. It was a memory of my family.” She scoffs. “Such a little thing compared to what was going on around me.”

"I once had a pair of shoes stolen…"

Esther smiles. It makes me feel closer to her. I can still remember looking forward to seeing her green scarf. Somehow, when I saw it, it gave me something to hope for, no matter how unrealistic.

"Tell me about you, Eli."

Where to begin? Then I have an idea. "Esther, mine is a long story, one that will take some time to tell. I have tomorrow off. Would you be willing to take the train with me into Munich tomorrow? We could see some places, what places remain to be seen, and I can tell you the story of my life."

"I would love that, Eli. Yes, I would love to join you tomorrow."

***

Somehow, surrounded by evidence of atrocities and pain, Esther and I, while caring for the weak and debilitated prisoners and working together in the kitchen commissary, find moments to share our stories and, most of all, our smiles. We also manage to escape for a few hours, just the two of us, to take walks by the nearby lake and go on short trips together. These are treasured times.

We share laughter, which is so important to us. Esther has a wonderful sense of humor and the patience to listen to my silly stories, which I invent just to see her laugh. I am in love with this intelligent woman and owner of herself. And she tells me she is in love with me.

A letter from my father's uncle actually arrives, offering me a job in Guatemala City, and I accept.

So, with so many lost years, what are we waiting for?

Our wedding, the first in the camp, takes place on July 3, 1946. Esther and I are married by the camp's rabbi, with David as my best man. Our guests are at least fifty prisoners and four American G I's who happen to be Jewish. The Yanks bring along musical instruments they've scavenged from the defunct Dachau orchestra, whose Jewish members were once forced to play for the Nazis.

At the conclusion of our wedding ceremony, the traditional cloth-wrapped glass is placed on the floor between Esther and me.

"Together?" I ask.

Smiling, she nods.

We trample the glass, careful of each other's feet—it breaks.

"Mazel Tov!" the crowd shouts, wishing us good luck.

Beny rushes up and stomps on the broken glass again. I guess to make sure it's really broken. He turns to our guests and yells loudly, "Mazel Tov!"

Laughter fills the room. American Gi's raise their musical instruments and start playing Horah, our traditional Jewish wedding dance.

Chairs are provided. Esther and I sit, and we are lifted up in the air. The crowd gathers around and starts dancing. Laughing, we're carried in a circle accompanied by the robust voices of our guests singing Hava Nagila.

The words "Hava Nagila," a Hebrew folk song, mean "Let's rejoice."

Epilogue

Many years have passed since Esther and I left Feldafing's displaced person camp and traveled to Guatemala City to work for my uncle, where we learned the trade of making and selling shoes.

Esther and I eventually opened our own shop, *Calzado Elias*, and it became successful.

We were blessed with three children: Jacob, Asher, and Jenny.

We built a three-bedroom villa on the outskirts of the city where our children grew up and then went off to college, acquired jobs in different parts of the world, and eventually married. They now have children of their own. And yet, despite having a successful, loving, and growing family, I felt something was missing in my life. I yearned to become closer to my Jewish faith.

When I first suggested we move to Israel, I was met with 'and give up all of our friends?' and 'leave the house we built?'

We finally overcame those misgivings, and in 1969, Esther and I moved to Israel, twenty-two years after our journey to Guatemala. We purchased an apartment in Ramat Eshkol, a newer neighborhood in Jerusalem, where I live today.

Esther, my beloved wife, passed away in October 2008 at the age of 86. I pray for her and miss her every day. I also pray for my children, Jacob Feinzilberg, Jenny Brodsky, and Asher Feinzilberg, my seven grandchildren and twenty-one great-grandchildren, and members of my family who were murdered during the Holocaust.

While living in Guatemala, whenever the subject of the Holocaust and Nazis came up, Esther and I would consider whether we should discuss the atrocities that took place in the concentration camps with the children. Knowing it would be painful to talk about and give our children nightmares, we decided against it. It was a decision we made at the time and I still don't know if it was the correct one.

This all changed once we made the move to Israel. In our neighborhood in Jerusalem, I found Holocaust survivors just like us who were openly speaking of their experiences and then, shockingly, heard that these truths were being denied by some in the world. Can you imagine? Do they think six million Jews just disappeared off the face of the earth? They don't know anything.

I couldn't stand by and allow that to happen. I joined an organization called AMCHA, a support group specifically for Holocaust survivors. The term Amcha is Hebrew for "your people" or "your nation." I now frequent this group several days a week, taking the bus from my apartment to our meetings.

I give talks to students and interested individuals. When I began relating my stories, I was surprised to discover that some of the younger ones knew little about the Holocaust. Even the middle-aged ones were foggy about the happenings inside the German concentration camps during World War II. Importantly, while they had been exposed to graphic pictures of gas chambers, crematoriums, and piles of corpses, they weren't aware of the root causes that created antisemitism and the hatred that propelled the Nazi regime to start their 'final solution.'

I am doing my best to correct their lack of education on this very important subject. I usually talk for over an hour and answer their many questions. Shortly after I began giving these lectures, I was surprised to learn I had begun appearing on the student's internet blogs.

I also give talks at Brigham Young University's Jerusalem campus, where I lecture every three months.

Over the years, I have seen my message start to spread. It is wonderful. I have spoken to thousands and thousands of schoolchildren, college students, politicians, and professionals. My story is for everyone. I talk of individual Jews I knew in the camps, their heroism, their sacrifices, and their love of their faith under the most trying circumstances.

I mention my meeting with General Dwight D. Eisenhower and other famous American generals after the war ended and my meeting with Benjamin Netanyahu, as well as the President of Israel, Reuven Rivlin, and the President of Germany, Frank-Walter Steinmeier, who met with me ahead of the World Holocaust Forum commemorating the liberating of Auschwitz.

When we met, the German media emphasized my life's story. Ironically, it felt surreal to see television segments of this meeting later in the German news of all places. I also speak with students at Hebrew University, the Knesset (Israel's parliament), the police department, the Israeli Army, and many other groups and institutions.

My daily schedule has become a habit. Almost every day, I wake up, have breakfast, go to the Jewish AMCHA center, and tell my story.

I am now having my speeches placed online, just like the new generation. I have been on television, and it appears the world is hungry to hear my story. And today's technology is helping to spread the word. It's amazing. Can you imagine?

When I get tired, I think of all those who did not survive. It is for them, I speak, and for my family and my faith.

I make a promise that in the years I have left, I will do everything I can to inform everyone of the horrors of the Holocaust. As a survivor, I feel God has chosen me, and others like me, to spread the truth so that it can be passed on to future generations. So that history will not repeat itself.

We can't allow this to happen. It is up to all of us.

There are two sayings we Jews have in reference to the Holocaust. Both are meaningful reminders of past persecutions and future aspirations. While the first is embedded in the minds of the living, the second is just as powerful as it reminds us to be ever vigilant, to recognize and fight antisemitism wherever it crops up and eradicate it.

Judaism is our legacy and will always remain so as long as we remember the powerful message in these simple words:

Never forget

Never again

The Feinzilberg Family Photos

FEINZILBERG FAMILY (1934) Adults- left to right: Sarah (aunt), Reizl (Sister), Golda Elka (Mother), Elias Joseph (only survivor), Guena (Sister), Yaacov (Father) - Children- left to right: Rivka Raquel (Sister), Hanche (Sister), Avigdor Nuto (Brother), Pearl (Sister)

Elias and Esther

Elias and Esther's wedding day in 1946 in Feldafing

Elias and Esther in Guatamala.

Second from left, former Prime Minister of Israel Golda Meir and Elias on the right. Taken in Guatemala

Elias and Esther in Guatemala with their children from left to right: Asher, Jenny, and Jacob

Esther and Elias in Israel, 1976

Elias (center) surrounded by students at Brigham Young University (BYU Jerusalem Campus), 2014

Elias with Israeli Prime Minister Netanyahu during Holocaust Memorial, 2017

Elias talking to the German President and his wife (2020)

Elias celebrates his 100th. Birthday (2017) in Jerusalem with mariachi music surrounded on the left by his son Jacob and on the right his granddaughter Noa.

Family and friends at Elias's 100th birthday party.

Photo taken by Helena Schätzle of Elias with one of his granddaughters, Dana. The picture won the Global Peace Photo Award in 2016 and was exhibited at the Austrian Parliament for one year, reminding the parliamentarians of their duty working for peace and justice. Since then, it has been shown in more than 12 exhibitions worldwide.

Elias 'Eli" Feinzilberg was born in Lodz, Poland, on October 22, 1917.
He passed away peacefully in his sleep on December 20, 2021, at the age of 104.

About the Author

Michael Brown is a retired Hollywood film editor who has won 3 Emmy Awards. His first novel, '**William & Lucy**.' won the 2012 Global eBook Award for Best Historical Novel of the Year (era 1500-1940). His historical family saga, '**The Girl Who Was Me Is Gone**,' was published in March 2020 by Penmore Press. His latest books, '**In the Company of Savages**,' '**Loving You is Crazy**,' and '**The Girl from Fisher Island**' are available on Amazon Books, as is this book, '**My Name is B-1259**.'

He lives in Austin, Texas, with his wife, Holly.

www.ingramcontent.com/pod-product-compliance
Lightning Source LLC
Chambersburg PA
CBHW071404090426
42737CB00011B/1345
9798218308964